The Juridical Nature of Unilateral Acts of States in International Law

Queen Mary Studies in International Law

Edited by

Malgosia Fitzmaurice
Phoebe Okowa
Sarah Singer

VOLUME 20

The titles published in this series are listed at *brill.com/qmil*

The Juridical Nature of Unilateral Acts of States in International Law

By

Eva Kassoti

BRILL
NIJHOFF

LEIDEN | BOSTON

Library of Congress Cataloging-in-Publication Data

Kassoti, Eva, author.
The juridical nature of unilateral acts of states in international law / by Eva Kassoti.
pages cm. -- (Queen Mary studies in international law ; volume 20)
Based on author's thesis (doctoral - University of Bristol Law School, Bristol, England, 2014), issued under title: Unilateral juridical acts and sources of international law.
Includes bibliographical references and index.
ISBN 978-90-04-26068-9 (hardback : alk. paper) 1. Unilateral acts (International law) I. Title.

KZ1262.J87K37 2015
341.26--dc23

2015026695

This publication has been typeset in the multilingual "Brill" typeface. With over 5,100 characters covering Latin, IPA, Greek, and Cyrillic, this typeface is especially suitable for use in the humanities.
For more information, please see www.brill.com/brill-typeface.

ISSN 1877-4822
ISBN 978-90-04-26068-9 (hardback)
ISBN 978-90-04-30076-7 (e-book)

This book is printed on acid-free paper.

Contents

Acknowledgments

This book is based on my Ph.D thesis and it would have never been completed without the help of many people. First and foremost, I wish to thank my supervisor Professor Patrick Capps; his expertise and guidance made this project possible. Furthermore, I would like to thank my examiners, Professor Malgosia Fitzmaurice and Professor Malcolm Evans, whose insightful comments helped me turn the thesis into a book.

Throughout the process of writing this book, I have tested the limits of patience of a number of close friends. For their continuing assistance, advice, encouragement and, at times, sheer faith, I would like to heartily thank Adale Robertson, Olympia Bekou, Mando Rachovitsa and Lisa Louwerse. I would also like to thank my first international law teacher, Dr Costas Antonopoulos of Democritus University of Thrace, who encouraged me to pursue further studies in the field of international law and provided much guidance.

Finally, my gratitude is extended to my family. Besides supporting me financially, they have tolerated long absences for more years than I care to remember. For this reason this book is dedicated to them.

List of Abbreviations

AJIL	American Journal of International Law
Ann. Surv. Int'l & Comp. L.	Annual Survey of International and Comparative Law
Aufl.	Auflage
BYIL	British Yearbook of International Law
Cal. L. Rev.	California Law Review
CD	Conference on Disarmament
Chi.- Kent J. Int'l & Comp. L.	Chicago-Kent Journal of International and Comparative Law
Duq. L.R.	Duquesne Law Review
ECOSOC	United Nations Economic and Social Council
EJIL	European Journal of International Law
Emph.	Emphasis
EU	European Union
fn.	footnote
et seq.	*et sequentia*
GA	United Nations General Assembly
German L.J.	German Law Journal
GOJIL	Goettingen Journal of International Law
Hague Recueil International	Recueil des Cours de l' Academie de Droit
Harvard ILJ	Harvard International Law Journal
i.e.	*id est*
Ibid.	*Ibidem*
ICJ	International Court of Justice
ICJ Reports	International Court of Justice Reports of Judgements, Advisory Opinions and Orders
ICJ Statute	Statute of the International Court of Justice
ICLQ	International and Comparative Law Quarterly
ILC	International Law Commission
ILM	International Legal Materials
JIL	Journal of International Law
LJIL	Leiden Journal of International Law
LGDJ	Librairie Generale de Droit et de Jurisprudence
LNTS	League of Nations Treaty Series
LOSC	United Nations Convention on the Law of the Sea
M. Nijhoff	Martinus Nijhoff
Mass. (Pick.)	Pickering's Massachusetts Reports

NILR	Netherlands International Law Review
NNWS	Non-nuclear-weapon States
No.	Number
NPT	Treaty on the Non-Proliferation of Nuclear Weapons
NPT Review (and Extension) Conference	Review (and Extension) Conference of the Parties to the Treaty on the Non-Proliferation of Nuclear Weapons
NYU J. Int'l L. & Pol.	New York University Journal of International Law and Politics
NWFZS	Nuclear Weapon Free Zones
NWS	Nuclear Weapon States
Ohio St. L.J.	Ohio State Law Journal
OSCE	Organization for Security and Co-operation in Europe
Oxford JLS	Oxford Journal of Legal Studies
p./pp.	page/s
para./s	paragraph/s
PCA	Permanent Court of Arbitration
PCIJ	Permanent Court of International Justice
PLO	Palestine Liberation Organization
PPNN Issue Review	Programme for Promoting Nuclear Non-Proliferation Issue Review
RdC	Recueil des Cours
Rep. of Int'l. Arbitral Awards	Reports of International Arbitral Awards
Res.	Resolution
rev.	revised
RGDIP	Revue Générale de Droit International Public
SC	United Nations Security Council
SCR	Canada Supreme Court Records
Suppl.	Supplement
tr./s	translator/s
Tul. L. Rev	Tulane Law Review
U.C. Davis J. Int'l L. & Pol'y	University of California Davis Journal of International Law and Policy
UK	United Kingdom
UN	United Nations
UN Doc.	United Nations Document
UNESCO	United Nations Educational, Scientific and Cultural Organization

UNTS	United Nations Treaty Series
US	United States of America
US Govt. Print. Off.	United States Government Printing Office
USSR	Union of Soviet Socialist Republics (Soviet Union)
Vol.	Volume
Va. J. Int'l L.	Vanderbilt Journal of International Law
VS	versus
Yale J. Int'l Law	Yale Journal of International Law
YIL	Yearbook of International Law
Yrbk	Yearbook

Table of Cases

i International Court of Justice

a *Cases*

Aegean Sea Continental Shelf Case, Greece vs Turkey, ICJ *Reports* 1978, p. 3.

Anglo-Norwegian Fisheries Case, UK vs Norway, ICJ *Reports* 1951, p. 116; Dissenting Opinion of Judge Read, p. 186.

Anglo-Iranian Oil Co. Case, UK vs Iran, ICJ *Reports* 1952, p. 93; Dissenting Opinion of Judge Read p. 142.

Asylum Case, Colombia vs Peru, ICJ *Reports* 1950, p. 266.

Case concerning Application of the Convention on the Prevention and Punishment of the Crime of Genocide, Bosnia vs Yugoslavia, ICJ *Reports* 1996, p. 595.

Case concerning Armed Activities on the Territory of the Congo (New Application: 2002), DRC vs Rwanda, ICJ *Reports* 2006, p. 6.

Case concerning Border and Transborder Armed Actions, Nicaragua vs Honduras, ICJ *Reports* 1988, p. 69.

Case concerning Military and Paramilitary Activities in and against Nicaragua, Nicaragua vs US, ICJ *Reports* 1984, p. 392.

Case concerning Military and Paramilitary Activities in and against Nicaragua, Nicaragua vs US, ICJ *Reports* 1986, p. 14.

Case concerning Pulp Mills on the River Uruguay, Argentina vs Uruguay, ICJ *Reports* 2010, p. 14.

Case concerning Pulp Mills on the River Uruguay, Order of 13 July 2006, Argentina vs Uruguay, ICJ *Reports* 2006, p. 113.

Case concerning Sovereignty over Pedra Blanca/Pulau Batu Puteh, Middle Rocks and South Ledge, Malaysia vs Singapore, ICJ *Reports* 2008, p. 12.

Case concerning the Frontier Dispute, Burkina Faso vs Mali, ICJ *Reports* 1986, p. 554.

Case concerning the Land and Maritime Boundary between Cameroon and Nigeria, Cameroon vs Nigeria, ICJ *Reports* 1998, p. 275; Dissenting Opinion of Judge Weeramantry, p. 362; Dissenting Opinion of Judge Koroma, p. 377.

Case concerning the Land and Maritime Boundary between Cameroon and Nigeria, Cameroon vs Nigeria, ICJ *Reports* 2002, p. 303.

Case concerning the Temple of Preah Vihear, Cambodia vs Thailand, ICJ *Reports* 1961, p. 17.

Case concerning the Temple of Preah Vihear, Cambodia vs Thailand, ICJ *Reports* 1962, p. 6; Separate Opinion of Judge Alfaro, p. 39; Dissenting Opinion of Judge Spender, p. 101.

Case of Certain Norwegian Loans, France vs Norway, ICJ *Reports* 1957, p. 9; Separate Opinion of Judge Lauterpacht p. 34.

Certain Activities Carried Out by Nicaragua in the Border Area, Order of 8 March 2011, Costa Rica vs Nicaragua, *ICJ Reports* 2011, p. 6.

Certain Activities Carried Out by Nicaragua in the Border Area, Order of 22 November 2013, Costa Rica vs Nicaragua, *ICJ Reports* 2013, p. 354.

Case concerning the Continental Shelf, Libya vs Malta, *ICJ* Reports 1985, p. 13.

Corfu Channel Case, UK vs Albania, *ICJ Reports* 1948, p. 15.

Delimitation of the Maritime Boundary on the Gulf of Maine Area, US vs Canada, *ICJ Reports* 1984, p. 246.

Fisheries Jurisdiction Case, Spain vs Canada, *ICJ Reports* 1998, p. 432.

Interhandel Case, Switzerland vs US, *ICJ Reports* 1959, p. 6; Dissenting Opinion of Judge Lauterpacht, p. 95.

Maritime Delimitation and Territorial Questions between Qatar and Bahrain, Qatar vs Bahrain, *ICJ Reports* 1994, p. 112.

North Sea Continental Shelf Cases, Germany vs Denmark, Germany vs Netherlands, *ICJ Reports* 1969, p. 3; Separate Opinion of Judge Ammoun, p. 101.

Nuclear Tests Case, Australia vs France, *ICJ Reports* 1974, p. 253; Dissenting Opinion of Judge De Castro p. 372.

Nuclear Tests Case, New Zealand vs France, *ICJ Reports* 1974, p. 457.

Questions relating to the Obligation to Prosecute or Extradite, Belgium vs Senegal, *ICJ Reports* 2012, p. 422; Separate Opinion of Judge Cançado Trindade, p. 487.

Questions Relating to the Obligation to Prosecute or Extradite, Order of 28 May 2009, Belgium vs Senegal, *ICJ Reports* 2009, p. 139.

Questions Relating to the Seizure and Detention of Certain Documents and Data, Order of 3 March 2014, Timor-Leste vs Australia, available at http://www.icj-cij.org/docket/files/156/18078.pdf; Separate Opinion of Judge Cançado Trindade available at http://www.icj-cij.org/docket/files/156/18082.pdf.

Questions Relating to the Seizure and Detention of Certain Documents and Data, Public Sitting held on 22 January 2014, CR 2014/4, p. 8.

South West Africa Cases, Ethiopia vs South Africa, Liberia vs South Africa, *ICJ Reports* 1962, p. 319; Joint Dissenting Opinion of Judge Spender and Judge Fitzmaurice, p. 465.

South West Africa Cases, Ethiopia vs South Africa, Liberia vs South Africa, *ICJ Reports* 1966, p. 6.

b *Advisory Opinions*

Accordance with International Law of the Unilateral Declaration of Independence in respect of Kosovo, Advisory Opinion, ICJ Reports 2010, p. 403; Declaration by Judge Simma, p. 478; Separate Opinion of Judge Yusuf, p. 618.

International Status of South West Africa, ICJ Reports 1950, p. 128; Separate Opinion of Judge Read, p. 164.

Legality of the Threat or Use of Nuclear Weapons, Advisory Opinion, ICJ Reports 1996, p. 226.

c *State Correspondence*

Verbatim Record of the Public Sitting held on Tuesday 1 December 2009, at 10 a.m., at the Peace Palace, in the *Kosovo Advisory Opinion*, CR 2009/24, available at http://www.icj-cij.org/docket/files/141/15710.pdf.

Verbatim Record of the Public Sitting held on 4 December 2009, at 10 a.m., at the Peace Palace, in *Kosovo Advisory Opinion*, CR 2009/28, available at: http://www.icj-cij.org/docket/files/141/15718.pdf.

Verbatim Record of the Public Sitting held on Tuesday 8 December 2009, at 10 a.m., at the Peace Palace, in the *Kosovo Advisory Opinion*, CR 2009/30, available at http://www.icj-cij.org/docket/files/141/15726.pdf.

Verbatim Record of the Public Sitting held on Wednesday 9 December 2009, at 10 a.m., at the Peace Palace, in the *Kosovo Advisory Opinion*, CR 2009/31, available at http://www.icj-cij.org/docket/files/141/15728.pdf.

Verbatim Record of the Public Sitting held on Thursday 10 December 2009, at 10 a.m., at the Peace Palace, in *Kosovo Advisory Opinion*, CR 2009/32, available at http://www.icj-cij.org/docket/files/141/15734.pdf.

Written Comments by Serbia in the *Kosovo Advisory Opinion*, 14 July 2009, available at http://www.icj-cij.org/docket/files/141/15686.pdf.

Written Statement of Serbia in the *Kosovo Advisory Opinion*, 15 April 2009, available at http://www.icj-cij.org/docket/files/141/15642.pdf.

ii Permanent Court of International Justice

Case concerning certain German Interests in Polish Upper Silesia, Germany vs Poland, *PCIJ Series A*, 1926, No. 7, p. 4.

Case of the Free Zones of Upper Savoy and the District of Gex, France vs Switzerland, *PCIJ Series A/B*, 1932, No. 46, p. 96.

Case of the S.S. "Wimbledon," UK, France, Italy, Japan vs Germany, *PCIJ Series A*, 1923, No. 1, p. 14.

Legal Status of Eastern Greenland Case, Denmark vs Norway, *PCIJ Series A/B*, 1933, No. 53, p. 22; Dissenting Opinion of Judge Vogt, p. 97.

Minority Schools in Albania, Advisory Opinion, *PCIJ Series A/B*, 1935, No. 64, p. 4.

Polish Postal Service in Danzig Advisory Opinion, *PCIJ Series B*, No. 11, 1926, p. 6.

Rights of Minorities in Upper Silesia (Minority Schools) Case, Germany vs Poland, *PCIJ Series A*, 1928, No.15, p. 4.

The Case of the S.S. Lotus, France vs Turkey, *PCIJ Series A*, 1927, No. 10, p. 4.

The Mavrommatis Palestine Concessions, Greece vs UK, *PCIJ Series A*, 1924, No. 2, p. 6.

iii Permanent Court of Arbitration

Arbitration under the Timor Sea Treaty of 20 May 2002, (*Timor-Leste* vs *Australia*), PCA, available at http://www.pca-cpa.org/showpage.asp?pag_id=1403.
Dispute concerning Access to Information under Article 9 of the OSPAR Convention, (*"OSPAR" Arbitration*) (*Ireland vs UK*), PCA, Final Award, 02 July 2003, available at http://www.pca-cpa.org/showpage.asp?pag_id=1158.

iv Other Arbitration Awards

Island of Palmas Case, 2 Rep. of Int'l. Arbitral Awards 829 (1928).
Opinion No. 10, Arbitration Commission, EC Conference on Yugoslavia, 92 ILR 206 (1992).

v Special Court for Sierra Leone

Proseutor v. Kallon and Kamara, Case No. SCSL-2004-15-AR72(E) and SCSL-2004-16-AR72(E), Appeals Chamber, Decision on Challenge to Jurisdiction: Lome Accord Amnesty, 13 March 2004, available at http://www.transcrim.org/07%20SCSL%20-%202004%20-%20Kallon%20Kamara.

vi World Trade Organization

Case Concerning Sections 301–310 of the Trade Act of 1974, WT/DS152/R, Report of the Panel (Dec. 22, 1999), available at http://www.wto.org/english/tratop_e/dispu_e/cases_e/ds152_e.htm.

vii Other

Caglar vs Billingham (Inspector of Taxes) 108 *ILR* 510 (1996).
Cave vs Mills, 7 *Hurlstone & Norman* 913 (1862).
Mills vs Wyman, 20 *Mass.* (3 *Pick.*) 207 (1825), available at http://grammar.ucsd.edu/courses/lign105/student-court-cases/mills.pdf.
Reference re Secession of Quebec Case, 2 *SCR* 217 (1998).

Table of Treaties

Additional Protocol II to the Treaty for the Prohibition of Nuclear Weapons in Latin America and the Caribbean, 14 February 1967, available at http://disarmament.un.org/treaties/t/tlateloco_p2.

Charter of the United Nations, 26 June 1945, San Francisco, 1 UNTS XVI (1945).

Convention for the Protection of the Marine Environment of the North-East Atlantic, 22 September 1992, available at http://www.ospar.org/content/content.asp?menu=00340108070000_000000_000000.

Convention on the Prevention and Punishment of the Crime of Genocide, 9 December 1948, available at http://www.icrc.org/ihl.nsf/full/357?OpenDocument.

Convention Respecting the Free Navigation of the Suez Maritime Canal, 29 October 1888, 3(2) AJIL (Supp.) 1909, p. 123–127.

Covenant of the League of Nations, 28 April 1919, Paris, available at www.yale.edu/lawweb/avalon/leagcov.htm.

Cyprus Treaty of Guarantee, 16 August 1960, Nicosia, 382 UNTS 8.

Declaration on the Suez Canal and the arrangements for its operation issued by Egypt, 24 April 1957, 265 UNTS 299.

Hague Convention (III) Relative to the Opening of Hostilities, 18 October 1907, The Hague, available at http://www.forces.gc.ca/jag/training/publications/law_of_armed_conflict/collection _of_docs_on_loac_2005_en.pdf.

Hague Convention (V) *on the Rights and Duties of Neutral Powers and Persons in Case of War on Land*, 18 October 1907, The Hague, available at http://www.yale.edu/lawweb/avalon/lawofwar/hague05.htm.

Montevideo Convention on Rights and Duties of States, 26 December 1933, Montevideo, 165 LNTS 19 (1934).

Statute of the International Court of Justice, 26 June 1945, San Francisco, available at http://www.icj-cij.org/documents/index.php?p1=4&p2=2&p3=0.

Statute of the International Law Commission, 21 November 1947, available at http://untreaty.un.org/ilc/texts/instruments/english/statute/statute_e.pdf.

Statute of the Permanent Court of International Justice, 16 December 1920, available at www.worldcourts.com/pcij/eng/documents/1920.12.16_statute.htm#_Toc160729737.

Treaty Concerning the Establishment of the Republic of Cyprus, 16 August 1960, Nicosia, 382 UNTS 215.

Treaty for the Prohibition of Nuclear Weapons in Latin America and the Caribbean, 14 February 1967, available at http://www.nti.org/media/pdfs/Treaty_of_Tlatelolco.pdf?_=1316643635.

Treaty on the Non-Proliferation of Nuclear Weapons, 1 July 1968, 729 UNTS 161.

United Nations Convention against Torture and other Cruel and Inhuman or Degrading Treatment or Punishment, 10 December 1984, available at http://www2.ohchr.org/english/law/cat.htm.

United Nations Convention on the Law of the Sea, 10 December 1982, Montego Bay, 1833 UNTS 3. 21 ILM 1261 (1982).

Vienna Convention on the Law of Treaties, 22 May 1969, Vienna, 1155 UNTS 331, 8 ILM 679 (1969).

Table of Legislation

i National Legislation

Bulgarian Obligations and Contracts Act of 1950.
Dutch Civil Code (*Burgerlijk Wetboek*).
Estonian Civil Code (*Tsiviilseadustiku Üldosa Seadus*).
French Civil Code (*Code Civil*).
German Civil Code (*Bürgerliches Gesetzbuch*).
Greek Civil Code (*Αστικός Κώδικας*).
Italian Civil Code (*Codice Civile*).
Scottish Requirements of Writing (Scotland) Act of 1995.
Slovak Civil Code (*Občiansky Zakonnìk*).
Spanish Civil Code (*Código Civil*).

Table of Other Documents

i UN Documents

a *General Assembly*

GA, Declaration on the Rights of Indigenous Peoples, UN Doc. A/Res/61/295 (2007).

GA, Final Document of the Tenth Special Session of the General Assembly, UN Doc. A/RES/S-10/2 (1978).

GA, Res. 3210 (XXIX), UN Doc. A/RES/3210 (1974).

GA, Res. 3237 (XXIX), UN Doc. A/RES/3237 (1974).

GA, Res. 43/177, UN Doc. A/RES/43/177 (1988).

GA, Res. 51/160, UN Doc. A/RES/51/160 (1997).

GA, Res. 67/19, UN Doc. A/RES/67/19 (2012).

b *Security Council*

SC, 974th Meeting, UN Doc. S/PV.974 (15 November 1961).

SC, Res. 169, UN Doc. S/RES/169 (1961).

SC, Res. 216, UN Doc. S/RES/216 (1965).

SC, Res. 217, UN Doc. S/RES/217 (1965).

SC, Res. 255, UN Doc. S/RES/255 (1968).

SC, Res. 541, UN Doc. S/RES/541 (1983).

SC, Res. 984, UN Doc. S/RES/984 (1995).

SC, Res. 1244, UN Doc. S/RES/1244 (1999).

c *Other UN Organs*

ECOSOC, Study of the Legal Validity of the Undertakings Concerning Minorities, UN Doc. E/CN.4/367 (1950).

d *NPT Review Conference*

Consideration of Proposed Agreement on the Prohibition of the Use or Threat of Use of Nuclear Weapons Against Non-Nuclear-Weapon States Parties to the Treaty on the Non-Proliferation of Nuclear Weapons (Proposal by Nigeria), Fourth NPT Review Conference, UN Doc. NPT/CONF.IV/17 (1990).

Decision 2: Principles and Objectives for Nuclear Non-Proliferation and Disarmament, 1995 NPT Review and Extension Conference, UN Doc. NPT/CONF.1995/32 (Part I), Annex (1995).

Developments with Regard to Effective International Arrangements to Assure Non-Nuclear-Weapon States Against the Use or Threat of Use of Nuclear Weapons, 1995 NPT Review and Extension Conference, UN Doc. NPT/CONF.1995/6 (1995).

Summary Record of the 3rd Plenary Meeting, 1995 NPT Review and Extension Conference, UN Doc. NPT/CONF.1995/SR.3 (1995).

Summary Record of the 4th Meeting of Committee 1, First NPT Review Conference, UN Doc. NPT/CONF/C.1/SR.4 (1975).

Summary Record of the 5th Meeting of Committee 1, Second NPT Review Conference, UN Doc. NPT/CONF.II/C.I/5 (1980).

Summary Record of the 6th Meeting of Committee 1, Second NPT Review Conference, UN Doc. NPT/CONF.II/C.I/SR.6 (1980).

Summary Record of the 7th Plenary Meeting, First NPT Review Conference, UN Doc. NPT/CONF/SR.7 (1975).

Summary Record of the 8th Plenary Meeting, First NPT Review Conference, UN Doc. NPT/CONF/SR.8 (1975).

Summary Record of the 8th Plenary Meeting, Second NPT Review Conference, UN Doc. NPT/CONF.II/SR.8 (1980).

Summary Record of the 9th Plenary Meeting, First NPT Review Conference, UN Doc. NPT/CONF/SR.9 (1975).

Summary Record of the 9th Plenary Meeting, Second NPT Review Conference, UN Doc. NPT/CONF.II/SR.9 (1980).

Summary Record of the 11th Plenary Meeting, Second NPT Review Conference, UN Doc. NPT/CONF.II/SR.11 (1980).

Working Paper Submitted by Egypt on Security Assurances to Non-Nuclear-Weapon States, 1995 NPT Review and Extension Conference, UN Doc. NPT/CONF.1995/MC.I/WP.4 (1995).

e *Conference on Disarmament*

Joint Declaration by the Ministers for Foreign Affairs of Brazil, Egypt, Ireland, Mexico, New Zealand, Slovenia, South Africa and Sweden, 1998 Conference on Disarmament, UN Doc. CD/1542 (1998).

Report of the Ad Hoc Committee on Effective International Arrangements to Assure Non-Nuclear-Weapon States against the Use or Threat of use of Nuclear Weapons, 1993 Conference on Disarmament, UN Doc. CD/1219 (1993).

Report of the Ad Hoc Committee on Effective International Arrangements to Assure Non-Nuclear-Weapon States against the Use or Threat of use of Nuclear Weapons, 1994 Conference on Disarmament, UN Doc. CD/1275 (1994).

Working Paper Submitted by the Syrian Arab Republic on Behalf of Member States of G-21 on Prevention of an Arms Race in Outer Space, 2012 Conference on Disarmament, UN Doc. CD/1940 (30 August 2012).

Working Paper Submitted by the UK, UN Doc. CD/177 (10 April 1981).

f *Correspondence from UN Member States*

Letter dated 6 April 1995 from the Permanent Representative of the Russian Federation to the United Nations addressed to the Secretary-General, UN Doc. S/1995/261.

Letter dated 6 April 1995 from the Permanent Representative of the United Kingdom of Great Britain and Northern Ireland to the United Nations addressed to the Secretary-General, UN Doc. S/1995/262.

Letter dated 6 April 1995 from the Chargé d'affaires a.i. of the Permanent Mission of the United States of America to the United Nations addressed to the Secretary-General, UN Doc. S/1995/263.

Letter dated 6 April 1995 from the Permanent Representative of France to the United Nations addressed to the Secretary-General, UN Doc. S/1995/264.

Letter dated 6 April 1995 from the Permanent Representative of China to the United Nations addressed to the Secretary-General, UN Doc. S/1995/265.

Letter dated 16 November 1988 from the Deputy Permanent Observer of the Palestine Liberation Organization to the United Nations addressed to the Secretary-General, UN Docs. A/43/827, S/20278 (1988).

g *International Law Commission*

Analytical Guide to the Work of the ILC, 1949–1997, (1998), available at http://untreaty.un.org/ilc/guide/9_9.htm.

Brierly J.L., Report on the Law of Treaties, UN Doc. A/CN.4/23, *Yrbk of the ILC* 1950, Vol. II, p. 222.

Documents of the 23rd session: Survey of International Law and Other Documents, UN Doc. A/CN.4/SER.A/1971/Add.l, *Yrbk of the ILC* 1971, Vol. II.

Draft Articles on Responsibility of States for Internationally Wrongful Acts, with Commentaries, UN Doc. A/56/10, *Yrbk of the ILC* 2001, Vol. II, p. 59.

Draft Articles on the Law of Treaties, with Commentaries, *Yrbk of the ILC* 1966, Vol. II, p. 262.

Fitzmaurice G., Report on the Law of Treaties, UN Doc. A/CN.4/101, *Yrbk of the ILC* 1956, Vol. II, p. 104.

Lauterpacht H., Report on the Law of Treaties, UN Doc. A/CN.4/63, *Yrbk of the ILC* 1953, Vol. II, p. 90.

Pellet A., Third Report on Reservations to Treaties, UN Doc. A/CN.4/491, p. 221.

Report of the ILC on the Work of Its 11th Session, UN Doc. A/CN.4/122, *Yrbk of the ILC* 1959, Vol. II.

Report of the ILC on the Work of Its 18th Session, UN Doc. A/CN.4/SER.A/1966/Add.l, *Yrbk of the ILC* 1966, Vol. II.

Report of the ILC on the Work of Its 48th Session, UN Doc. A/CN.4/SER.A/1996/Add.l, *Yrbk of the ILC* 1996, Vol. II

Report of the ILC on the Work of Its 50th session, UN Doc. A/53/10, *Yrbk of the ILC* 1998, Vol. II.

Report of the ILC on the Work of Its 51st session, UN Doc. A/54/10, *Yrbk of the ILC* 1999, Vol. II.
Report of the ILC on the Work of Its 52nd Session, UN Doc. A/55/10, *Yrbk of the ILC* 2000, Vol. II.
Report of the ILC on the Work of Its 53rd Session, UN Doc. A/56/10, *Yrbk of the ILC* 2001, Vol. II.
Report of the ILC on the Work of Its 55th Session, UN Doc. A/58/10, *Yrbk of the ILC* 2003, Vol. II.
Report of the ILC on the Work of Its 57th Session, UN Doc. A/60/10, *Yrbk of the ILC* 2005, Vol. II.
Report of the ILC on the Work of Its 58th Session, UN Doc. A/61/10, *Yrbk of the ILC* 2006, Vol. II.
Rodríguez Cedeño V., Eighth Report on Unilateral Acts of States, UN Doc. A/CN.4/557, p. 119.
Rodríguez Cedeño V., Fifth Report on Unilateral Acts of States, UN Doc. A/CN.4/525, p. 91.
Rodríguez Cedeño V., First Report on Unilateral Acts of States, UN Doc. A/CN.4/486, p. 319.
Rodríguez Cedeño V., Fourth Report on Unilateral Acts of States, UN Doc. A/CN.4/419, p. 115.
Rodríguez Cedeño V., Ninth Report on Unilateral Acts of States, UN Doc. A/CN.4/569, p. 147.
Rodríguez Cedeño V., Second Report on Unilateral Acts of States, UN Doc. A/CN.4/500, p. 195.
Rodríguez Cedeño V., Sixth Report on Unilateral Acts of States, UN Doc. A/CN.4/534, p. 53.
Rodríguez Cedeño V., Third Report on Unilateral Acts of States, UN Doc. A/CN.4/505, p. 247.
Summary Records of the 19th Session, UN Doc. A/CN.4/Ser.A/1967, *Yrbk of the ILC* 1967, Vol. I.
Summary Record of the 2525th Meeting, UN Doc. A/CN.4/SR.2525, *Yrbk of the ILC* 1998, Vol. I.
Summary Record of the 2526th Meeting, UN Doc. A/CN.4/SR.2526, *Yrbk of the ILC* 1998, Vol. I.
Summary Record of the 2527th Meeting, UN Doc. A/CN.4/SR.2527, *Yrbk of the ILC* 1998, Vol. I.
Summary Record of the 2603rd Meeting, UN Doc. A/CN.4/SR.2603, *Yrbk of the ILC* 1999, Vol. I.
Summary Record of the 2722nd Meeting, UN Doc. A/CN.4/SR.2722, *Yrbk of the ILC* 2002, Vol. I.
Summary Record of the 2726th Meeting, UN Doc. A/CN.4/SR.2726, *Yrbk of the ILC* 2002, Vol. I.

Summary Record of the 2771st Meeting, UN Doc. A/CN.4/SR.2771, *Yrbk of the ILC* 2003, Vol. I.

Summary Record of the 2772nd Meeting, UN Doc. A/CN.4/SR.2772, *Yrbk of the ILC* 2003, Vol. I.

Summary Record of the 2813th Meeting, UN Doc. A/CN.4/SR.2813, *Yrbk of the ILC* 2004, Vol. I.

Summary Record of the 2818th Meeting, UN Doc. A/CN.4/SR.2818, *Yrbk of the ILC* 2004, Vol. I.

Summary Record of the 2853rd Meeting, UN Doc. A/CN.4/SR.2853, 6 September 2005, available at http://untreaty.un.org/ilc/guide/9_9.htm.

Summary Record of the 2854th Meeting, UN Doc. A/CN.4/SR.2854, 4 August 2005, available at http://untreaty.un.org/ilc/guide/9_9.htm.

Summary Record of the 2855th Meeting, UN Doc. A/CN/SR.2855, 15 September 2005, available at http://untreaty.un.org/ilc/guide/9_9.htm.

Unilateral Acts of States: Replies from Governments to the Questionnaire: Report of the Secretary-General, UN Doc. A/CN.4/511, p. 265.

Waldock H., First Report on the Law of Treaties, UN Doc. A/CN.4/144, *Yrbk of the ILC* 1962, Vol. II, p. 27.

Waldock H., Fourth Report on the Law of Treaties, UN Doc. A/CN.4/177, *Yrbk of the ILC* 1965, Vol. II, p. 3.

ii League of Nations Documents

Resolution adopted by the Council of the League of Nations, on February 21st, 1921 in 2 *Official Journal of the League of Nations* 112 (1921).

iii Reports

Cartwright J., Whittaker S., *Proposals for Reform of the Law of Obligations and the Law of Prescription; English Translation of Avant-projet de Réforme du Droit des Obligations et de la Prescription (2005)*, 2007, available at http://www.justice.gouv.fr/art_pix/rapportcatatla0905-anglais.pdf.

Conference on Yugoslavia Arbitration Commission (Badinter Commission): Opinions on Questions Arising from the Dissolution of Yugoslavia, January 11 and July 4, 1992, 31 *ILM* 1488 (1992).

Fleck D., Second Report on Legal Aspects of Nuclear Disarmament, International Law Association Committee on Nuclear Weapons, Non Proliferation and Contemporary International Law, Washington Conference Report (2014), available at http://www.ila-hq.org/en/committees/index.cfm/cid/1025.

Institut de Droit International, Examen de l'organisation et des Statuts de la Societe des Nations, Rapport de Adatchi et Ch. De Visscher, 30 *Annuaire* 22 (1923).

Report of the Independent International Fact-Finding Mission on the Conflict in Georgia, September 2009, Vol. II, available at http://rt.com/files/politics/georgia-started-ossetian-war/iiffmcg-volume-ii.pdf.

Von Bar C., Clive E., Schulte-Nölke H., *Principles, Definitions and Model Rules of European Private Law, Draft Common Frame of Reference* (DCFR), prepared by the Study Group on a European Civil Code and the Research Group on EC Private Law (*Acquis* Group), 2009, available at http://ec.europa.eu/justice/contract/files/european-private-law_en.pdf.

UK Government, Securing Britain in an Age of Uncertainty: The Strategic Defence and Security Review, October 2010, available at https://www.gov.uk/government/publications/the-strategic-defence-and-security-review-securing-britain-in-an-age-of-uncertainty.

US Department of Defense, Nuclear Posture Review Report, April 2010, available at: http://www.defense.gov/npr/docs/2010%20Nuclear%20Posture%20Review%20Report.pdf.

iv Miscellaneous

Address of the President of the United States delivered at a joint session of the two Houses of Congress, 08/01/1918, *Foreign Relations of the United States* (1918), Supp. I, p. 12.

Announcement of US Support for the United Nations Declaration on the Rights of Indigenous Peoples: Initiatives to Promote the Government-to-Government Relationship & Improve the Lives of Indigenous Peoples, available at http://www.state.gov/documents/organization/153223.pdf.

Canada's Statement of Support on the United Nations Declaration on the Rights of Indigenous Peoples, available at http://www.aadnc-aandc.gc.ca/eng/1309374239861/1309374546142.

Cicero M.T., *Pro Murena: Speech in Defense of Lucius Licinius Murena*, 63 BC, available at: http://www.perseus.tufts.edu/hopper/text?doc=Cic.+Mur.+36&fromdoc=Perseus%3Atext%3A1999.02.0019.

Crimea Parliament Declares Independence From Ukraine Ahead of Referendum, *RT*, 11 March 2014, available at rt.com/news/crimea-parliament-independence-ukraine-086/.

EC Guidelines on the Recognition of New States in Eastern Europe and in the Soviet Union, 16 December 1991, available at http://207.57.19.226/journal/Vol4/No1/art6.html.

Fihn B., The Conference on Disarmament and Negative Security Assurances, March 2011, available at http://www.unidir.org/files/publications/pdfs/the-conference-on-disarmament-and-negative-security-assurances-369.pdf.

Harper D., *Online Etymology Dictionary*, available at http://dictionary.reference.com.

Harvard Draft Convention on the Law of Treaties, 29 *AJIL* 657 (Suppl.) 1935.

Mikhelidze N., The Geneva Talks Over Georgia's Territorial Conflicts: Achievements and Challenges, prepared for the Istituto Affari Internazionali (IAI) in the Framework of the Observatory on the Caucasus, November 2010, available at http://www.iai.it/pdf/DocIAI/iai1025.pdf.

OSCE, Final Act of the Conference on Security and Co-operation in Europe, adopted in Helsinki on 1 August 1975, also known as the Helsinki Final Act, available at http://www.osce.org/mc/39501.

President of Georgia's Address to European Parliament Members: Georgia Makes 'Unilateral Pledge' of Non-Use of Force, 23 November 2010, available at http://www.usa.mfa.gov.ge/index.php?lang_id=ENG&sec_id=595&info_id=8979.

Proclamation of Germany concerning the Extension of the Breadth of Its Territorial Sea, 11 November 1994, available at www.un.org/Depts/los/LEGISLATIONANDTREATIES/europe.htm.

Q&A: 'New Context' for Geneva Talks after Non-Use of Force Pledges, *Civil Georgia*, 15 December 2010, available at http://www.civil.ge/eng/article.php?id=22960.

Resolution on Basic Directions of Georgia's Foreign Policy, 7 March 2013, available at http://www.civil.ge/eng/article.php?id=25828.

Scottish Law Commission, Memorandum No. 35, Constitution and Proof of Voluntary Obligations: Unilateral Promises, 10 March 1977, available at http://www.scotlawcom.gov.uk/publications/discussion-papers-and-consultative-memoranda/1970-1979/.

Statement by the Ministry of Foreign Affairs of Georgia regarding the unscheduled large-scale military drills by the Russian Armed Forces in the Black Sea region, 29 March 2013, available at http://uk.mfa.gov.ge/index.php?lang_id=ENG&sec_id=595&info_id=18005.

UK Foreign Office Policy Document No. 148, 57 *BYIL* 614 (1986), paras. II.18–22.

US Arms Control and Disarmament Agency, *Documents on Disarmament* (1968), available at http://www.un.org/disarmament/publications/documents_on_disarmament/1968/DoD_1968.pdf.

Weingerl A., Definition of Unilateral Acts of States, presented at the 2004 Florence Founding Conference of the European Society of International Law, available at http://www.esil-sedi.eu/english/florence_agora_papers.html.

Who Recognized Kosova as an Independent State? The Kosovar People Thank You! available at: www.kosovothanksyou.com.

Introduction

But since men are a wicked lot and will not keep their promises to you, you likewise need not keep yours to them.

N. MACHIAVELLI, *The Prince, Ch. XVIII.*

The nature of promises, Linda, is that they remain immune to changing circumstances.

F. UNDERWOOD, *House of Cards, Ep. 1, Ch. 1.*

1 Purpose of the Present Study

One of the most striking features of modern international relations has undoubtedly been the rise of unilateralism in almost every field of international activity.[1] The term 'unilateralism', according to Dupuy, is commonly used in international law literature to denote two concepts: one of them is legal, while the other, essentially political.[2] Unilateralism, from a legal point of view, refers to the performance of unilateral acts with legal effects on the international plane. However, from a political-theory point of view, the term denotes the recourse to unilateral action, by some States in the conduct of their foreign policy.[3] Over the past few years, a considerable amount of literature has been published on the political dimension of unilateralism.[4] Nevertheless, the legal dimension of unilateralism and its potential impact on the structure of the international legal order, and more specifically on the doctrine of the sources of international law, have been largely left at the margins of scholarly attention.

This book focuses on the legal aspects of unilateralism, as defined by Dupuy. Unilateral acts in the form of written or oral statements, *communiqués* or declarations have always been part and parcel of international life. Nevertheless,

1 See –, Unilateralism in International Law: A United States – European Symposium, 11 *EJIL* 3 (2000), p. 3 *et seq*, held by the Michigan's Centre for International Law in 1999.

2 P.M. Dupuy, The Place and Role of Unilateralism in Contemporary International Law, 11 *EJIL* 19 (2000), p. 20.

3 *Ibid.*

4 See for example J.B. Attanasio, J.J. Norton (eds.), *Multilteralism v. Unilateralism: Policy Choices in a Global Society*, (London: British Institute of International and Comparative Law, 2004); B.F. Podliska, *Acting Alone: A Scientific Study of American Hegemony and Unilateral Use-of-force Decision Making*, (Lanham: Lexington Books, 2010).

 | DOI 10.1163/9789004300767_002

the recent technological advancements in the field of telecommunications have mainstreamed the use of unilateral acts as a means by which a State may interact with other subjects of international law. Almost all modern textbooks on international law make a brief reference to the question of unilateral acts[5] and, as will be discussed shortly, some works that deal generally with the phenomenon of unilateral acts have also been published. However, a systematic study of the legal nature of such acts has not yet been undertaken.

The aim of the present work is to fill this gap in the literature and to examine the legal nature of unilateral acts of States in international law. One of the most problematic aspects of unilateral acts is the question as to whether and under which circumstances acts of unilateral origin may be considered as having binding effects in international law – this is, in fact, a contested issue in and of itself. As Chapter 1 demonstrates, the debate surrounding unilateral acts has primarily focused on the extent to which these acts may constitute a new source of law – not on their legal nature. Therefore, any discussion of the legal nature of unilateral acts must include an exposition of the problems encountered when conceptualising these acts within the current doctrine of the sources of international law and an examination of how these conceptual problems have been handled in legal theory.

In this light, the purpose of the present work is two-fold: first, it purports to define the legal nature of unilateral acts. Specifically, it seeks to establish the criteria for characterising an act as a 'unilateral juridical act'[6] under international law. The present author argues that there are two main elements that comprise the legal nature of unilateral juridical acts: (i) the element of unilateralism and (ii) the element of the intention to create legal effects on the international plane.

While in the case of acts of a contractual nature the emphasis is on the interlocking of intentions,[7] this study demonstrates that, in the case of unilateral acts, the intention of the author State is autonomous in the production of the ensuing effects. Thus, it is asserted that the element of unilateralism refers to the ability of unilateral acts to create legal effects irrespective of any kind of

5 See for example D.J. Harris, *Cases and Materials on International Law*, 7th ed., (London: Sweet & Maxwell, 2010), p. 45; M. Shaw, *International Law*, 7th ed., (Cambridge: Cambridge University Press, 2014), pp. 86–7; J. Crawford, *Brownlie's Principles of Public International Law*, 8th ed., (Oxford: Oxford University Press, 2012), p. 415.

6 The term 'juridical act' is employed throughout the book to denote legal acts, namely acts that have binding effects on the international plane. For a detailed discussion of the term 'juridical' and of the theory of international juridical acts in international law, see *infra* Chapter 5.

7 See *infra* Chapter 4.

acceptance or reliance by the addressee. Furthermore, the element of intention is defined as the manifest or objective will – as opposed to the real or subjective will – of a State to create legal effects by means of a unilateral act.[8]

According to the present author, analysing unilateral acts in the abstract has been the reason why many of the attempts to conceptualise them thus far have failed. Therefore, the present work advocates that a contextual approach to unilateral acts is a condition *sine qua non* for any meaningful discussion of the phenomenon. For this reason, the context in which such acts occur will serve as a point of reference for ascertaining both their legal and unilateral nature. The term 'context' is specifically used throughout the book to connote the factual circumstances and the legal environment in which unilateral acts occur. Based on both State and judicial practice, this work argues that a list of indicators can be compiled that would be of great assistance in determining whether a given act is a unilateral juridical act. These include: the absence of a treaty law context; the absence of a rule requiring reciprocity; the absence of a context of negotiations; the existence of circumstances that preclude the conclusion of an international agreement; the absence of a pattern of offer/acceptance; the content of the act; its publicity; the forum in which the act was made; and the authority who made the act on behalf of the State.[9]

The present work, while highlighting the special role played by the factual and legal circumstances surrounding the making of unilateral acts, also enters a caveat against over-reliance on context. Thus, it is maintained that context does not oust the need for unilateralism and intent. Nevertheless, this work also maintains that the above indicators are of great probative value – they can assist in accurately determining whether a given act should be accorded the status of a unilateral juridical act.

Since most unilateral acts are created and operate in a 'less-than-formal environment', establishing the element of intention is often an arduous task, which is why context is emphasised in this study. The phrase 'less-than-formal environment' is employed to refer to two characteristics of unilateral acts: their lack of a standardised form and the informal processes in which such acts usually originate. To illustrate the added difficulties caused by unilateral acts being formulated in such an environment this study focuses on the problem of establishing the existence of a legal act in general. Thus, comparisons are drawn throughout the book between unilateral acts and international agreements with a particular focus on the factors that may enable the identification of the intention to create legal effects in each case.

8 See *infra* Chapter 6.

9 See *infra* Chapters 4, 5 and 6.

By way of contrast to unilateral acts, this study argues that in modern State-practice the task of establishing the existence of an international agreement is relatively easy. Nowadays most agreements are adopted within such a formal setting of negotiations (and in such a standard form) that there is little doubt as to their legal status. Similarly, the use of standard legal terminology, such as "State-parties agree" or "undertake", as well as the inclusion of dispute settlement clauses facilitate the task of ascertaining the authors' intention to create legally binding obligations.[10] On this basis, the identification of an international instrument as an international agreement, and especially as a multilateral international agreement, does not, as a rule, pose great difficulties. The same does not hold true for unilateral acts. According to the present author, apart from certain types of unilateral acts, such as acts of recognition and protest, whose content and legal effects have been standardised through State-practice, most unilateral acts occur in an environment where standardised form and formality of the creating process are largely absent. Thus, the book claims that in such an informal environment it is necessary to look at the legal and factual context surrounding the act in order to ascertain whether it is, in fact, a unilateral juridical act.

A contextual approach to unilateral acts does not in any way diminish their legal character, but, on the contrary, is a *standard tool for identifying the existence of legal acts in less-than-formal scenarios.*[11] While the intention to create legal effects may be relatively easily identifiable in the majority of international agreements, the situation is different for instruments concluded under less formal circumstances. Context still plays a major role in determining the legal identity of instruments that do not correspond to the archetypal type of agreements often encountered in State-practice, *i.e.* agreements containing express provisions regarding their legal status, agreements which have been drafted in the standard form and language of legal rights and obligations and agreements concluded with the formalities usually reserved for binding legal instruments.

The continuing relevance of the contextual approach adopted by the present author is illustrated by the proliferation of 'soft-law instruments'[12] (instruments of dubious legal status) in modern international State practice. More specifically, the present work takes a closer look at instruments, usually of

10 J. Klabbers, *The Concept of Treaty in International Law*, (The Hague: Kluwer Law International, 1996), p. 72.

11 See *infra* Chapter 5.

12 For a definition of soft-law instruments see generally A. Boyle, Some Reflections on the Relationship of Treaties and Soft Law, 48 *ICLQ* 901 (1999).

bilateral nature, the designation, content and creating process of which, do not readily show whether the instrument was intended to create legal effects. The book argues that international judicial bodies, whenever confronted with instruments of doubtful normative effect, often take into account the context surrounding the creation of these instruments in order to ascertain their legal identity. Chapters 5 and 6 demonstrate that the International Court of Justice, as well as other international courts and tribunals, routinely have recourse to a number of indicators by which they can determine whether a certain instrument is an international agreement. Thus, the book concludes that international legal practice is anything but unfamiliar with the contextual approach employed here.

In addition, this study purports to demonstrate that unilateral acts and international agreements may come under 'international juridical acts' that comprise acts of both bi/multilateral and unilateral origin that express the manifest intention of their author/s to become bound. The aforementioned proliferation of soft law instruments and the declining importance of form and formalities have made the distinction between legal and non-legal acts in international law more important than ever, as this work will reveal. Although some lawyers have attempted to develop a theory of international juridical acts that would facilitate distinction between legal and non-legal acts irrespective of their origin, these attempts have been rather sporadic.[13] Consequently, the theory of international juridical acts remains largely underdeveloped. However, the book maintains that, in practice, international courts and tribunals actually treat unilateral acts and international agreements as two facets of the same phenomenon – international juridical acts. In this way the book proves, with reference to case-law, the continuing relevance of the theory of international juridical acts in determining the legal nature of international acts.

2 Methodology

The book adopts a doctrinal approach, focusing on library-based research.[14] The main sources used are judicial practice and academic literature – although references to relevant State practice have been made, where necessary. This was a deliberate choice – as it will be explained in Chapter 1, the topic has

13 See for example J.H.W. Verzijl, *International Law in a Historical Perspective, Vol. VI: Juridical Facts as Sources of International Rights and Obligations*, (Leiden: Sijtoff, 1973).

14 On methodology see generally R. Cryer, T. Hervey, B. Sokhi-Bulley, *Research Methodologies in EU and International Law*, (Oxford: Hart Publishing, 2011).

sparked strong debate and virtually all instances of unilateral acts in State practice have been controversial.

It is also important to note the frequent reliance on the *Nuclear Tests Case*[15] throughout the book. The numerous references to the Court's judgment does not imply that there are no other occasions in which the Court upheld the binding force of a unilateral act. On the contrary, in a series of subsequent judgments the Court has confirmed that, under certain conditions, unilateral acts may produce legal effects on the international plane.[16] However, as the only judgment in which the Court addressed the question of unilateral acts in international law at length – a fact that has been recognised both in doctrine[17] and in the work of the ILC on the topic[18] – the *Nuclear Tests* judgment is of crucial importance to the theory of unilateral acts. For this reason, the judgment has been given a prominent place in the book.

3 Contribution to International Legal Scholarship

The framework, structure and analysis of this book (hopefully) offer a new and original perspective to the on-going debate concerning unilateral acts. Presently, there are two major conceptual works on unilateral acts; both are books – one, written in French in 1962, by Eric Suy[19] and the other published recently in English by Christian Eckart.[20] There are significant differences between the present work and these two books. Firstly, Suy's work was written in a time when international judicial practice on unilateral acts was very limited. Although some relevant judicial practice existed prior to 1974, the

15 *Nuclear Tests Cases*, Australia vs France, *ICJ Reports* 1974, p. 253; *Nuclear Tests Cases*, New Zealand vs France, *ICJ Reports* 1974, p. 457. The Court's judgements in these two cases are almost identical. Hereinafter, all references made to the *Nuclear Tests Case* will concern the case between Australia and France.

16 See for example the *Case concerning Military and Paramilitary Activities in and against Nicaragua*, *ICJ Reports* 1986, p. 14; the *Case concerning the Frontier Dispute*, *ICJ Reports* 1986, p. 554; and the *Case concerning Armed Activities on the Territory of the Congo (New Application: 2002)*, *ICJ Reports* 2006, p. 1.

17 C. Eckart, *Promises of States under International Law*, (Oxford: Hart Publishing, 2012), p. 12.

18 See Guiding Principle 1, 3, 7 and 10 and the commentaries thereto of the Guiding Principles applicable to unilateral declarations of States capable of creating legal obligations in Report of the ILC on the Work of Its 58th Session, UN Doc. A/61/10, *Yrbk of the ILC* 2006, Vol. II. Hereinafter referred to as the 2006 Guiding Principles.

19 E. Suy, *Les Actes Juridiques Unilateraux en Droit International Public*, (Paris: LGDJ, 1962).

20 C. Eckart, *supra* note 17.

discussion on unilateral acts only really started in earnest after the judgment of the International Court of Justice in the *Nuclear Tests Case*.[21] Consequently, Suy's work is largely theoretical and does not take modern judicial practice into account. By contrast, the present work offers an up-to-date account of all relevant case-law of international courts and tribunals thereby providing a holistic picture of unilateral acts.

Secondly, although Eckart's monograph[22] has provided the most up-to-date examination of the topic thus far, there are three major differences between his book and the work of the present author. First, the two works have a different focus. Eckart's book is focused on unilateral acts as instruments of international rights and obligations and thus, his work, while making references to the legal character of unilateral acts, is broader in scope and covers areas such as revocability, modification and validity of unilateral acts.[23] Conversely, the present study adopts a practical approach and argues that the main problem of unilateral acts is determining whether an act of a seemingly unilateral origin is, in fact, a unilateral act with binding effects on the international plane. For this reason the present study does not merely define the essentials of the legal nature of unilateral acts, but also provides a list of indicators that facilitate the determination of the existence of these elements in any given case. This does not mean that questions of revocability, modification or validity are not important; but simply that, in the opinion of the present author, the International Law Commission has satisfactorily tackled these issues in its work on the topic.[24]

The prominent space the present author affords to the relevant work of the ILC on unilateral acts is a further difference between the present study and Eckart's treatment of the subject. Although Eckart makes some references to the Commission's efforts to codify the legal regime applicable to unilateral acts, his book contains no detailed consideration of the topic. However, the present work contains a specific chapter focused on the work of the ILC and its final product, the 2006 Guiding Principles.[25] The examination contained therein not only elucidates the failings and achievements of the Commission in the area, but also the difficulties faced by the Commission in its decade-long struggle with unilateral acts. Such a searching exposition of the ILC's work is necessary in order to provide a thorough understanding of the reasons

21 *Nuclear Tests Cases*, *supra* note 15.

22 C. Eckart, *supra* note 17.

23 *Ibid.*, pp. 251 *et seq.*

24 See the *Analytical Guide to the Work of the ILC, 1949–1997*, (1998), available at http://untreaty.un.org/ilc/guide/9_9.htm.

25 See the 2006 Guiding Principles, *supra* note 18.

underpinning the weaknesses of the 2006 Guiding Principles. A final difference between the present work and Eckart's book relates to the overall framework of discussion of unilateral acts. The current study aims to place unilateral acts within the general framework of international juridical acts and prove the merits of the relevant theory as a tool for ascertaining the legal nature of acts irrespective of their origin (bi/multilateral or unilateral).

Finally, although Chapter 3 is devoted to providing a detailed account of the relevant work of the ILC, a discussion about the contributions of the present work would not be complete without a brief reference to the differences between the work of the ILC and the present author on the topic. The International Law Commission scrutinised unilateral acts of States for ten years, from 1996 to 2006.[26] Despite the fact that the culmination of the ILC's work was initially envisaged to be the adoption of draft articles, which would then become the basis for a Convention on the subject[27] (much like the Vienna Convention on the Law of Treaties),[28] this did not materialise. Rather, the final product was a set of Guiding Principles applicable to unilateral declarations of States capable of creating legal obligations,[29] which however do not provide practical, detailed instructions regarding the determination of the juridical nature of unilateral acts. The book reviews the relevant work of the ILC and the 2006 Guiding Principles and aims to bridge this gap.

4 Scope and Delimitation of the Study

The topic of unilateral acts of States is vast. The need for clarity (and space limitations) dictates that the subject be delimited from the outset. Chapter 1 will show that unilateral acts pose a number of different problems to international lawyers – such as the source of their binding force, their relation to the recognised sources of international law, and their legal nature. It will be also demonstrated that these problems do not apply to the whole gamut of acts commonly designated as 'unilateral' in practice. More particularly, it will be shown that unilateral acts based on pre-existing norms of customary or treaty law are not problematic because they are formulated within well-known legal

26 *Analytical Guide*, *supra* note 24.

27 See the ILC's mandate to assist in the codification of unilateral acts in GA, Res. 51/160, UN Doc. A/RES/51/160 (1997).

28 *Vienna Convention on the Law of Treaties*, 22 May 1969, Vienna, 1155 UNTS 331, 8 ILM 679 (1969).

29 See the 2006 Guiding Principles, *supra* note 18.

regimes (customary or treaty law). Therefore, any questions relating to their binding nature or to the source of their legal force may be answered by having recourse to the rules applicable to that regime. For this reason, unilateral acts that are formulated in execution of a treaty provision or on the basis of a customary rule will not be the primary focus of the present work. Rather, Chapter 1 will demonstrate that, in practice, problems mainly arise in relation to unilateral acts that are not themselves mandated or otherwise permitted by other pre-existing legal obligations of either treaty or customary law character. Henceforth, these acts shall be called 'voluntary acts' and the exploration of their legal nature, namely the conditions under which they may produce legal effects on the international plane, will be the main focus of the remainder of this book.

Furthermore, the present work is limited to unilateral, voluntary acts of States. Consequently, unilateral acts of non-State entities, such as international organisations, individuals or groups, will not be examined. Although such acts are excluded from the purview of this study, it does not mean that international organisations do not possess the power to formulate unilateral acts with legal effects on the international plane or that such acts are of minor importance.[30] However, there are substantial differences between unilateral acts performed by international organisations and unilateral acts performed by States and therefore, the two categories of acts should be studied separately.

More specifically, while the rules regulating the formulation of unilateral acts of States are based on general international law, when it comes to international organisations, the rules applicable to their unilateral acts are contained in the constituent treaties of such organisations or in instruments based on such treaties.[31] In his first report (in which the exclusion of unilateral acts of international organisations from the ambit of the ILC's work was proposed) the Special Rapporteur stated:

> In all such cases, the unilateral acts concerned are performed as a result of the competence which States themselves have conferred on the body and of which they may become the object. Unilateral authoritative acts, which continue to be important in international law, are regulated by the law peculiar to each international organization or body.[32]

---

30 See generally, M. Virally, *Unilateral Acts of International Organisations*, in M. Bedjaoui (ed.), *International Law: Achievements and Prospects*, (Paris: UNESCO, 1991), p. 241.

31 V. Rodríguez Cedeño, First Report on Unilateral Acts of States, UN Doc. A/CN.4/486, p. 319, paras. 33–4.

32 *Ibid.*, para. 38.

While virtually all other attempts to delimit the topic were met with fierce criticism, it is worth noting that, there was general agreement with the Special Rapporteur's decision to exclude unilateral acts of international organisations.[33]

Unilateral acts of other non-State entities are also excluded from the scope of this study. Unlike international organisations, there is little evidence to suggest that other non-State actors, such as individuals or groups, have the capacity to create legal effects on the international plane by means of unilateral acts in the same way that States do. Rather, in the view of this author, the pronouncement of the Permanent Court in the *Wimbledon Case*[34] that the right to enter into international engagements is an attribute of State sovereignty[35] is also applicable to obligations that originate from unilateral acts. Accepting the possibility that non-State entities can create rights and obligations through their unilateral acts would, in turn, mean acknowledging that these entities have a law-making role in international law – something recognised neither by international judicial practice,[36] nor by the opinion of the majority of scholars.[37] However, it should be noted that there is an on-going debate regarding the binding effects of unilateral declarations in which non-State armed groups indicate their agreement to abide by international humanitarian law obligations.[38] Although it has been suggested that there are potential advantages in

---

33 Report of the ILC on the Work of Its 50th session, UN Doc. A/53/10, *Yrbk of the ILC* 1998, Vol. II, p. 54, para. 153.

34 *Case of the S.S. "Wimbledon"*, *PCIJ Series A*, 1923, No. 1, p. 14.

35 *Ibid.*, p. 25.

36 See for example the Judgment of the Special Court for Sierra Leone in *Proseutor v. Kallon and Kamara*, Case No. SCSL-2004-15-AR72(E) and SCSL-2004-16-AR72(E), Appeals Chamber, Decision on Challenge to Jurisdiction: Lome Accord Amnesty, 13 March 2004, available at http://www.transcrim.org/07%20SCSL%20-%202004%20-%20Kallon%20 Kamara, paras. 45–50, in which the Court stated that an agreement between the Government of Sierra Leone and the Revolutionary United Front was not an international agreement because it was signed between a State and an armed groups. See more case-law cited in S. Sivakumaran, *The Law of Non-International Armed Conflict*, (Oxford: Oxford University Press, 2012), p. 109.

37 See generally K. Parlett, *The Individual in the International Legal System: Continuity and Change in International law*, (Cambridge: Cambridge University Press, 2011), pp. 324–5, where it is stated that non-State entities may have rights and obligations in international law only if and to the extent that those rights and obligations are created or recognised by States. See also R. Higgins, *Problems and Process: International Law and How We Use It*, (Oxford: Clarendon Press, 1994), p. 39. See *contra* R. McCorquodale, An Inclusive International Legal System, 17 *LJIL* 477 (2004).

38 S. Sivakumaran, *supra* note 36, pp. 113 *et seq.*

recognising such declarations as binding upon their authors,[39] it is generally acknowledged that their legal status is far from settled.[40] Such declarations will not be examined in this book due to the uncertainty as to whether declarations issued by non-State armed groups are indeed binding.

5 Structure

The present book consists of eight chapters. Chapter 1 examines the main problems pertaining to unilateral acts of States. It is shown that there is inconsiderable literature on the subject and that the existing literature has chiefly focused on the problem of conceptualizing unilateral acts within the framework of the modern doctrine on the sources of international law. It is also demonstrated that the attempts to solve the problem of the relation between unilateral acts and the sources of international law have been misguided to the extent that they do not take into account, and do not provide answers to, the preliminary problem of the legal nature of such acts. Furthermore, it is asserted that only by answering the question of the legal nature of unilateral acts (whether and under which circumstances such acts may produce legal effects on the international plane) one can provide a satisfactory answer to the question of the interplay between unilateral acts and the sources of international law. Therefore, the rest of the book will focus on solving the problem of the legal nature of unilateral acts.

Chapter 2 focuses on the classification of unilateral acts, as well as with questions of definition. The chapter begins by exploring different definitions of unilateral acts, concluding that the existing definitions are too narrow. Against this background, a definition of unilateral acts based on the elements comprising the legal nature of such acts, as these elements have been identified in judicial practice (unilateralism and the intention to become bound) is propounded. The chapter continues by exploring different classifications of unilateral acts to be found in the literature. The exploration of different typologies serves to acquaint the reader with the various types of unilateral acts and thus, put the discussion into context. Here, a number of different criteria for classification are critically analysed with an aim to arriving at a typology that best reflects the variety of content, effects, and legal environments in which such acts occur in practice. In this respect, it is argued that a classification on

39 A. Roberts, S. Sivakumaran, Lawmaking by Nonstate Actors: Engaging Armed groups in the creation of International Humanitarian Law, 37 *Yale J. Int'l L.* 108 (2011) at pp. 126–32.

40 *Ibid.*, p. 115; S. Sivakumaran, *supra* note 36, p. 109.

the basis of the legal context in which unilateral acts take place is preferable since it not only takes into account the circumstances surrounding the origins of the act but also the relevant rules of law.

Chapter 3 examines the work of the International Law Commission on the topic. In this chapter, the reports of the Special Rapporteur, the ensuing debate within the International Law Commission, as well as the final product (the 2006 Guiding Principles) are introduced, analysed and evaluated. It will be shown that, despite the commendable efforts of the Special Rapporteur and the Commission, the Guiding Principles adopted by the ILC fall short of providing genuine, practical guidance on distinguishing between juridical and political acts of unilateral origin. It is argued that this in turn necessitates the re-examination of the topic beyond the work of the ILC.

Chapter 4 explores the first of the elements of the legal nature of unilateral acts – unilateralism. This chapter examines the unilateral nature of acts commonly designated as 'unilateral' in practice with a view to establish a criterion for distinguishing between acts that are genuinely of unilateral nature and acts that may appear unilateral in form, but are in essence of a contractual character. It is argued that 'unilateralism' can be defined as the autonomy of the act to produce legal effects irrespective of any kind of acceptance or reliance on behalf of the addressee. Furthermore, the chapter analyses the relevant State and judicial practice and provides a list of indicators to facilitate the determination of the strictly unilateral nature of an act in practice. These include taking into account the existence of a treaty law context, of a rule that requires reciprocity, of a context of negotiations, of a pattern of offer/acceptance and of circumstances that would preclude the conclusion of an international agreement.

Chapters 5 and 6 enquire into the juridical nature of unilateral acts in order to identify a criterion for distinguishing between unilateral legal acts and unilateral acts with no legal effects on the international plane. It will be argued that the manifest intention of the author State to become bound is the determinant factor in conferring binding effects on an act – irrespective of its origin. Chapter 6 examines the relevant case-law and provides a list of indicators of the manifest intent to become bound that would assist the determination of the legal character of a unilateral act in practice. These include: the content of the act, its publicity, the forum in which the act was made and the authority who made the act on behalf of the State. This chapter will also identify two important similarities between unilateral acts and international agreements. It will be demonstrated that the same criterion for ascertaining their legal character (manifest intention to be bound) and the same means of ascertaining the existence of that criterion (interpretation of the act in accordance with its content and with the circumstances surrounding its making) is applicable to both unilateral acts and international agreements. On this basis, it is claimed that unilateral acts and international agreements are two aspects of the same phenomenon, namely that of international juridical acts.

Against this background, Chapters 7 and 8 deal with two specific types of unilateral acts, the legal nature of which remains highly controversial in the literature: unilateral declarations of independence and unilateral security assurances. Chapter 7 examines unilateral declarations of independence and argues that these declarations are legally neutral acts – an argument that comports both with the factual nature of the creation of States under international law and with relevant State practice. Chapter 8 discusses positive and negative security assurances provided in the form of unilateral undertakings. These assurances are tested against the background of the doctrine of unilateral juridical acts and it is argued that, despite their shortcomings in terms of scope and content, such assurances may be considered as binding undertakings to the extent that they express the manifest intention of their authors to become bound thereby. The final chapter of the book draws together the threads from earlier chapters, summarizing the main findings of the study.

CHAPTER 1

Prolegomena to a Discussion of Unilateral Juridical Acts in International Law

1 Introduction

This chapter will provide the canvas for the discussion of unilateral acts that will follow in the subsequent chapters and has three basic aims. First, it sets out to introduce the range of unilateral acts that will be the subject of the present study. It will be shown that the term 'unilateral', far from denoting a carefully delimited legal concept, has been used to collectively describe a large number of heterogeneous acts that exist in almost every field of international activity and constitute an important tool of modern State interaction. Secondly, the chapter will identify the specific problems pertaining to these acts in international law. In this respect, it will be asserted that, up until now, international lawyers have primarily engaged with unilateral acts insofar as to tackle the problem of the interplay of such acts with the recognised sources of international law. It is claimed that this problem cannot be satisfactorily resolved without first addressing the preliminary question of the legal nature of unilateral acts, namely the question as to whether and under which circumstances these acts may produce legal effects. Thirdly, this chapter purports to provide a brief summary of the main approaches to the problems relating to unilateral acts and to question whether and to what extent the already existing literature provides satisfactory solutions to these problems. For reasons of convenience and clarity, the various approaches will be divided in two categories according to the stance their authors adopt regarding the question whether or not unilateral acts constitute a new source of law – believers and deniers. It will be claimed that both believers and deniers are susceptible to the same mistake; attempting to provide an answer to the question of the interaction between unilateral acts and the sources of international law without first delimiting the legal nature of such acts. On this basis, it will be concluded that neither the former nor the latter may give an accurate account of the state of the law in relation to the realities on the ground of international practice and this, in turn, necessitates a re-examination of the topic.

 | DOI 10.1163/9789004300767_003

2 The Canvas: Unilateral Acts in International State and Judicial Practice

In international law, States frequently perform acts that, while not leading to the establishment of agreements, have important consequences on the international plane. Such acts are commonly described in theory as 'unilateral acts' and some examples of unilateral acts would include acts of recognition of Statehood, acts leading to the formation of customary rules, acts concerning the territorial status of a State, such as delimitation of the territorial sea or of the continental shelf, declarations of war, or of neutrality and declarations made under Art. 36.2 of the ICJ Statute.

Apart from these standardised forms in which unilateral acts commonly appear, a series of other instances have featured in the writings of several authors as unilateral legal acts, a term used to denote any act of unilateral origin that has legal effects on the international plane.[1] These include: the 1957 Egyptian declaration concerning the Suez Canal;[2] the declarations made by Albania, Latvia and Lithuania on the protection of minorities in their respective territories prior to their admission to the League of Nations;[3] the 1939 declarations of guarantee made by the UK regarding Greece and Romania;[4] the Chinese declarations concerning the railway rights of China and Japan in Manchuria;[5] and a number of negative security assurances given by nuclear weapon States.[6] Of course, there are also unilateral acts pertaining to the law of treaties, such as reservations, interpretative declarations, ratification, signature, and accession among others.

In terms of international jurisprudence, on a number of occasions both the PCIJ and the ICJ have acknowledged that unilateral acts may, under certain

1 V. Rodríguez Cedeño, First Report on Unilateral Acts of States, UN Doc. A/CN.4/486, p. 319, p. 332, para. 105.

2 M. Whiteman, *Digest of International Law*, Vol. III, (Washington D.C.: US Govt. Print. Off., 1963), pp. 1123–6.

3 K. Skubiszewski, *Unilateral Acts of States*, in M. Bedjaoui (ed.), *International Law: Achievements and Prospects*, (Paris: UNESCO, 1991), p. 225.

4 W. Fiedler, Unilateral Acts in International Law, in R. Berhardt (ed.), *Encyclopedia of Public International Law*, Vol. IV, (Amsterdam, Oxford: North-Holland, 1984), p. 1019.

5 T. Franck, Word Made Law: The Decision Of the ICJ in The Nuclear Tests Case, 69 *AJIL* 612 (1975), p. 615.

6 A. Rosas, Negative Security Assurances and Non-Use of Nuclear Weapons, 25 *Germ. Yrb. I.L.* 199 (1982), p. 208.

conditions, produce legal effects, for example in the *Eastern Greenland Case*[7] and, more importantly, in the *Nuclear Tests Case*.[8] More recent case-law of the World Court has confirmed the existence of a phenomenon such as unilateral acts with binding effects. In the *Nicaragua Case*,[9] in the *Frontier Dispute Case*[10] and more recently in the *Case concerning Armed Activities on the Territory of the Congo*,[11] the ICJ unequivocally asserted that legal relations may be borne out of acts of unilateral origin. Thus, it seems that international law, both in terms of judicial and State-practice is anything but unfamiliar with the concept of 'unilateral acts.'

Notwithstanding this, the question of the role of such acts in international law has remained unanswered. Although some important doctrinal works on the subject have been published over the years,[12] the legal regime applicable to these acts has not yet been clearly demarcated. As a result, the theory of unilateral acts is considerably underdeveloped in relation to the theory of international agreements. It should be also noted that the ILC struggled for nearly ten years to produce a draft convention codifying the rules applicable to unilateral acts of States.[13] As it will be explained in detail in the third chapter, irreconcilable tensions between the members of the Commission led to the abandonment of the codification project in 2006. Instead, the ILC adopted a set of Guiding Principles applicable to unilateral declarations of States capable of creating legal obligations.[14] However, as it will be argued in the relevant chapter, the 2006 Guiding Principles are of limited assistance in determining the legal nature of a unilateral act in practice.

---

7 *Legal Status of Eastern Greenland Case*, *PCIJ Series A/B*, 1933, No. 53, p. 22.

8 *Nuclear Tests Cases*, Australia vs France, *ICJ Reports* 1974, p. 253, New Zealand vs France, *ICJ Reports* 1974, p. 457. The Court's judgments in these two cases are almost identical. Hereinafter, unless otherwise stated, all references made to the *Nuclear Tests Case* will concern the case between Australia and France.

9 *Case concerning Military and Paramilitary Activities in and against Nicaragua*, Merits, *ICJ Reports* 1986, p. 14.

10 *Case concerning the Frontier Dispute*, *ICJ Reports* 1986, p. 554.

11 *Case concerning Armed Activities on the Territory of the Congo* (*New Application: 2002*), *ICJ Reports* 2006, p. 1.

12 E. Suy, *Les Actes Juridiques Unilateraux en Droit International Public*, (Paris: LGDJ, 1962); C. Eckart, *Promises of States under International Law*, (Oxford: Hart Publishing, 2012).

13 For an analytical guide on the work of the ILC on the topic of Unilateral Acts, see generally *Analytical Guide to the Work of the ILC, 1949–1997*, (1998), available at http://untreaty.un.org/ilc/guide/9_9.htm.

14 See the Guiding Principles applicable to unilateral declarations of States capable of creating legal obligations in Report of the ILC on the Work of Its 58th Session, UN Doc. A/61/10, *Yrbk of the ILC* 2006, Vol. II.

The evolution of a coherent doctrine on unilateral acts has also been hindered by the lack of a generally agreed definition. Currently, there is no international treaty defining unilateral acts. Similarly, no definition is to be found in customary international law. This has adversely affected the uniform treatment of the phenomenon by international lawyers, a number of whom, as it will be shown below, have questioned the very existence of unilateral acts as a legal institution.

A further hindrance to the development of the doctrine of unilateral legal acts is their heterogeneity. As the above examples show, unilateral acts exist in different fields of international activity and are used by States in very diverse contexts. A State may use a unilateral act to protest against the conduct of another State, to convey its intention to become bound by an international treaty, to undertake an obligation *vis-à-vis* another State/s, to recognise the existence of an entity as a sovereign State, or simply to score a point in the international political arena. Such difficulties have made international lawyers to treat unilateral acts more conveniently in the area of law in which they occur rather than as a separate genre of acts.[15] Nevertheless, and despite the way in which one chooses to deal with them, the fact remains that such acts pose a number of important problems for international lawyers. The next part of this chapter will discuss a number of problems that have been identified in theory as pertaining to unilateral acts.

3 The Problem of the Interplay between Unilateral Acts and the Recognized Sources of International Law

A review of the modern literature on unilateral acts reveals that they are mostly discussed in relation to the sources of international law.[16] More particularly, the problem of the basis of the binding force of the Ihlen Declaration in the context of the *Eastern Greenland Case*[17] and of the French statements in the *Nuclear Tests Case*[18] has sparked a fierce debate in the literature[19] about the

15 J. Crawford, *Brownlie's Principles of Public International Law*, 8th ed., (Oxford: Oxford University Press, 2012), p. 415.

16 See for example D.J. Harris, *Cases and Materials on International Law*, 7th ed., (London: Sweet & Maxwell, 2010), p. 49; M. Shaw, *International Law*, 7th ed., (Cambridge: Cambridge University Press, 2014), pp. 86–7.

17 *Eastern Greenland Case, supra* note 7.

18 *Nuclear Tests Case, supra* note 8.

19 See for example A. Pellet, *Article 38*, in A. Zimmermann, C. Tomuschat, K. Oelles- Frahm (eds.), *The Statute of The International Court of Justice: A Commentary*, 2nd ed., (Oxford:

possibility of such acts being sources of law outside Art. 38 of the ICJ Statute.[20] This part of the chapter endeavours to examine the relevant debate and elucidate how international lawyers have perceived the problem of the interplay between these acts and the recognized sources of international law as the key issue involving unilateral acts.

For this purpose, this section begins by introducing the debate about the extent to which Art. 38 of the ICJ Statute contains an exhaustive list of the sources of international law. Then, the Ihlen Declaration and the 1974 French statements will be briefly discussed in order to provide a practical understanding of the problems encountered in attempting to explain the source of their binding force by having recourse to the sources listed in Art. 38. The section concludes with an analysis of the already existing literature on the subject with a view to enquire whether and to what extent the aforementioned questions have been tackled.

3.1 *Sources of International Law and Art. 38.1 of the Statute of the International Court of Justice*

The term 'sources of the law' has been used with varying meanings in legal literature[21] and thus, any discussion about the sources requires that issues of terminology be settled from the outset. Since a detailed exposition of the varied concepts that have, at times, been described as 'sources of the law' would be beyond the ambit of the present chapter, it suffices here to note that the term in question has been mainly used to designate the following: at first, as Bos observes, the term may be used to designate the "recognized manifestations of law."[22] In other words, sources of the law are all the forms in which the law may become apparent in a given legal system.[23] Secondly, the term is used in the literature to connote the procedures and/or methods for the creation of legal rules.[24] Although both definitions are relevant, the term 'sources of the law' will be mainly used here in the latter sense.

Oxford University Press, 2012), p. 730, at pp. 763–7; A. Rubin, The International Legal Effects of Unilateral Declarations, 71 *AJIL* 1 (1977).

20 *Statute of the International Court of Justice*, 26 June 1945, San Francisco, available at http://www.icj-cij.org/documents/index.php?p1=4&p2=2&p3=0.

21 For the different meanings of the term sources, see for example, G.J.H. Van Hoof, *Rethinking the Sources of International Law*, (Deventer: Kluwer, 1983), pp. 57–60.

22 M.S. Bos, *A Methodology of International Law*, (Amsterdam: T.M.C. Asser Institute, 1984), p. 49.

23 *Ibid.*, pp. 48–51.

24 V.D. Degan, *Sources of International Law*, (The Hague: M. Nijhoff Publishers, 1997), p. 1. (See particularly fn. 1).

The question of the sources of the law lies at the heart of every legal system. In the absence of this concept, the whole existence of a legal system as a system, in the sense of an organized whole that may develop and adapt to changing circumstances, would be questionable. More particularly, in the absence of the concept of the sources, the law would be a body of random rules, which once distanced from the social and political circumstances that generated them, would be of no use to problem-solving in a rapidly changing international arena.[25] Furthermore, in the absence of a comprehensive list enumerating the ways in which a legal rule may come into being, the distinction between law and other disciplines, such as philosophy, morality and religion, would collapse, since it would not be possible to establish the validity of a norm *qua* legal norm.[26]

The question of the sources of the law is also central to the international legal system. Arguably, identifying the sources of the law in the international legal system is even more complex than identifying them in national legal systems since the latter benefit from the existence of central legislative authorities. Thus, while legislation or judicial decisions provide the sources of the law in municipal legal orders, in international law, the absence of a central legislative authority makes matters infinitely more complicated. As Higgins observes: "But we have become so preoccupied with jurisprudential debate about the sources of international law, that we have, I think, lost sight of the fact that it is an admission of an uncertainty at the heart of the international legal system."[27]

It has become almost sacrosanct to refer to Art. 38.1 of the ICJ Statute as the starting point in every discussion on the sources of international law. Art. 38, which repeats verbatim Art. 38 of the 1920 Statute of the Permanent Court of International Justice,[28] enumerates international agreements, custom and general principles of law as the main sources that the Court is called to apply in its decisions, while the teachings of the most qualified scholars and judicial decisions feature in the text of the article as subsidiary sources.

The literature on Art. 38, and more generally on the sources of international law, is vast and the topic remains one of the most fiercely debated in theory. One of the perennial questions surrounding Art. 38 is whether the list of

25 R. Higgins, *Problems and Process: International Law and How We Use It*, (Oxford: Clarendon Press, 1994), p. 3.

26 H.L.A. Hart, *The Concept of Law*, 2nd ed., (Oxford: Oxford University Press, 1961), pp. 13–5.

27 R. Higgins, *supra* note 25, p. 17.

28 *Statute of the Permanent Court of International Justice*, 16 December 1920, available at www.worldcourts.com/pcij/eng/documents/1920.12.16_statute.htm#_Toc160729737.

sources enumerated therein is exhaustive or not.[29] On the face of it, Art. 38 merely lists the sources that the ICJ is bound to apply in exercising its judicial functions and its wording does not allude to any sort of 'constitutional' declaration of the formal sources of international law. Nevertheless, it is widely held that the list of Art. 38 is "authoritative in general because it represents State-practice."[30]

However, to claim that international society has not changed since 1920, when the earliest form of Art. 38 first made its appearance in the international arena, would be absurd. On the contrary, change has been the only constant in the time elapsed between the early 20th and the early 21st century. More specifically, the scope of international law has been constantly expanding in order to accommodate a number of significant developments in international relations including the emergence of numerous new States in the aftermath of the decolonisation period, the emergence of non-State entities as international actors, such as international institutions and to a lesser extent individuals, as well as the increased concern about human rights and the environment. As a result, a number of specialised rules have been created and developed in order to regulate all these new areas of global activity. Whilst the substantive aspects of these developments have been discussed by and large in modern literature, their impact on the classic conceptions of law-making is far from certain.

Thus, on the one hand, a number of authors have suggested that international law has developed significantly since 1920 and such developments are not reflected in Art. 38.[31] On the other hand, changes in the international scenery do not necessarily imply an automatic change or addition of new sources. One could viably claim, and indeed many international lawyers have, that despite the ever-changing nature of the international world, the list of Art. 38 of the ICJ Statute continues to represent an exhaustive statement of the sources of international law.[32] Despite the position one adopts with respect to the completeness of Art. 38 of the ICJ Statute, authors of both schools of thought generally accept that resolutions of international organizations and unilateral acts of States are the most prominent candidates for the title of 'new sources of international law.' While there is a large amount of literature

29 G. Danilenko, *Law-Making in the International Community*, (London: M. Nijhoff, 1993), pp. 37–40.

30 R. Jennings, A. Watts (eds.), *Oppenheim's International Law*, Vol. 1: Peace, 9th ed., (London: Longman, 1992), p. 24.

31 See for example, A. Pellet, *supra* note 19, p. 763.

32 See for example H. Thirlway, *The Sources of International Law*, in M. Evans (ed.), *International Law*, 4th ed., (Oxford: Oxford University Press, 2014), p. 91, at p. 95.

regarding resolutions of international organizations, the same does not hold true for unilateral acts.

3.2 *The Problematic Relation between the Source/s of the Binding Force of Unilateral Acts and Art. 38.1 of the ICJ Statute: Some Examples from Judicial Practice*

Against this background, this section exemplifies the hurdles and frustrations of attempting to attribute the binding force of some unilateral acts to one of the sources enumerated in Art. 38.1 of the ICJ Statute. The exposition of these problems will facilitate a better understanding of the rationale underpinning proposals to treat unilateral acts as an independent source of international law.

A The Enigma of the Ihlen Declaration in the Context of the *Eastern Greenland Case*

The case concerned a dispute between Denmark and Norway over the sovereignty of Eastern Greenland.[33] In this case, the Permanent Court of Justice was, among others, faced with the question of the legal status of a Declaration made by the Norwegian Minister of Foreign Affairs, Mr. Ihlen, to his Danish Counterpart in the context of negotiations regarding the disputed territory. The Court found that it was: "...beyond all dispute that a reply of this nature given by the Minister of Foreign Affairs on behalf of his Government in response to a request by the diplomatic representative of a foreign Power, in regard to a question falling within his province, is binding upon the country to which the Minister belongs."[34] Thus, the Court concluded that, on the basis of this oral undertaking, Norway was obliged to refrain from contesting Danish sovereignty over the whole of Greenland.[35]

However, on the basis of the relevant dictum, the grounds upon which the binding nature of the declaration was based are not readily apparent. While the Court considered it "beyond all dispute" that the statement made by Mr. Ihlen created an obligation incumbent upon Norway, no formal source of the obligation was mentioned in the text of the judgment.

---

33 For a detailed account of the history of the dispute between Denmark and Norway over Greenland as well as of the claims advanced by the parties, see generally L. Preuss, The Dispute Between Norway and Denmark Over the Sovereignty of Eastern Greenland, 26 *AJIL* 469 (1932).

34 *Eastern Greenland Case*, *supra* note 7, p. 70.

35 *Ibid.*

Apart from the vagueness of the judgment itself, unravelling the enigma of the legal effects attributed to Ihlen's Declaration on the basis of the list of sources enumerated in Art. 38 of the Statute of the PCIJ[36] is also problematic. The binding character of the Ihlen Declaration does not seem, on the face of it at least, to result from the application either of a customary rule, or of a general principle. Furthermore, although the Declaration is widely cited as an example of an oral agreement,[37] this view is also problematic insofar as the Court made it tolerably clear that no bilateral engagement was created.[38] While the existence of a context of negotiations may cast some doubt upon the value of the *Eastern Greenland* judgment as one involving unilateral acts, in the *Nuclear Tests Case*, the problem of the source of the binding nature of unilateral acts is inescapable.

B The Enigma of the Statements made by France in the Context of the *Nuclear Tests Case*

The *Nuclear Tests Case*[39] involved a dispute concerning the holding of atmospheric nuclear tests by France in the region of the South Pacific. In 1973, the governments of New Zealand and Australia instituted proceedings against France before the International Court of Justice. Both applicants asked the Court not only for a declaration regarding the illegality of the tests in question, but also for a declaration specifying that the respondent was under an obligation to discontinue them.[40]

However, instead of dealing with the vexed question of the legality of holding nuclear tests, the Court took an altogether different route. Having taken into account a series of statements indicating the willingness of France to cease the tests in questions, made extrajudicially by French authorities, and having analysed the legal principles involved it concluded that the object of the dispute had become moot.[41] The ICJ reached this conclusion by interpreting the French statements as binding undertakings on behalf of France to

---

36 See Art. 38 of the *Statute of the Permanent Court of International Justice, supra* note 28.

37 See for example the literature cited in S. Wittich, *The PCIJ and the Modern International Law of Treaties*, in C. Tams, M. Fitzmaurice (eds.), *Legacies of the Permanent Court of International Justice*, (Dordrecht: M. Nijhoff, 2013), p. 89, at p. 117, fn. 130.

38 *Eastern Greenland Case, supra* note 7, p. 52.

39 *Nuclear Tests Case, supra* note 8.

40 The correct interpretation of the submissions made in the *Nuclear Tests Cases* for the purpose of ascertaining the true object and purpose of the applicants' claim is a highly contentious matter and one of the main reasons of dissent by Judges Onyema, Dillard, Arechaga and Waldock.

41 *Nuclear Tests Case, supra* note 8, p. 272.

cease the tests in question.[42] In one of its most controversial dicta, the Court stated that "it is well recognised that declarations made by way of unilateral acts, concerning legal or factual situations, may have the effect of creating legal obligations."[43]

What was the formal source of France's obligation? From an initial reading of the case, no source enumerated in Art. 38 of the Court's Statute seems to be directly relevant. First, no treaty relationship existed between the State undertaking the obligation and the beneficiary States; the Court, when upholding the binding character of the French statements, made it clear that these undertaking were of a strictly unilateral nature.[44] Furthermore, even if one postulates the French statements as an offer for the conclusion of an international agreement, the response of the applicants may not, by any stretch of the imagination, be construed as acceptance thereof. Far from accepting the French statements as having settled the dispute, both Australia and New Zealand expressed their doubts regarding their binding nature.[45] On the other hand, the possibility of the Court having relied upon a customary rule seems equally remote, since the Court did not prove the existence of such a rule. In the same vein, the Court does not seem to have relied upon a general principle in order to justify the effects attributed to the French statements.

3.3 *Overview of the Relevant Literature*

A Deniers: Rubin and Thirlway

In his commentary to the ICJ's judgment in the *Nuclear Tests Case*, Rubin[46] dismissed the whole concept of unilateral legal acts on the ground that, in reality, international law does not attribute any binding force to such acts. More specifically, he argued that prior to the Court's ruling there was no real support either in State practice or in theory for the proposition that unilateral acts may, under certain conditions, create legal effects.[47] On this basis, Rubin went on to

42 *Ibid.*, pp. 268–70.

43 *Ibid.*, p. 267, para. 43.

44 *Ibid.*, para. 43.

45 *Ibid.*

46 A. Rubin, *supra* note 19.

47 *Ibid.*, p. 24. As seen above, the same author denied that the relevant instances of 'unilateral acts' in the earlier case-law of the PCIJ constituted valid examples of unilateral legal acts as those were described by the ICJ in the *Nuclear Tests Case*. In Rubin's opinion, the binding effects of all those early examples may be more conveniently explained by having recourse to other legal phenomena, such as treaties, estoppel etc. The same opinion is also shared by D.J. Harris: "There seems little evidence to support the rule stated by the Court whereby a state may be bound by a unilateral public pronouncement intended by

suggest that the decision of the Court was *ultra vires*.[48] More particularly, he argued that none of the sources of international law enumerated in Art. 38.1 of the Court's Statute may be used in order to justify the binding force attributed to unilateral acts, since no evidence of a rule to the effect that the Court propounded in the *Nuclear Tests Case* may be found in either customary law, or in any applicable treaty, or, indeed, in any general principle of law.[49] Thus, in his opinion, by upholding the binding force of unilateral acts and by considering this concept applicable to the case, the Court used a source of law not enumerated in Art. 38.1 of its Statute.[50] On this basis, Rubin concluded that the Court violated its obligation under the Statute to decide the cases submitted to it exclusively in accordance with the sources contained therein.[51]

The same opinion, although expressed in milder terms, has been shared by Hugh Thirlway. Using the same case as a framework for discussing the concept of unilateral acts, Thirlway points to its exceptional character. In his opinion, the Court in the *Nuclear Tests Case* wished to settle the dispute without having to rule on the politically sensitive question of the legality of the nuclear tests under customary international law.[52] In the same vein as Rubin, Thirlway considers one of the most controversial aspects of the case to be the formal source of the obligations that the Court found incumbent upon France. In the absence of any direct link between those obligations and any of the recognised sources of international law, Thirlway questioned whether unilateral acts might be regarded as a new source of law.[53] The author answered this to the negative. More particularly, Thirlway maintained that, under normal circumstances, unilateral acts create no legal effects of their own accord.[54] International State practice shows that the normal consequence of a unilateral act is either that the act will be accepted by the State to which it is addressed and thus, it will

it to be binding without more." See D.J. Harris, *Cases and Materials on International Law*, 6th ed., (London: Sweet & Maxwell, 2004), p. 798. (However, it is interesting to compare this to the relevant passage in the latest edition of Harris' textbook: " Although there was at the time little evidence to support it, the rule stated by the Court whereby a State may be bound by a unilateral public pronouncement intended by it to be binding without more has now taken root." D.J. Harris, *supra* note 16, p. 49.)

48 A. Rubin, *ibid.*, p. 28.

49 *Ibid.*

50 *Ibid.*, p. 29.

51 *Ibid.*

52 H. Thirlway, *supra* note 32, p. 112. See also H. Thirlway, *The Sources of International Law*, (Oxford: Oxford University Press, 2014), p. 51.

53 *Ibid.*

54 *Ibid.*

become the basis for an agreement, or that the act will be ignored and thus it will produce no effects.[55] Therefore, to generalise and create a theory on unilateral acts based on the *Nuclear Tests Case* would not be, in Thirlway's view, an approach reflecting the reality of international State practice.

In light of the above, it becomes apparent that both Rubin's and Thirlway's criticism of the *Nuclear Test* judgment is focused on the problems arising from the application of the modern doctrine on the sources of international law to unilateral acts. Rubin and Thirlway were primarily concerned with the question of the formal source of France's obligations to cease the nuclear tests in the South-Pacific region. Both lawyers approached this question by following a rigid approach to the sources of international law, which may be summarised as follows: in their opinion, the first paragraph of Art. 38 of the ICJ Statute represents a complete and exhaustive list of the sources of international law.[56] Thus, both lawyers consider the assertions that Art. 38 represents an out-of-date catalogue of sources ill founded.[57] In their view, all 'candidates' for new sources of international law are conceptually derived from other recognised sources and thus, they do not constitute a new source of law, but merely prove the widening scope of the already existing sources.[58] Following this approach means that no obligations may result for States from sources other than those listed in Art. 38.

B Believers: Pellet and Virally

By way of contrast to Rubin and Thirlway, other international lawyers, such as Pellet, have accepted the possibility that new sources of international law have come into existence since the adoption of the ICJ Statute. According to Pellet, the Court takes cognizance of and relies on sources other than those listed in Art. 38.1 of its Statute – and more particularly on unilateral acts of States and international organisations – in its practice.[59] Similarly, Virally argues that: "Article 38 of the Statute of the International Court does not list unilateral acts of states among the sources of law it enumerates. But this does not mean that such acts cannot give rise to international rules of law."[60] According to Virally, in most cases, unilateral acts are discussed in the context of the other two

55 *Ibid.*

56 *Ibid.*, p. 119; A. Rubin, *supra* note 19, pp. 28–9.

57 *Ibid.*

58 *Ibid.*

59 A. Pellet, *supra* note 19, p. 763.

60 M. Virally, *The Sources of International Law*, in M. Sorensen (ed.), *Manual of Public International Law*, (London: Macmillan, 1968), p. 116 at p. 154.

major sources of international law – custom and international agreements[61] – in the sense that, in most cases, unilateral acts pertain either to the application of a customary rule, or to the creation, performance or termination of an international agreement. However, Virally also acknowledges that, in some cases, unilateral acts have an independent legal significance for the author State, as is the case with acts of recognition or acts of renunciation, as well as with acts by which a State directly undertakes an international obligation.[62] Thus, both Pellet and Virally view unilateral acts as sources of international law existing independently of Art. 38 of the ICJ Statute.[63]

4 The Unresolved Problem of the Legal Nature of Unilateral Acts

The foregoing exposition showed that the modern debate on unilateral acts largely revolves around the question of the relationship between such acts and Art. 38.1 of the ICJ Statute. According to which side of the argument they fall on, international lawyers may be classed as either believers or deniers of the status of such acts as independent sources of international law. However, exactly which acts do these lawyers have in mind when they defend or deny the character of unilateral acts as an independent source of the law?

Given the variety of unilateral acts, the problem of the relation between these acts and the sources of international law does not pervade the whole spectrum of acts commonly described as 'unilateral' in practice. More specifically, acts that occur in the context of treaty-making, such as acts of ratification, accession or signature, do not raise any specific questions of binding force to the extent that they are covered by the *pacta sunt servanda* rule.[64] Similarly, acts that derive their legal validity from the existence of a customary rule of international law are not problematic. Furthermore, not all acts commonly designated as unilateral are necessarily of a truly unilateral character, thus making the question of their binding force as 'unilateral acts' largely obsolete. For example, a unilateral declaration made by a State under Art. 36.2 of the ICJ Statute is operative only when it interlocks with a similar declaration made by another State.[65]

61 *Ibid.*, p. 155.

62 *Ibid.*

63 *Ibid.*; A. Pellet, *supra* note 19, p. 763.

64 See generally, M. Lachs, *Pacta Sunt Servanda*, in R. Berhardt (ed.), *Encyclopedia of Public International Law*, Vol. VII, (Amsterdam, Oxford: North-Holland, 1984), p. 364.

65 See Art. 36.2 of the ICJ Statute, *supra* note 20.

However, both believers and deniers make the mistake of treating such acts as a homogeneous phenomenon in their attempt to provide an all-encompassing answer to the question of the basis of their binding force. If one were to accept the believers' position, namely that "unilateral acts are an independent source of international law", then, in the absence of a definition, we must accept that *all* unilateral acts (even those pertaining to treaties or to the formation/application of customary law) may constitute an independent source of law – which is simply not the case. Similarly, to flatly deny that some unilateral acts may constitute a source of rights and obligations for their author would be to dismiss a growing body of State and judicial practice – which may not be ignored merely on the ground that it conflicts with Art. 38.1 of the ICJ Statute. Upon closer inspection, the question as to whether unilateral acts may constitute a source of law existing independently of Art. 38 really only arises in relation to acts described as 'voluntary' in the introduction to this book (acts that are not themselves mandated or otherwise permitted by other pre-existing legal obligations of either treaty or customary law character). Therefore, it is imperative to delimit the range of unilateral acts that are actually problematic before examining their relation to the sources of law.

However, even this clarification is not enough in order to answer the question of the relationship between (voluntary) unilateral acts and the sources of international law. This is so because the binding effects of these unilateral acts in international law are highly disputed. A number of lawyers, such as Koskenniemi,[66] Rubin[67] and Giganti,[68] have shed doubt on the legal character of such acts. In their view, voluntary unilateral acts do not exist as a legal phenomenon and the binding effects that different international courts have attributed to them at times may be explained by having recourse to other phenomena, such as estoppel.[69] In this light, it becomes evident that the question as to whether unilateral acts constitute an independent source of law may not be properly answered before first ascertaining the legal nature of such acts, namely before ascertaining whether and under which circumstances unilateral acts may create binding effects in international law. Therefore, the rest of the book will endeavour to determine the legal nature of unilateral acts.

66 M. Koskenniemi, *From Apology to Utopia: The Structure of International Legal Argument*, re-issued with Epilogue, (Cambridge: Cambridge University Press, 2005), p. 345 *et seq.*

67 A. Rubin, *supra* note 19, p. 28.

68 A. Giganti, The Effect of Unilateral State Acts in International Law, 2 *NYUJ Int'l L.& Pol.* 333 (1962), pp. 344–51.

69 *Ibid.*, p. 351.

There are further reasons underpinning the need to clarify the regime governing unilateral acts. According to the commentary accompanying Art. 12 of the International Law Commission's Articles on State Responsibility,[70] the breach of obligations assumed by means of a unilateral act may engage the responsibility of a State in the same way as breaches of obligations under customary international law or under an international treaty.[71] This, however, leads to a paradoxical situation in which, while the secondary rules governing the breach of an international obligation are clearly defined, the legal regime applicable to the very assumption of obligations by means of a unilateral act is far from clear.[72] Thus, if it is accepted that, in international law, obligations may also arise by way of unilateral acts, it is in the best interest of States to know where the line between a political and a legal act is drawn.

Taking into consideration that recent improvements in the telecommunication technologies have made it easier for States to communicate their views on a variety of issues of international significance, the lack of a sufficiently developed regime governing unilateral acts is bound to create confusion as to the obligations incumbent upon a State at any given time. Thus, the development of a doctrine of unilateral legal acts is central to the promotion of stability and legal certainty in international relations. As the ILC noted in its 1997 report in which the reasons for codifying such acts were offered: "In the interest of legal security and to help bring certainty, predictability and stability to international relations and thus, strengthen the rule of law, an attempt should be made to clarify the functioning of this kind of acts and what the legal consequences are, with a clear statement of the applicable law."[73]

70 See the ILC's Draft Articles on Responsibility of States for Internationally Wrongful Acts, with Commentaries, UN Doc. A/56/10, *Yrbk of the ILC* 2001, Vol. II, p. 59.

71 According to Art. 12 of the ILC Draft Articles, *ibid.*, p. 126, para. 3: "There is a breach of an international obligation by a State when an act of that State is not in conformity with what is required of it by that obligation, regardless of its origin or character." With regard to the latter phrase, the relevant part of the commentary accompanying Art. 12 reads: "As this phrase indicates, the articles are of general application. They apply to all international obligations of States, whatever their origin may be. International law obligations may be established by a customary rule of international law, by a treaty or by a general principle applicable within the international legal order. *States may assume international obligations by a unilateral act.*" (Emph. added).

72 The same point is made by A. Weingerl in the first page of his paper on the Definition of Unilateral Acts of States, presented at the 2004 Florence Founding Conference of the European Society of International Law, available at http://www.esil-sedi.eu/english/florence_agora_papers.html.

73 V. Rodríguez Cedeño, *supra* note 1, p. 3.

5 Conclusion

The aim of the present chapter was to provide the framework within which the discussion of unilateral acts will take place and to identify the main research question that the rest of the book will address. It was shown that, while unilateral acts are a commonly used tool of modern State interaction, the doctrine of unilateral acts in international law remains largely underdeveloped. Moreover, it was demonstrated that the hitherto debate has mainly focused on the question whether these acts may be regarded as a source of international law not listed under Art. 38 of the ICJ Statute. It was argued that, depending on their answer, international lawyers may fall into two categories: believers or deniers of the status of unilateral acts as an independent source of law. The chapter went on to provide an overview of the arguments adduced by both believers and deniers and it was claimed that both approaches are misguided to the extent that they do not take into account the heterogeneity of unilateral acts. In this respect, it was argued that the question as to whether these acts are an independent source of law is only meaningful for voluntary unilateral acts. In light of the doubts expressed in theory regarding the binding effects of voluntary unilateral acts, it was further supported that the question of the relation between unilateral acts and the recognized sources of international law may not be properly answered without first answering the preliminary question of their legal nature. It was also shown that establishing the legal nature of unilateral acts is of paramount importance for the purpose of providing clarity and stability in international relations. The chapter concluded by arguing that the key issue relating to unilateral acts is the elucidation of their legal nature and therefore this issue will be the focus of the rest of this book.

CHAPTER 2

Classification of Unilateral Acts

1 Introduction

This chapter purports to examine the different classifications of unilateral acts to be found in legal literature with a view to arriving at a typology that best reflects the variety of circumstances in which such acts occur in practice. The chapter will begin by discussing the difficulties inherent in the classification of unilateral acts. It will be argued that the lack of a widely agreed definition is the most serious obstacle to their systematisation. A number of definitions of unilateral acts that have been proposed in theory will be critically analysed and rejected on the ground that they are too narrow. The chapter will then provide an alternative definition of unilateral acts on the basis of the essential elements of their legal nature (unilateralism and the intention to create legal effects). Against this backdrop the chapter will continue by exploring different classifications of unilateral acts that exist in the literature. It will be argued that a classification on the basis of the legal context in which unilateral acts occur is preferable since it takes into account both the circumstances surrounding the making of the act and the effect of relevant legal rules.

At this point, one ought to bear in mind that the exploration of typologies of unilateral acts herein is by no means exhaustive; there is a considerable amount of literature on the different types of unilateral acts[1] and almost every author who dealt with the phenomenon proposed a different classification, or, at least, a variation of the existing ones. However, due to space constraints, this chapter will focus on the typologies most commonly encountered in the literature.

2 The Difficulties of Classifying Unilateral Acts

From the outset, it should be noted that there is a degree of difficulty inherent in any attempt of systematizing such a heterogeneous group of acts as

1 For a comprehensive account of the different classifications of unilateral acts to be found in the literature, see V. Rodríguez Cedeño, Fifth Report on Unilateral Acts of States, UN Doc. A/CN.4/525, p. 91.

 | DOI 10.1163/9789004300767_004

unilateral acts. In international law unilateral acts are as various as they are numerous.[2] States frequently use unilateral acts in the form of declarations, *communiqués*, or otherwise, to convey to other States or to the international community at large, a wide array of factual or legal situations. There are unilateral acts pertaining to the law of international personality, such as recognition of States or proclamation of independence; unilateral acts pertaining to the territorial status of States, such as acts of territorial or sea delimitation; unilateral acts pertaining to the judicial settlement of international disputes, such as declarations accepting the compulsory jurisdiction of the ICJ, or declarations made in the course of judicial proceeding. In light of the great diversity in which unilateral acts manifest themselves in international law, the hurdles of identifying common denominators upon which the grouping of such acts could be based become apparent. More particularly, the fact that unilateral acts are so diverse, both in terms of content and effects, and in terms of formulation, allows for only a few general criteria to be discerned.

Another corollary to the heterogeneity of unilateral acts that further frustrates the task of classification is the lack of an all-encompassing definition. International jurisprudence is of no avail in this matter. The ICJ, far from dwelling on issues of definition, has been more concerned with the particular circumstances under which binding force may be attributed to a unilateral act. Doctrine has also largely failed to produce a precise and all-embracing definition. At best, most definitions have been too general in scope to provide any degree of orientation. As Fiedler observes "attempts to reach a general definition by way of abstraction have failed because of the versatility of the various categories that need to be summarized under a common heading."[3] Thus, for example, Regaldies describes unilateral acts as "an expression of will envisaged in public international law as emanating from a single subject of law and resulting in the modification of the legal order."[4] For Jacque unilateral acts "emanate from a single expression of will and create norms intended to apply to subjects of law who have not participated in the formulation of the act."[5]

2 J. Combacau, S. Sur, *Droit International Public*, (Paris: Montchrestien, 1993), p. 213.

3 W. Fiedler, *Unilateral Acts in International Law*, in R. Berhardt (ed.), *Encyclopaedia of Public International Law*, Vol. IV, (Amsterdam, Oxford: North-Holland, 1984), p. 1018, at p. 1018.

4 F. Regaldies, Contribution a la etude de l' acte juridique unilateral et droit international public, 15 *Revue Juridique Themis* 417 (1980–1), at p. 417, as quoted in V. Rodríguez Cedeño, *supra* note 1, p. 99, para. 57.

5 J-P. Jacque, *A Propos de la Promesse Unilaterale*, in P. Reuter (ed.), *Melanges offerts a Paul Reuter: Le droit International: Unite et Diversite*, (Paris: A. Pedone, 1981), p. 239, as quoted in V. Rodríguez Cedeño, *ibid.*

According to the ILC, unilateral declarations "publicly made and manifesting the will to be bound may have the effect of creating legal obligations."[6]

However, in light of the wide spectrum of acts that the term 'unilateral acts' may be ascribed to, the aforementioned definitions are problematic. More closely observed, these definitions seem to be too narrow. In Jacque's and in Regaldie's definitions the intention of the author State is the determinant factor in attributing legal effects to unilateral acts. However, intention is only one of the elements to be considered in ascertaining the legal nature of a unilateral act; of equal importance here are the context in which the act occurred and the effect of relevant rules of law.[7] Thus, for example, in the case of recognition, the intention of the recognizing State alone is not enough to establish that the recognized State will be validly considered, *vis-à-vis* the recognizing one, as an international person, namely as a person that possesses all rights and duties that complement the attribution of Statehood under international law.[8] More importantly, the lawful grant of recognition is subject to the observance of customary rules on recognition, such as the obligation not to recognize the annexation of territory by use of force.[9] Similarly, the definition

6 Guiding Principle 1 of the Guiding Principles applicable to unilateral declarations of States capable of creating legal obligations in Report of the ILC on the Work of Its 58th Session, UN Doc. A/61/10, *Yrbk of the ILC* 2006, Vol. II, p. 369. For a detailed account of the various attempts to arrive at a generally agreed definition within the Commission, see C. Eckart, *Promises of States under International Law*, (Oxford: Hart Publishing, 2012), p. 18, fn. 3.

7 J. Crawford, *Brownlie's Principles of Public International Law*, 8th ed., (Oxford: Oxford University Press, 2012), p. 415.

8 These include the ability to conclude treaties and the acquisition of immunity from the jurisdiction of the courts of the recognising States. For a discussion of the most important consequences of recognition of new States see R. Jennings, A. Watts (eds.), *Oppenheim's International Law*, 9th ed., Vol. 1: Peace, (London: Longman, 1992), p. 130 and pp. 158–60.

9 See *Opinion No. 10*, Conference on Yugoslavia Arbitration Commission (Badinter Commission): Opinions on Questions Arising from the Dissolution of Yugoslavia, January 11 and July 4, 1992, 31 ILM 1488 (1992), para. 4, in which it is stated that "...while recognition is not a prerequisite for the foundation of a State and is purely declaratory in its impact, it is nonetheless a discretionary act that other States may perform when they choose and in a manner of their own choosing, subject only to compliance with the imperatives of general international law, and particularly those prohibiting the use of force in dealings with other States or guaranteeing the rights of ethnic, religious or linguistic minorities." An example of the application of the rule of non-recognition of entities that came about by means of illegal occupation is the case of Northern Cyprus. In 1974, Turkey invaded Northern Cyprus and, 9 years later, an entity by the name of Turkish Republic of Northern Cyprus was declared to have been established in that area. In response to this declaration, the UN Security Council issued a resolution proclaiming the invalidity of the Turkish declaration and calling upon

provided by the ILC fails to accurately describe unilateral acts. More particularly, the Commission's definition lacks any reference to the unilateral nature of these acts and, taken at face value, it seems to suggest that publicity is one of the requirements for the act to be legally valid. However, such a conclusion is not justified on the basis of the relevant judicial practice.[10] As it will be explained in detail in Chapter 6, although publicity is an indicator of the manifest intention of the author to become bound by means of a unilateral act, the fact that an act was not made publicly does not mean that it may not create legal effects. Upon contemplation, the weaknesses of the aforementioned definitions result from the fact that they attempt to describe in the abstract a phenomenon as diverse as unilateral acts.

In the opinion of the present author, the heterogeneity of unilateral acts makes it impossible to arrive at a generic definition, similar to that given to international agreements under Art. 2.1 of the Vienna Convention on the Law of Treaties.[11] Rather, it is submitted that unilateral acts should be defined on the basis of the essential elements of their legal nature. Such a definition would have the benefit of accurately describing unilateral acts while being broad enough to take into account the diverse legal environments in which these acts occur in practice. This approach is also justified by the actual practice of international judicial bodies in relation to other legal acts. When called upon to determine whether a certain instrument is an international agreement or not, international judges do not generally attempt to fit the instrument into the definition of the Vienna Convention. Instead, they focus on the existence of the elements of an international agreement, taking always into account the legal and factual context within which the instrument in question came into being.[12]

What are, then, the essential elements of the legal nature of unilateral acts upon which the definition of unilateral acts may be based? The Court in the *Nuclear Tests Case*[13] identified the element of unilateralism and the element of

---

Member – States to refrain from recognizing the entity in question. See SC, Res. 541, UN Doc. S/RES/541 (1983).

10 For the same criticism, see C. Eckart, *supra* note 6, pp. 239–42.

11 *Vienna Convention on the Law of Treaties*, 22 May 1969, Vienna, 1155 UNTS 331, 8 ILM 679 (1969).

12 J. Klabbers, *The Concept of Treaty in International Law*, (The Hague: Kluwer Law International, 1996), p. 72; M. Fitzmaurice, The Identification and Character of Treaties and Treaty Obligations Between States in International Law, 73 *BYIL* 141 (2002), p. 168.

13 *Nuclear Tests Cases*, Australia vs France, *ICJ Reports* 1974, p. 253, New Zealand vs France, *ICJ Reports* 1974, p. 457. The Court's judgments in these two cases are almost identical.

the intention of the author State to become bound as the essentials of the legal nature of unilateral acts. According to the Court:

> It is well recognized that declarations made by way of unilateral acts, concerning legal or factual situations, may have the effect of creating legal obligations. When it is the intention of the State making the declaration that it should become bound according to its terms, that intention confers upon the declaration the character of a legal undertaking, the State being thenceforth legally required to follow a course of conduct consistent with the declaration.[14]

There is also consensus in doctrine that unilateralism and the intention to be bound are the essential elements of the legal nature of unilateral acts.[15]

Against this background, the next section will focus on the attempts that have been made in the literature to classify unilateral acts. It will be shown that the content of a unilateral act, its legal effects and the purpose for which the act is formulated have featured in doctrine as the main criteria for classification.

3 Review of the Systems of Classification of Unilateral Acts to be Found in the Literature

3.1 *Unilateral Acts from the Standpoint of Their Content*

A large number of the authors who engaged in the systematization of unilateral acts favored a material criterion, insofar as they attempted to categorize unilateral acts on the basis of their content. Thus, Heilborn's study of unilateral acts focuses on the acts of recognition, protest, renunciation and notification.[16] In addition to these four, Cassese also distinguished promise as a separate

---

Hereinafter, unless otherwise stated, all references made to the *Nuclear Tests Case* will concern the case between Australia and France.

14 *Ibid.*, para. 43.

15 C. Eckart, *supra* note 6, pp. 38–40; V. Rodríguez Cedeño, First Report on Unilateral Acts of States, UN Doc. A/CN.4/486, p. 319, at pp. 335–6, paras. 133–151.

16 P. Heilborn, *Das System Des Volkerrechts, Entwickelt aus den Volkerrechtlichen Begriffen*, (Berlin: Springer, 1896), as quoted in J.H.W. Verzijl, *International Law in a Historical Perspective, Vol. VI: Juridical Facts as Sources of International Rights and Obligations*, (Leiden: Sijtoff, 1971), p. 105.

category.[17] Similarly, Pellet and Daillier – following a material criterion – conclude that the main types are recognition, protest, notification, promise and waiver.[18] Suy, in his monograph on unilateral acts, deals with recognition, promise, protest, renunciation and notification as well as with acts that contribute to the formation of customary rules.[19] Other authors, while choosing the content of the act as a criterion for classification, have grouped unilateral acts under different headings. Thus, in the ninth edition of *Oppenheim's International Law*, notification, protest and renunciation feature as distinct types of unilateral acts, while the generic category of 'declaration' has been introduced to cover a wide array of acts irrespective of their specific content.[20] Overall, however, it seems that there is consensus in the doctrine as to the existence of a basic core of material acts that include recognition, protest, waiver, notification and promise.

It is noteworthy at this point to mention that the above grouping of the acts on the basis of their content is also reflected in the answers given by States to a questionnaire concerning some aspects of the phenomenon of unilateral acts prepared by the ILC.[21] Thus, for example, Argentina stated that "a clear distinction must be drawn among the four traditional kinds of unilateral acts: promise, waiver, recognition and protest"[22] while El Salvador opined that notification, recognition, protest, waiver, promise, declaration, appeal and resolution are the most important types of unilateral acts.[23] Although no determinate conclusions may be drawn from such comments, especially in light of the different views expressed by other States and of the small number of States that actually took part in the survey,[24] it seems that, in the opinion of some States at least, classification according to a material criterion is a valid one.

---

17 A. Cassese, *International Law*, 2nd ed., (Oxford: Oxford University Press, 2005), pp. 184–5.

18 P. Daillier, A. Pellet, *Droit International Public*, (Paris: LGDJ, 1999), p. 358.

19 E. Suy, *Les Actes Juridiques Unilateraux en Droit International Public*, (Paris: LGDJ, 1962), as quoted in K. Zemanek, *Unilateral Legal Acts Revisited* in K. Wellens (ed.), *International Law: Theory and Practice: Essays in Honour of Eric Suy*, (The Hague: M. Nijhoff, 1998), p. 209 at p. 210.

20 Such as acts that constitute exercise of a power granted by a treaty provision or by a customary rule. See R. Jennings, A. Watts, *supra* note 8, pp. 1188–93.

21 See the V. Rodríguez Cedeño, Fourth Report on Unilateral Acts of States, UN Doc. A/CN.4/419, p. 115, at p. 124, para 62.

22 Unilateral Acts of States: Replies from Governments to the Questionnaire: Report of the Secretary-General, UN Doc. A/CN.4/511, p. 265, at p. 275.

23 *Ibid.*

24 *Ibid.*; The Netherlands for example stated that "the contents of unilateral statements are not restricted to certain categories of subject matter. The Netherlands therefore considers

However, a material approach to the question of classification is not devoid of problems. Before embarking upon the analysis of the specific problems encountered in classifying unilateral acts in accordance with their content, it would be useful here to take a brief look at the so-called 'traditional unilateral acts' in order to put the discussion in context. These, as mentioned above, include recognition, protest, promise, waiver or renunciation, and notification. According to doctrine, recognition of a factual situation is a unilateral act "whereby the recognizing State indicates a willingness to acknowledge the factual situation and to bring about certain legal consequences of that acknowledgement."[25] Recognition in international law is often discussed within the framework of recognition of States or Governments.[26] However, there is a great variety of other situations that may call for recognition, such as recognition of a right, or recognition of a national liberation movement as representing a people fighting against alien occupation.[27] Thus, depending on the facts or situation that the act of recognition comes to acknowledge, its legal effects may vary. However, beyond these specific effects to be judged *in concreto* and in accordance with the content of a given act, the typical minimum effect of recognition is estoppel;[28] in other words, the minimum effect of

---

the contents of the statement of secondary importance for the purpose of producing legal effects. Of greater relevance are formal criteria such as the unambiguity of the statement and the objectified intention of producing legal effects, that is to say an intention that can be demonstrated objectively." *Ibid.*, p. 276.

25 D.P. O' Connell, *International Law*, 2nd ed., (London: Stevens, 1970), p. 128; see also R. Jennings, A. Watts, *supra* note 8, pp. 128–30.

26 Generally on recognition see: H. Lauterpacht, *Recognition in International Law*, (Cambridge: Cambridge University Press, 1947); T. Chen, *The International Law of Recognition*, (London: Stevens, 1951).

27 For example, the UN General Assembly has recognised the Palestine Liberation Organisation (PLO) as representing the people of Palestine and has granted it permanent observer status within the UN. See GA, Res. 3210 (XXIX), UN Doc. A/RES/3210 (1974), and GA, Res. 3237 (XXIX), UN Doc. A/RES/3237 (1974). It should be noted that after the Palestinian Declaration of Independence of 15 November 1988 (see Letter dated 16 November 1988 from the Deputy Permanent Observer of the Palestine Liberation Organization to the United Nations addressed to the Secretary-General, UN Docs. A/43/827, S/20278 (1988)), the GA decided that the designation 'Palestine' will be used in place of the designation 'PLO' in the UN system, see GA, Res. 43/177, UN Doc. A/RES/43/177 (1988). On 29 November 2012, the GA decided to upgrade Palestine to 'non-member observer State' status. See GA, Res. 67/19, UN Doc. A/RES/67/19 (2012).

28 G. Schwarzenberger, *International Law as applied by International Courts and Tribunals*, Vol. I, 3rd ed., (London: Stevens, 1957), p. 127.

recognition is that the recognizing State is debarred from challenging the fact or situation it has previously accepted.[29]

Another unilateral act which features in theory as belonging to the so-called 'traditional' unilateral acts is waiver or renunciation.[30] Waiver is a unilateral act under which the waiving State willingly abandons a claim or a right.[31] However, such unilateral abandonment of a right cannot be lightly presumed. The ICJ in the *Certain Norwegian Loans Case* insisted that a waiver "cannot be inferred; on the contrary it must be expressly declared."[32] Protest, on the other hand, is a unilateral act whereby the protesting State formally objects to acts or conduct of another State.[33] Its purpose and effects vary according to the intention of the protesting State. Through a protest, a State may wish to indicate that it reserves its rights with respect to the action against which the protest is lodged, and more particularly, in the case of unlawful action, its right to demand compensation.[34] Protest may also indicate the unwillingness of the protesting State to recognize or accept the conduct in question, or any ensuing consequences, as legitimate.[35] Finally, protest in the context of applicability of customary rules of international law is of special significance. If a State proves that it has manifestly and consistently objected to a customary norm at the stage of formation, it may later successfully claim that it is not bound thereby. Thus, for example, in the *Asylum Case*[36] the Court concluded that even if the Colombian Government had succeeded in establishing the existence of a customary rule giving the State granting the asylum the right to unilaterally qualify an offence in matters of diplomatic asylum, this rule could not be invoked

29 In the context of recognition of States, see for example Art. 6 of the *Montevideo Convention on Rights and Duties of States*, 26 December 1933, Montevideo, 165 LNTS 19 (1934), under which recognition, once granted, cannot be later withdrawn.

30 For the semiotic difference between the terms 'waiver' and 'renunciation', see R. Jennings, A. Watts, *supra* note 8, p. 1195, fn. 1.

31 See for example the *Corfu Channel Case, ICJ Reports* 1948, p. 15 at p. 27, in which the ICJ interpreted a statement of the Albanian Government as a waiver of the right to subsequently raise an objection against the admissibility of the UK Application.

32 *Case of Certain Norwegian Loans, ICJ Reports* 1957, p. 9 at p. 26.

33 K. Skubiszewski, *Unilateral Acts of States*, in M. Bedjaoui (ed.), *International Law: Achievements and Prospects*, (Paris: UNESCO, 1991), p. 221, at p. 227.

34 I. McGibbon, Some Observations on the Part of Protest in International Law, 30 *BYIL* 293 (1953), p. 298.

35 *Ibid.*

36 *Asylum Case, ICJ Reports* 1950, p. 266.

against Peru, since Peru had repudiated it by refraining to ratify two regional conventions giving effect to that rule.[37]

Promise holds a prominent place in the writings of scholars who follow a material criterion in the classification of unilateral acts. Promise constitutes a unilateral transaction under which the promising State undertakes to perform an act or to behave in a certain manner.[38] An oft-cited example of promise in international law is to be found in the *Nuclear Tests Case*. As briefly discussed in the first chapter, this case involved a series of public announcements indicating the intention of France not to hold any further nuclear tests in the South Pacific which were interpreted as constituting a promise.[39] Judicial practice and doctrine have laid stress on the intention of the promising State, the circumstances surrounding the making of the promise and the authority of the person acting on behalf of the author State as important elements in determining the character of an act as a promise.[40] Furthermore, the ICJ has acknowledged the binding force of promissory unilateral acts on a number of occasions.[41] Finally, another unilateral act that belongs to the group of classic material acts is notification. According to theory, notification is "the act by which a State makes other States cognizant of a certain action it has performed."[42] In some cases, international law prescribes a duty of notification; thus, for example, under Art. 2 of the Hague Convention concerning the Commencement of Hostilities, the existence of a state of war must be duly notified to neutral Powers.[43]

---

37 *Ibid.*, p. 277. See also the *Anglo-Norwegian Fisheries Case*, *ICJ Reports* 1951, p. 116 at p. 131, in which the Court upheld the lawfulness of the straight baseline system used by Norway despite the British contention that the adoption of such a system violates the 10-mile rule, *i.e.* a customary rule dictating that the length of straight lines must not exceed 10 miles. The Court having established that the 10-mile rule is not actually a rule of general international law concluded that in any case the rule in question "is inapplicable as against Norway inasmuch as she has always opposed any attempt to apply it to the Norwegian Coast."

38 V.D. Degan, *Sources of International Law*, (The Hague: M. Nijhoff, 1997), p. 287.

39 *Ibid.*

40 See generally S. Garbone, Promise in International Law: A Confirmation of its Binding Force, 1 *Italian YIL* 166 (1975).

41 See for example the *Nuclear Tests Case*, Australia vs France, *supra* note 13, para. 46; *Case concerning Military and Paramilitary Activities in and against Nicaragua*, Merits, *ICJ Reports* 1986, p. 14, para. 261; *Case concerning the Frontier Dispute*, *ICJ Reports* 1986, p. 554, para. 39; *Case concerning Armed Activities on the Territory of the Congo Case*, (*New Application 2002*), *ICJ Reports* 2006, p. 6, para. 50.

42 A. Cassese, *supra* note 17, p. 184.

43 *Hague Convention (III) Relative to the Opening of Hostilities*, 18 October 1907, The Hague, available at http://www.forces.gc.ca/jag/training/publications/law_of_armed_conflict/collection_of_docs_on_loac_2005_en.pdf.

Having recited the so-called 'traditional' unilateral acts, the discussion will now turn to the specific problems encountered in adopting a material approach to the question of classification of unilateral acts. At first, it seems that such a typology is not representative of the multitude of unilateral acts to be found in State practice. As seen above, following a material criterion, doctrine has produced a list of five basic types of unilateral acts; these include recognition, waiver or renunciation, protest, promise and notification. However, in light of the wide spectrum of acts that the term 'unilateral acts' covers, the idea of subsuming them in five broad categories seems problematic; in practice, a number of unilateral acts exist that cannot be classed in any of these categories. For instance, under which category would declarations of war or neutrality fall? Furthermore, under which heading would a declaration accepting the jurisdiction of an international judicial body come? Would negative security guarantees[44] given by nuclear weapon States be better treated as promises or as waivers? Therefore, it seems that classification in the proposed categories falls short of accurately reflecting the variety of unilateral acts to be found in State practice.

Of course, one could plausibly argue that while such a typology is not useful, the idea upon which it is based, *i.e.* the criterion of content, could still be a valid one. In other words, an argument could be advanced that by following a criterion of content, other material acts, alongside the ones that have largely engaged the attention of scholars, could be added so as to arrive at a classification reflective of State-practice. Nevertheless, it seems that such a proposition is also problematic. At first, the variety of unilateral acts existing on the international plane is such that by following a criterion of content, a disproportionate number of categories would emerge. Thus, beyond recognition, waiver, promise, protest and notification, one would also have to add declarations of war, declarations of neutrality, declarations accepting the jurisdiction of an international body, declarations made in the course of judicial proceedings, *etc.* However, creating so many categories of unilateral acts would defeat the very purpose of the task of classification – which is to develop a coherent and coordinated system in which to discuss the function of unilateral acts in international law.

Furthermore, even if the proposition is accepted that all unilateral acts occurring on the international plane could fit into the aforementioned categories problems still persist, as even within the realm of 'traditional' unilateral acts a certain degree of obscurity lies. While in theory the boundaries between

44 A. Rosas, Negative Security Assurances and Non-Use of Nuclear Weapons, 25 *Germ. Yrb. I.L.* 199 (1982), p. 208.

these categories are clearly delimited, in practice, the content of an act is often ambiguous and thus, the assignment of an act to a certain category becomes a matter of interpretation. As Fiedler observes commenting upon the obscurity of the terms employed to describe the different types of unilateral acts: "on closer examination, it is apparent that even a promise, a commonly employed term, is associated with considerable legal uncertainty."[45] An illustrative example here is the *Eastern Greenland Case*.[46] As discussed in the previous chapter, the case concerned, among others, the binding force of an oral declaration made by the Norwegian Foreign Minister, Mr Ihlen. The question arising here is how to categorise Ihlen's Declaration following a material criterion. Some commentators have treated the Declaration as a classic example of a promise in international law.[47] However, the Declaration could also be seen as recognition of the Danish sovereignty over Eastern Greenland,[48] or even as a waiver of Norway's rights on the territory. Therefore, it becomes apparent that, since the content of a unilateral act is often ambiguous, a typology based on the criterion of content is doomed to consistently produce conflicting results.

Finally, another problem relating to the classification of unilateral acts in categories of recognition, waiver, promise, notification, *etc.* is that such a classification tends to confuse form with content.[49] The most notable examples here are notification and declaration. As seen above, authors, who have largely followed a material criterion for the classification of unilateral acts, often enumerate notification and declaration among them. However, both these terms seem to apply more to the form rather than to the substance of a unilateral act. Indeed, a notification or a declaration may have any content. Thus, for example, through a notification, a State may wish to communicate to other States its intention to acquire a permanent neutrality status,[50] to extend its territorial

45 W. Fiedler, *supra* note 3, p. 1018.

46 *Legal Status of Eastern Greenland Case, PCIJ Series A/B*, 1933, No. 53, p. 22.

47 See, for example, J.W. Garner, The International Binding Force of Unilateral Oral Declarations, 27 *AJIL* 493 (1933), at p. 496. See also the Dissenting Opinion of Judge Vogt in the *Eastern Greenland Case, supra* note 46, p. 97 at p. 118 in which he asserts the character of the Declaration as a promise. However, it needs to be noted that the character of the Ihlen Declaration as a unilateral act is disputed and according to the present author, the Declaration constitutes an oral agreement rather than a unilateral act. The Ihlen Declaration will be discussed in detail in Chapter 4.

48 D. Carreau, *Droit International*, (Paris: A. Pedone, 1988), p. 209.

49 J. Combacau, S. Sur, *supra* note 2, p. 94.

50 For example, on the 26th of October 1955 the Austrian Parliament adopted a Constitutional Law declaring Austria's permanent neutrality. Subsequently, Austria notified foreign governments of its enactment in order to gain international recognition as a permanently

sea,[51] or to refrain from participating in judicial proceedings instituted against it.[52] Similarly, unilateral declarations are an everyday instrument of State interaction relating to a wide variety of legally relevant facts or situations. Thus, for instance, through a declaration, a State may reaffirm its obligations under an already existing treaty,[53] it may assume new ones,[54] or it may simply make its position clear about an important point of international law.[55] In general, it seems that both declaration and notification are tools used so widely and in so diverse contexts that they have become dissociated from any specific content. Therefore, to include them into a classification based on a material criterion would create unnecessary confusion.

In summary, this part of the chapter explored the criterion of content as a criterion for classification of unilateral acts. It has been shown that, on the basis of a material criterion, the literature largely agrees that the main types of unilateral acts include recognition, protest, promise, waiver or renunciation

---

neutral State. See B.R. Havel, An International Law Institution in Crisis: Rethinking Permanent Neutrality, 61 *Ohio St. L.J.* 167 (2000), at p. 206. See also A. Verdross, Austria's Permanent Neutrality and the United Nations Organization, 50 *AJIL* 61 (1956). More recently, Malta and Costa Rica followed Austria's example declaring their permanent neutrality and notifying other States thereof. For Malta's declaration of permanent neutrality see C. Rousseau, Chronique des Faits Internationaux, 85 *RGDIP* 411 (1981). For Costa Rica's declaration of permanent neutrality, see F.C. Cruz, Costa Rica's Constitutional Jurisprudence, its Political Importance and International Human Rights Law: Examination of Some Important Decisions, 45 *Duq. L. Rev.* 557 (2007), fn. 32.

51 See for example the Proclamation of Germany concerning the Extension of the Breadth of Its Territorial Sea, 11 November 1994, available at www.un.org/Depts/los/LEGISLATIONANDTREATIES/europe.htm.

52 For example, in the *Nuclear Tests Case*, France notified the Applicants and the Registry of the Court of its unwillingness to participate in the proceedings and to appoint an agent on the ground that the jurisdiction of the Court was ill-founded. See *Nuclear Tests Case*, *supra* note 13, para. 13. Similarly, on the 18th of January 1985, the US formally notified the Registry of the Court of the US intention not to participate in any further proceedings in connection with the *Nicaragua Case*. See M.N. Leich, Contemporary Practice of the United States relating to International Law, 79 *AJIL* 431 (1985), at pp. 438–9.

53 See for example the Advisory Opinion of the ICJ in the case, *International Status of South West Africa*, *ICJ Reports* 1950, p. 128, at p. 135, in which the Court held that a declaration made by the Union of South Africa before the League Of Nations "constituted recognition by the Union Government of the continuance of its obligations under the Mandate and not a mere indication of the future conduct of that Government."

54 See for example the *Nuclear Tests Case*, *supra* note 13, para. 53.

55 See for example the UK Foreign Office Policy Document No. 148, 57 *BYIL* 614 (1986), paras. II.18–22, in which the UK supported the existence of an exception to the general rule of non-intervention on humanitarian grounds.

and notification. This section continued with a brief analysis of these types of acts in order to determine how theory perceives their nature and function within international law. Further, the section focused on the specific problems encountered in classifying unilateral acts in accordance with their content. At first, it was argued that the multitude of circumstances under which States have recourse to unilateral acts is such that it makes any effort of classifying them in accordance with their content intrinsically difficult. It was shown that a number of unilateral acts exist that escape classification in terms of categories of recognition, protest and the like, including declarations of war or of neutrality.

Moreover, it was argued that, although in theory the content and legal effects of different material acts seem easily distinguishable, in practice, there are a number of unilateral acts that may fit in more than one category. Thus, for example, in the *Eastern Greenland Case*, Ihlen's declaration may be treated as recognition, waiver or even promise. Finally, the section turned to the confusion between form and content of the act that may result from analysing unilateral acts in terms of the aforementioned categories. More particularly, it was shown that the inclusion of notification and declaration in a typology based upon a material criterion is erroneous, since both these terms are associated in practice more with the form of the act rather than with its specific content. In this light, it was concluded that basing a typology of unilateral acts solely upon a material criterion fails to take into account both the great diversity of unilateral acts and the different legal environments in which such acts occur.

3.2 *Unilateral Acts from the Standpoint of Their Legal Effects*

In order to circumvent the problems arising from basing a typology of unilateral acts on the criterion of content, some authors have attempted to examine unilateral acts from the standpoint of their legal effects. Thus, Jacque classified unilateral acts in three main categories: acts through which a State undertakes an obligation, acts through which a State waives a right and acts through which a State reaffirms a right.[56]

The Special Rapporteur of the ILC on unilateral acts of States also used legal effects as a criterion for classification. Since the purpose of the Commission was to codify unilateral acts, the classification of these acts was considered instrumental in that process.[57] Thus, the task of creating a suitable typology fell to the Special Rapporteur. Since classification of unilateral acts was an issue to

56 J-P. Jacque, *Elements pour une theorie de l'acte juridique en droit international public*, (Paris: LGDJ, 1972), p. 336.

57 See V. Rodríguez Cedeño, *supra* note 1, para. 137.

which the Special Rapporteur devoted much of his attention, it would be pertinent here to summarize his approach before examining his conclusions.

In his fourth report, the Special Rapporteur, Cedeño, dedicated a whole section on the issue of classification of unilateral acts.[58] Having rejected a number of typologies proposed in theory, Cedeño proceeded to enquire whether a criterion of legal effects could be used. To this end, he examined the legal effects of unilateral acts most commonly found in State practice, *i.e.* the legal effects of promise, protest, waiver and recognition. According to his view, promise is a unilateral act by which a State undertakes to behave in a certain manner; therefore, it is an act through which a State assumes an obligation in international law.[59] Similarly, a waiver is an act which creates obligations for the waiving State, since through a waiver, a State does not only abandon a prior claim or right, but also undertakes an obligation "no longer to contest the rights that another State has acquired through the waiver."[60] Furthermore, recognition is another unilateral act by which a State undertakes obligations; through recognition, a State accepts certain claims, facts or legal situations and thereby, it acknowledges that they may be invoked against it.[61] In contrast to other material acts, protest is not an act by which a State unilaterally commits to conduct itself in a certain manner. Rather, through a protest, a State seeks to prevent the emergence of a legal situation that would be contrary to its own rights or interests. Thus, through a protest "the author State in no way undertakes an obligation; on the contrary, it seeks to reaffirm a right by preventing another State from acquiring it."[62] Having examined these four 'classic' unilateral acts, Cedeño concluded that, by following a criterion of legal effects, two main types of unilateral acts may be discerned: acts by which a State reaffirms a right and acts by which a State undertakes an obligation.[63]

From the outset, it seems that there is one basic drawback in classifying unilateral acts on the basis of their legal effects: namely the possible overlap between the aforementioned categories. Indeed, the spectrum of acts examined by the Special Rapporteur is unduly restricted to the so-called 'classic' acts. However, if more unilateral acts are put to the test, it quickly becomes apparent that some of them may fall under both categories. For instance, a declaration of neutrality is a unilateral act whereby a State both undertakes

58 See V. Rodríguez Cedeño, *supra* note 21, paras. 44–100.

59 *Ibid.*, para. 79.

60 *Ibid.*, para. 86.

61 *Ibid.*, para. 91.

62 *Ibid.*, para. 94.

63 *Ibid.*, para. 98.

obligations and reaffirms its rights: a neutral State is bound to respect international law rules regarding neutrality in the outbreak of hostilities between other States.[64] However, at the same time, through a declaration of neutrality, a State reaffirms its sovereign rights of self-determination in issues of war and peace.[65] Thus, a distinction between acts that create obligations and acts that reaffirm rights does not seem to be correct to the extent that it fails to take into account acts that may fall within both categories.[66]

Classifying unilateral acts on the basis of their legal effects has further problems. As seen above, the categories proposed are only two, namely acts that create obligations for the author State and acts through which a State reaffirms its rights. However, State practice shows that there are some unilateral acts that actually create rights for the author State. For instance, through the proclamation of an Exclusive Economic Zone (EEZ), coastal States not only assume obligations but also acquire new rights. For example, according to Art. 61 of the United Nations Convention on the Law of the Sea,[67] coastal States are under an obligation to conserve living resources in their EEZ. On the other hand, by establishing an EEZ, coastal States also acquire certain rights. According to Art. 56 of the LOSC, coastal States have sovereign rights to a number of activities for the economic exploitation and exploration of the zone.

However, it would be erroneous to assume that such sovereign rights preexist or are simply re-affirmed through, the act of proclamation; on the contrary, the act of proclamation creates these sovereign rights in favour of the coastal State. In the words of O. Vicuna: "Although the language used by Articles 56 and 57 of the Convention seems to suggest the existence of ipso facto rights that would not require express proclamation, inasmuch as they confirm that the coastal State has certain rights, an interpretation along those

64 A neutral State is bound, for instance, to prohibit belligerents from moving troops or convoys of either munitions of war or supplies across its territory. See Art. 5 of the *Hague Convention* (V) *on the Rights and Duties of Neutral Powers and Persons in Case of War on Land,* 18 October 1907, The Hague, available at http://www.yale.edu/lawweb/avalon/lawofwar/hague05.htm.

65 B.R. Havel, *supra* note 50, fn. 17.

66 This point was also raised by some members of the ILC who questioned the classification proposed by the Special Rapporteur. In their view, such classification failed to take into account acts that could fall under both categories, such as declarations of war or of neutrality. See the Report of the ILC on the Work of Its 53rd Session, UN Doc. A/56/10, *Yrbk of the ILC* 2001, Vol. II, para. 236.

67 *United Nations Convention on the Law of the Sea,* 10 December 1982, Montego Bay, 1833 UNTS 3. 21 ILM 1261 (1982). Hereinafter referred to as LOSC.

lines would not seem reasonable."[68] If the contrary proposition was accepted, it would mean that the duties related to the proclamation of an EEZ would be incumbent upon all coastal States, irrespective of their wish to establish that zone or not.[69] However, international law, as it stands today, does not impose any such obligation upon coastal States. On the contrary, it falls within the discretion of each coastal State to decide whether it wishes to proclaim an EEZ and consequently, to undertake the concomitant duties or enjoy the concomitant rights. Therefore, under international law, the establishment of an EEZ is of constitutive character.

The creation of sovereign rights for the coastal State through the proclamation of an EEZ serves as an example to illustrate that some unilateral acts may also create new rights in favour of the author State. There are more instances of State practice that confirm this proposition. For example, the acceptance of the compulsory jurisdiction of the ICJ is also a unilateral act that creates both rights and obligations for the declarant State. By making a declaration under Art. 36.2 of the ICJ Statute, a State both acquires the right to initiate proceedings before the Court against any State that has accepted the same obligation, and undertakes the duty to accept the compulsory jurisdiction of the Court in all legal disputes referred to therein.[70] Therefore, it seems that a rigid distinction between unilateral acts that create obligations and unilateral acts through which rights are re-affirmed fails to demonstrate the variety of legal effects that a unilateral act may have in practice.

This section examined the possibility of following a legal effects criterion for the classification of unilateral acts. It was shown that, according to this criterion, theory has distinguished between unilateral acts whereby a State assumes obligations and unilateral acts whereby a State reaffirms rights. However, it was argued that this distinction does not reflect the variety of legal effects that unilateral acts may have. On the contrary, a survey of State practice demonstrates that there are unilateral acts, such as declarations of war or of neutrality, which may fall under both categories. Furthermore, this typology fails to take into account unilateral acts that create rights in favour of the author State, such as the establishment of an EEZ zone. For all these reasons, a classification on the basis of the criterion of legal effects is not a satisfactory one.

---

68 O. Vicuna, *The Exclusive Economic Zone: Regime and Legal Nature under International Law*, (Cambridge: Cambridge University Press, 1989), p. 40.

69 *Ibid.*

70 See generally C. Tomuschat, *Article 36*, in A. Zimmermann, C. Tomuschat, K. Oelles-Frahm (eds.), *The Statute of The International Court of Justice: A Commentary*, 2nd ed., (Oxford: Oxford University Press, 2012), p. 633.

3.3 *The Problems of the Aforementioned Systems of Classification*

The foregoing analysis showed that both typologies examined thus far have one problem in common; they are all unduly focused upon a specific element of the unilateral act and fail to take into account the circumstances surrounding the making of the act and the effect of relevant rules of law. More particularly, it was shown that classification on the basis of the criterion of content is too rigidly attached to unilateral acts that have come to acquire an independent status in international law through a process of repetition (such as recognition, protest, waiver), while it neglects acts that occur in other contexts (such as unilateral acts in the custom-forming process or unilateral acts that pertain to the law of treaties). Furthermore, classification on the basis of the legal effects of the unilateral act was deemed dissatisfactory to the extent that it does not take into account unilateral acts that may create rights for the author State on the basis of a relevant rule of law allowing for such rights to come into existence.

3.4 *Unilateral Acts from the Standpoint of the Legal Context in Which They Occur or of the Purpose They Serve*

Modern authors, such as Virally and Zemanek, have attempted to address the abovementioned shortcomings. To this end, they came up with classifications that take into account both the purpose and the general legal context in which the act arises. More particularly, Zemanek makes an important distinction between 'adjunctive' and 'autonomous' unilateral acts.[71] In his view, all unilateral acts that constitute elements of a larger law-creating process belong to the category of adjunctive unilateral acts (such as acts pertaining to the custom or treaty-making process) and therefore, they have to be discussed in the context of these processes.[72] On the other hand, autonomous unilateral acts are "communications under, not about, rules of the existing international order and intend to confirm or to change the legal position of the author State in the application of the respective rule of international law."[73] According to Zemanek, all unilateral acts performed with the intention to establish rights and/or obligations for the author State fall into this category. Virally made a similar taxonomy. He classified unilateral acts into acts that are part of the treaty-making process, acts that contribute

71 K. Zemanek, *supra* note 19, p. 210.

72 *Ibid.*

73 K. Zemanek, The Law-Making Processes of the International System, 266 *Hague Recueil* 131 (1997), at pp. 193–4.

to the formation of custom and acts that have an independent significance in international law.[74]

On this basis, three categories of unilateral acts may be discerned: unilateral acts that lead to the formation or application of customary law, unilateral acts in the treaty-making process and autonomous unilateral acts. To the first category belong unilateral acts that, coupled with the residual elements of custom, may lead to the creation of general or regional rules of customary law. In other words, unilateral acts serve, within this context, as precedents for the formation of customary rules. This has essentially been the case with the law of the sea. The unilateral practice of the great naval powers of the 18th century led gradually to the formation of customary rules that were later codified in the LOSC.[75] A related question here is whether these acts encompass unilateral statements or declarations alongside physical acts. In other words, could unilateral statements be considered as having the same precedential value as actual practice in the formation of customary rules?

Until quite recently, the answer given by judicial practice and doctrine was negative; the traditional approach to custom considered it to be based solely upon the actual practice of States.[76] Characteristic of this approach is the following passage from the Dissenting Opinion of Judge Read in the *Anglo-Norwegian Fisheries Case*: "Customary international law is the generalisation of the practice of States. This cannot be established by citing cases where coastal States have made extensive claims, but have not maintained their claims by the actual assertion of sovereignty over trespassing foreign ships."[77] However, recent changes in the structure of the international community, such as the

---

74 M. Virally, *The Sources of International Law*, in M. Sorensen (ed.), *Manual of Public International Law*, (London: Macmillan, 1968), p. 116 at p. 155. Note, however, that the classifications proposed by Zemanek and Virally are not identical. For example, while Zemanek includes in the category of unilateral acts, acts that apply a customary rule, Virally treats such acts as forming a discrete category. Furthermore, while Virally treats declarations made under Art. 36.2 of the ICJ Statute within the context of unilateral acts in the treaty-making process, Zemanek treats such declarations within the context of autonomous unilateral acts.

75 V.D. Degan, Unilateral Act as a Source of Particular International Law, 1 *Finnish YIL* (1994), Vol. 5, p. 149, at p. 149.

76 See A. D'Amato, *The Concept of Custom In International Law*, (Ithaca: Cornell University Press, 1971), pp. 50–1; H. Thirlway, *Customary International Law and Codification: An Examination of the Continuing Role of Custom in the Present Period of Codification of International Law*, (Leiden: Sijtoff, 1972), p.58.

77 Dissenting Opinion of Judge Read in the *Anglo-Norwegian Fisheries Case*, *supra* note 37, p. 186 at p. 191.

emergence of a number of new States in the aftermath of the decolonisation process and the increased interaction between States within the framework of international *fora*, have altered traditional conceptions of State practice for the purpose of ascertaining the emergence of a customary rule.[78] Under the current scheme, the concept of State practice has expanded to include unilateral statements or declarations, to the extent that they reflect the official position of States on issues of legal significance.[79] The ICJ seems to share the same approach and, in its judgements, weight has been attached not only to material acts of States, but also to their views, as proof of the existence of a customary rule.[80] In this light, the more correct approach would be to include both material acts of States and unilateral statements in the category of unilateral acts in the custom-making process inasmuch as "they reflect views of States…on the content or legal quality of rules of conduct emerging in the international community."[81]

Finally, Zemanek also included acts that apply a customary rule in the category of unilateral acts in the context of customary law.[82] In other words, apart from acts that lead to the formation of custom, acts that apply a customary rule, and thus confirm its existence, are also to be discussed within the general framework of unilateral acts in the context of customary international law. Virally, on the other hand, treated unilateral acts that involve the application of a customary rule as belonging to (and forming) a category of their own.[83]

However, Zemanek's approach seems more convincing especially in light of the way in which customary rules come into existence and evolve in

78 G.M. Danilenko, *Law-Making in the International Community*, (Dordrecht: M. Nijhoff, 1993), p. 85.

79 *Ibid.*, p. 87. See also M. Akehurst, Custom as a Source of International Law, 47 *BYIL* 1 (1974–5), at pp. 1–3.

80 For example, in the *Asylum Case*, the Court referred not only to the State-practice relating to the exercise of diplomatic asylum, but also to "the official views expressed on various occasions." See the *Asylum Case*, *supra* note 36, at p. 277. Furthermore, in the *North Sea Continental Shelf Cases*, the Court treated Truman's Proclamation concerning the sovereign rights of coastal States over the continental shelf "as the starting point of the positive law on the subject." *North Sea Continental Shelf Case*, *ICJ Reports* 1969, p. 3, at pp. 32–3. See also the *Case concerning the Continental Shelf*, in which the Court in order to examine the practice of States regarding the use of the proportionality principle as a criterion for the delimitation of the continental shelf, took into account "the public expression of their views at the United Nations Conference on the Law of the Sea." See the *Case concerning the Continental Shelf*, *ICJ Reports* 1985, p. 13, at p. 45.

81 G.M. Danilenko, *supra* note 78, p. 86.

82 K. Zemanek, *supra* note 19, pp. 194–5.

83 M. Virally, *supra* note 74, p. 156.

international law. At the municipal law level, the distinction between acts leading to the adoption of the rule and acts that constitute application of the rule can be made more easily. However, in the sphere of international law, neither a legislative authority, in the form of a body entrusted with the task to enact laws, nor a formalized legislative process exists. Accordingly, it is difficult to determine the exact time when a trend or a generalized practice ripens into a customary rule and consequently, treat all acts occurring after that time as mere instances of application of the rule. Thus, in international law, the line between acts that create a rule and acts that confirm it through application is often blurred.[84] Furthermore, the application of a customary rule in international law is not a static process; far from evidencing adherence to a rigid set of rules, application of a customary rule often involves changes that will gradually result in the modification of the initial content of the rule.[85] In the words of Zemanek: "a date when the formation of custom ends and its validity begins cannot be established."[86] On this basis, insisting upon a distinction between acts that lead to the formation of custom and acts that apply it seems to be meaningless. Therefore, it would be best to include not only acts that have a bearing on the formation of a customary rule, but also acts that apply such a rule in the category of unilateral acts in the custom-forming process.

Under the proposed classification, another category of unilateral acts would comprise all acts that are elements of the treaty-making process. Here belong all unilateral acts that pertain to the establishment, entry into force or termination of international agreements. Such acts are essentially part of an international agreement and the evaluation of their nature and legal effects will have to be made under that light. Most questions regarding the function of unilateral acts in the treaty-making process are tackled within the framework of the Vienna Convention on the Law of Treaties. Thus, for example, the

84 K. Zemanek, *supra* note 19, p. 195.

85 A pertinent example here is the rule on the breadth of the territorial sea. In the 18th century, the rule was that a State could establish the breadth of its territorial sea up to a limit of 3 nautical miles. The three-mile limit rule originated from the idea that the distance in which a canon mounted on the shore could fire was three miles from the coastline (the so-called canon-rule). However, claims for a wider territorial sea in the 19th and 20th century led to the modification of the three-mile limit rule. Nowadays, most coastal States claim a 12-mile territorial sea. As a result, it is generally agreed that the customary rule on the breadth of the territorial sea has changed and that the 12-mile limit rule is now in force. This modification is reflected in Art. 3 of LOSC which provides that "every State has the right to establish the breadth of its territorial sea up to a limit not exceeding 12 nautical miles." J. Crawford, *supra* note 7, p. 260.

86 K. Zemanek, *supra* note 19, p. 195.

definition and legal effects of the acts of ratification, signature, accession, suspension, termination and denunciation of international treaties are regulated under the relevant provisions of the Convention.[87]

Nevertheless, there are unilateral acts pertaining to the law of treaties the full scope of which is not clearly defined under the Convention; this is the case, for example, with interpretative declarations. Although such declarations are commonly employed in practice, they are not defined in the text of the Vienna Convention. However, there have been attempts to define the legal scope of interpretative declarations outside the framework of the Vienna Convention. Thus, for example, in the view of the Special Rapporteur of the ILC on reservations to treaties, Pellet, an interpretative declaration is a "unilateral declaration, however phrased or named, made by a State or an international organisation whereby that State or international organisation purports to clarify the meaning or scope attributed by the declarant to the treaty or to certain of its provisions."[88] Since an interpretative declaration essentially establishes the understanding of the meaning of the treaty or some of its provisions for the declarant, it is generally accepted that it will become a tool in the interpretation of the treaty provided that other States do not formally object thereto.[89] In general, for unilateral acts in the treaty-making process, the contractual element is strong; much will depend upon the reaction of other States parties and acceptance, even in a tacit manner, is important for these acts to produce legal effects.

However, interpretative declarations or reservations are not the only unilateral acts concerning treaties. In his survey, Pellet identified a number of other acts that, although seemingly performed in connection to a treaty, in reality, have no legal relationship to it.[90] Such acts include unilateral declarations whereby the declarant undertakes obligations that go beyond the terms of the treaty.[91] These may not be plausibly regarded as being part of an international

87 See Arts. 2, 12, 14 and 54–56 of the Vienna Convention, *supra* note 11.

88 See the A. Pellet, Third Report on Reservations to Treaties, UN Doc. A/CN.4/491/Add. 4, p. 221, para. 361.

89 A. Aust, *Modern Treaty Law and Practice*, 3rd ed., (Cambridge: Cambridge University Press, 2013), pp. 115–8. See also the examples referred to therein.

90 A. Pellet, *supra* note 88, para. 366. Other examples given by Pellet include: "(b) A declaration that can be construed as an offer to add a new provision to the treaty; (c) A "declaration of non-recognition", when the declaring State does not intend to prevent application of the treaty in its relations with the unrecognized entity."

91 A typical example of a declaration whereby the declarant, instead of restricting, expands the obligations assumed under a treaty is the one made by South Africa upon entering the General Agreement on Tariffs and Trade in 1948. For a discussion of the legal effects of this

agreement; in contrast to reservations or interpretative declarations, which constitute acts that may not produce effects unless in relation to a given treaty, such acts may well exist outside the sphere of the treaty. As Pellet notes: "They could have been made under any circumstances, they have no effect on its [the treaty's] implementation, nor do they seek to."[92] Consequently, the regime of the Vienna Convention is not applicable to them. Such unilateral acts are best treated within the context of autonomous unilateral acts, a topic that will be discussed next.

According to the criterion of context in which the act occurs, a third category of unilateral acts is autonomous unilateral acts. Autonomy here is a term of art that applies to unilateral acts that, although having legal effects on the international plane, are not elements of the treaty or custom-forming processes. Therefore, such acts will have to be evaluated within the sub-system of international law in which they occur. According to Zemanek and Virally, different types of unilateral acts may fall under this category. At first, acts that have come to acquire an independent legal status in international law (having been standardized in form through a process of repetition)[93] belong to this category. These include all 'traditional' unilateral acts, such as recognition, protest, waiver, *etc.* Furthermore, acts that lead directly to the creation of obligations for the author State, such as unilateral acts of a gratuitous character also belong to this category. These acts are autonomous to the extent that they create obligations for the author State in accordance with its intention and without the existence of a larger contractual framework. Thus, for example, the statements made by France in the context of the *Nuclear Tests Case* are autonomous inasmuch as the declarant State intended to become bound according to the content of its statements and irrespective of the existence of a *quid pro quod.*

Finally, Zemanek adds declarations made under Art. 36.2 of the ICJ Statute[94] to the category of autonomous unilateral acts. As seen earlier, there is a strong contractual element in declarations accepting the compulsory jurisdiction of the ICJ, in the sense that, such declarations will produce legal effects only *vis-a-vis* States that have accepted the same obligation by making reciprocal declarations under Art. 36.2. Thus, some authors, such as Virally, have treated declarations accepting the compulsory jurisdiction of the Court in the context

---

declaration see Addendum 3 of A. Pellet, Third Report on Reservations to Treaties, UN Doc. A/CN.4/491/Add.3, p. 221, paras. 213–7.

92 A. Pellet, *supra* note 88, para. 373.

93 K. Zemanek, *supra* note 19, p. 198.

94 *Ibid.*

of unilateral acts in the treaty-making process.[95] However, although its is true that the contractual element is strong in the case of declarations accepting the compulsory jurisdiction of the Court, the fact that such declarations constitute in essence unilateral acts of State sovereignty[96] may not be neglected. More particularly, their unilateral character – the fact that, instead of arising from a contractual situation, they are products of a unilateral drafting process – renders the regime governing international treaties proper partly inapplicable to them.

Thus, for example, in the *Anglo-Iranian Oil Co. Case*, the Court, taking into account the unilateral character of Iran's Declaration, concluded that principles commonly employed in the interpretation of an international treaty proper are inapplicable to the interpretation of declarations made under Art. 36.2 of its Statute. In the words of the Court:

> It [the Government of the United Kingdom] asserts that a legal text should be interpreted in such a way that a reason and a meaning can be attributed to every word in the text. It may be said that this principle should in general be applied when interpreting the text of a treaty. But the text of the Iranian Declaration is not a treaty text resulting from negotiations between two or more States. It is the result of unilateral drafting by the Government of Iran, which appears to have shown a particular degree of caution when drafting the text of the Declaration.[97]

The Court, then, went on to examine other elements that it considered more appropriate to the interpretation of a unilaterally drafted instrument and put primary emphasis upon the intention of the declarant State.[98] The ICJ

95 M. Virally, *supra* note 74, p. 155.

96 See the *Fisheries Jurisdiction Case*, in which the Court stated that "a declaration of acceptance of the compulsory jurisdiction of the Court, whether there are specified limits set to that acceptance or not, is a unilateral act of State sovereignty." *Fisheries Jurisdiction Case*, Spain vs Canada, *ICJ Reports* 1998, p. 432, para. 46.

97 *Anglo-Iranian Oil Co. Case*, *ICJ Reports* 1952, p. 93 at p. 105.

98 *Ibid.* More particularly, the Court considered that, in the light of the denunciation by Iran of all treaties with other States relating to the regime of capitulations, it was unlikely that it was the intention of Iran in accepting the Court's jurisdiction to submit disputes concerning these unilaterally denounced treaties to the jurisdiction of the Court. Note, however, that Judge Read disagreed with the majority of the Court on this point. In his view, the unilateral nature of a declaration made under Art. 36.2 did not justify departure from principles of interpretation applied to international treaties proper. In his own words: "I am unable to accept the contention that the principles of international law which

has consistently adhered to the position adopted in the *Anglo-Iranian Oil Co. Case*.[99]

This gives rise to a *sui generis* position; although a declaration accepting the compulsory jurisdiction of the Court produces effects only if it coincides with a reciprocal declaration, its unilateral character prevents it from being treated on the same footing as an international treaty proper.[100] Therefore, it seems more appropriate to follow Zemanek's approach and treat declarations made under Art. 36.2 of the ICJ Statute as forming a category of their own within the

govern the interpretation of treaties cannot be applied to the Persian Declaration [the Iranian Declaration], because it is unilateral. Admittedly it was drafted unilaterally. On the other hand, it was related, in express terms, to Article 36 of the Statute, and to the declarations of other States which had already deposited, or which might in the future deposit, reciprocal declarations. It was intended to establish legal relationships with such States, consensual in their character, within the regime established by the provisions of Article 36." See the Dissenting Opinion of Judge Read in the *Anglo-Iranian Oil. Co. Case, ibid.*, p. 142 at p. 142.

99 The Court has, on a number of occasions, stressed the relevance of the intention of the author State and of the circumstances antecedent to the making of the declaration in the interpretation of declarations accepting the compulsory jurisdiction of the Court, as well as of reservations contained therein. Thus, for example, in the *Aegean Sea Continental Shelf Case*, the Court stated that it followed from its jurisprudence that, in interpreting a reservation included in the Greek Declaration, "regard must be paid to the intention of the Greek Government at the time when it deposited its instrument of accession to the General Act; and it was with that jurisprudence in mind that the Court asked the Greek Government to furnish it with any available evidence of explanations of the instrument of accession given at that time." See *Aegean Sea Continental Shelf Case, ICJ Reports* 1978, p. 3, at p. 29. Furthermore, in the *Fisheries Jurisdiction Case* (Spain v. Canada), the Court confirmed that it will interpret "a declaration including a reservation contained therein in a natural and reasonable way, having due regard to the intention of the State concerned at the time when it accepted the compulsory jurisdiction of the Court. The intention of the State ,may be deduced not only from the text of the relevant clause, but also from the context in which the clause is to be read, and an examination of the evidence regarding the circumstances of its preparation and the purposes intended to serve." See the *Fisheries Jurisdiction Case*, Spain vs Canada, *supra* note 96, para. 49.

100 Thus, for example, in the *Fisheries Jurisdiction Case*, the Court, in response to Spain's contention that legal rules relating to the interpretation of declarations made under Art. 36.2 of the Court's Statute may coincide with those governing the interpretation of treaties, stated that the regime of the Vienna Convention on the Law of Treaties "may only apply analogously to the extent compatible with the sui generis character of the unilateral acceptance of the Court's jurisdiction." See the *Fisheries Jurisdiction Case*, Spain vs Canada, *ibid.*, para. 46.

larger framework of autonomous unilateral acts, instead of treating them as elements of the treaty-making process.

There are some clear benefits in accepting the context in which the act occurs as a criterion for the classification of unilateral acts. First, following such a typology offers the researcher a considerable degree of flexibility. Instead of narrowly focusing on one element of the unilateral act, a classification along the lines proposed by Zemanek and Virally takes into account the fact that unilateral acts may exist in different areas of international law, thereby making it easier both to concentrate on the unique features that each category may have, and to deduce elements commonly shared by all. Furthermore, following this classification allows us to pay due attention to the effect of relevant rules of law. Thus, for example, rules relating to the formation and application of custom in international law are relevant in the understanding of the nature and effects of unilateral acts in the context of customary law. Similarly, the regime of the Vienna Convention on the Law of Treaties governs most aspects of unilateral acts pertaining to the treaty-making process. Finally, the category of autonomous unilateral acts offers the opportunity to examine acts of independent legal significance within the sub-system of law in which they arise. In sum, this classification is preferable because it offers a comprehensive account of the various effects of unilateral acts while paying due attention to the context in which the act occurs, including the surrounding circumstances and more importantly the effect of relevant rules of law.

In summary, this section examined the possibility of using the context in which the act occurs as a criterion for classifying unilateral acts. It was shown that, on the basis of the legal context in which the act occurs, doctrine has generally agreed that there are three types of unilateral acts: unilateral acts in the context of customary international law, unilateral acts in the treaty-making process and autonomous unilateral acts. To the first category belong unilateral acts in the form of both material acts and unilateral statements that relate to the formation or application of customary rules. To the category of acts in the treaty-making process belong all unilateral acts pertaining to the law of treaties, such as ratification or interpretative declarations. Finally, acts having an independent significance in international law, such as recognition or declarations made under Art. 36.2 of the ICJ Statute, fall under the category of autonomous unilateral acts. The section then focused on the benefits of following such a classification. More particularly, it was shown that this typology is preferable since it offers a flexible, yet solid, framework for the classification of unilateral acts by paying attention both to the circumstances antecedent to the making of the act and to the effect of relevant rules of law.

4 Conclusion

This chapter examined different typologies of unilateral acts that have been suggested in the literature in order to pinpoint the one which best reflects the multitude of legal environments in which these acts take place in practice. It was shown that the task of classification is impeded by the heterogeneousness of unilateral acts and the lack of a generally agreed definition. Moreover it was argued that the existing definitions do not accurately describe the phenomenon of unilateral acts and therefore, an alternative definition based on the elements of the legal nature of these acts (unilateralism and the intention of the author to become bound) was proposed. It was asserted that this definition enjoys the benefit of accurately describing unilateral acts while being broad enough to take into account the diverse contexts in which these acts occur. The chapter continued by examining different classifications of unilateral acts against the background of State practice. It was argued that classifications based on the criteria of content and legal effects are dissatisfactory to the extent that they treat unilateral acts in isolation from the legal environment in which they occur. Finally, the chapter turned to the criterion of the context in which the act arises. It was argued that classification of unilateral acts on the basis of this criterion is preferable since it takes into consideration the circumstances surrounding the making of the act and the effect of relevant rules of law. Having provided a typology of unilateral acts, and thus, familiarised the reader with the range of acts that may fall within the category of unilateral acts, the next chapter will focus on the work of the ILC on the topic with a view to ascertain whether and to what extent the Commission tackled satisfactorily the question of the legal nature of unilateral acts.

CHAPTER 3

The Work of the International Law Commission on Unilateral Acts of States

1 Introduction

The purpose of this chapter is to present and critically analyse the work of the International Law Commission on unilateral acts of States and the final product of the Commission's work, the 2006 Guiding Principles.[1] In doing so, this chapter also aims to highlight the differences between the treatment of the topic by the ILC and the present work and thus, to show why it is important to re-examine the question of unilateral acts herein. It is clear that this book would not have been complete if the Commission, which is composed of eminent jurists, or "persons of recognized competence", had been ignored.[2] It has been accepted that the reports prepared by the Commission are "at least in the category of writings of the more qualified publicists"[3] in terms of sources of international law. Furthermore, as the product of a decade-long engagement with the subject, the texts prepared by the Commission provide a natural starting point for the exploration of unilateral acts.

This chapter will begin with a brief, historical overview of the Commission's work on the topic. It will then briefly introduce the 2006 Guiding Principles in order to put the discussion in context. Next, the main difficulties encountered by the ILC and the main issues that dominated the debate within the Commission will be analysed. Two substantive arguments are advanced. The first relates to the reasons that ultimately led to the abandonment of the codification project in 2006. It is asserted that the change of approach by the Special Rapporteur from a general approach to a case-by-case analysis of individual unilateral acts led to a general loss of interest with the topic

1 Guiding Principles Applicable to Unilateral Declarations of States Capable of Creating Legal Obligations with Commentaries Thereto, in Report of the ILC on the Work of Its 58th Session, UN Doc. A/61/10, *Yrbk of the ILC* 2006, Vol. II, p. 369. Hereinafter referred to as the 2006 Guiding Principles.

2 Art. 2.1 of the *Statute of the International Law Commission*, 21 November 1947, available at http://untreaty.un.org/ilc/texts/instruments/english/statute/statute_e.pdf.

3 H. Lauterpacht, *The Function of the Commission and the Selection of Topics for Codification*, in E. Lauterpacht (ed.), *International Law, Being the Collected Papers of Hersch Lauterpacht*, Vol. I, (Cambridge: Cambridge University Press, 1970), p. 445, at p. 445.

 | DOI 10.1163/9789004300767_005

within the ILC. This was compounded by two further difficulties – repeatedly voiced skepticism about the feasibility of the project, as well as the Special Rapporteur's over-reliance on the Vienna Convention on the Law of Treaties.[4] The second substantive argument is that disagreements within the Commission led to three major weaknesses of the final product: the failure to distinguish between unilateral juridical and unilateral political acts; the failure to define the element of the unilateral nature of unilateral acts (unilateralism); and the failure to establish clear boundaries between estoppel and unilateral acts.

The chapter will conclude by highlighting the differences between the work of the ILC on unilateral acts and this book. It will be claimed that, by way of contrast to the methodological approach favoured by the Special Rapporteur in his later reports, this work addresses the most problematic aspect of unilateral acts in practice: that of the definition of their legal nature. Moreover, it will be argued that this book moves beyond the work of the ILC by examining the context in which unilateral juridical acts usually occur and by pinpointing a list of factors that normally indicate the existence of the essential elements of the legal nature of unilateral acts (unilateralism and the intention to create binding obligations) in practice.

2 The Work of the ILC on Unilateral Acts of States

2.1 *Historical Overview*

The interest of the ILC in unilateral acts can be dated back to 1967, when a reference was made to the subject in the ILC's future organization of work. Tammes, member of the Commission at the time, stated that:

> So far as the sources of international law were concerned, the Commission had recently completed a very far-reaching and comprehensive draft on the law of treaties, and it would be difficult to suggest another source of international law that was as wide in scope. A limited counterpart to the law of treaties could, however, be found in the topic of unilateral acts, concerning which ample research and practice were available and which greatly needed clarification and systematization.[5]

4 *Vienna Convention on the Law of Treaties*, 22 May 1969, Vienna, 1155 UNTS 331, 8 ILM 679 (1969).

5 Statement by Tammes in Summary Records of the 19th Session, UN Doc. A/CN.4/Ser.A/1967, *Yrbk of the ILC* 1967, Vol. I, p. 179, para. 6.

The topic re-surfaced in the agenda of the Commission's long-term programme of work in 1971.[6] The complexities, as well as the great practical value, of such a study were highlighted in the 1971 Report:

> A study which examined the subject, or its different branches, and concluded with a series of definitions of the main forms of unilateral acts and their respective legal effects under international law, together with a succinct commentary, might prove to be of considerable practical value to States in their dealings with one another; at the moment no comparable agreed text exists to which reference can easily be made.[7]

In 1996 the Commission felt ready to undertake a full study of the topic with the aim of codifying the legal regime applicable to these acts; in its report of the same year, it was stated that, amongst other subjects proposed, unilateral acts would be a proper one for immediate consideration.[8] The following year the Commission appointed Cedeño as the Special Rapporteur on Unilateral Acts. In his nine reports to the Commission,[9] Cedeño attempted to provide an in-depth overview of the topic before the Commission decided to discontinue the project of codification in 2006 by adopting a set of Guidelines applicable to unilateral declarations.[10]

It was well-accepted at the time that the topic of unilateral acts of States was one of the most complicated and divisive ever tackled by the ILC. For example, Dugard admitted that the topic was unlike any other the Commission had dealt with in the past.[11] Similarly, Melescanu acknowledged the difficult and delicate nature of the subject, "as important to international law as reservations to treaties."[12] Furthermore, the quality of the reports prepared by Cedeño often attracted negative feedback; in his comments following the presentation

6 Review of the Commission's Long-term Programme of Work in Documents of the 23rd Session: Survey of International Law and Other Documents, UN Doc. A/CN.4/SER.A/1971/Add.l, *Yrbk of the ILC* 1971, Vol. II, p. 60 *et seq.*

7 *Ibid.*, para. 283.

8 Report on the Long-term Programme of Work in Report of the ILC on the Work of Its 48th Session, UN Doc. A/CN.4/SER.A/1996/Add.l, *Yrbk of the ILC* 1996, Vol. II, p. 141.

9 Unilateral Acts of States in *Analytical Guide to the Work of the ILC, 1949–1997*, (1998), available at http://untreaty.un.org/ilc/guide/9_9.htm.

10 See the 2006 Guiding Principles, *supra* note 1.

11 See the statement by Dugard in Summary Record of the 2722nd Meeting, UN Doc. A/CN.4/SR.2722, *Yrbk of the ILC* 2002, Vol. I, p. 76, para. 57.

12 See the statement by Melescanu in Summary Record of the 2771st Meeting, UN Doc. A/CN.4/SR.2771, *Yrbk of the* ILC 2003, Vol. I, p. 140, para. 11.

of the fifth report, Pellet went as far as to state that "the Special Rapporteur was rather like a broken record, repeating the same things and, by doing so, forcing Commission members...to repeat themselves in turn."[13]

The project also suffered due to the heated exchanges and greatly divergent views that followed the presentation of literally every aspect of the nine reports submitted by the Special Rapporteur. As it will be discussed in detail in a later section of this chapter, terse exchanges between Koskenniemi and Pellet were a standard feature after 2002.[14] As a result, the undertaking was twice nearly abandoned. In 2003, Koskenniemi cast doubt on the very existence of unilateral acts as a legal institution.[15] His remarks triggered an extended discussion regarding the feasibility of the project.[16] Although different views were expressed, it was generally felt that the topic was too important to be abandoned.[17] Again in 2004, the presentation of the seventh report of the Special Rapporteur was met with comments that came close to calling for discontinuance. According to Addo, opinions were extremely divided on the scope of the subject matter and thus, the Commission was locked in a stalemate.[18] Addo admitted that he was tempted to propose that the Commission should abandon the topic, but he did not do so, out of consideration for the work done up until that point.[19] The decision to establish a Working Group chaired by Pellet was adopted in order to break the impasse and help the Commission move forward.[20]

The hope that the establishment of a Working Group would facilitate progress and resolve the disagreements within the Commission was not realized. By 2005, the fatigue with the topic was obvious. In light of long-standing

13 See the statement by Pellet in Summary Record of the 2726th Meeting, UN Doc. A/CN.4/SR.2726, *Yrbk of the ILC* 2002, Vol. I, p. 99, para. 11.

14 See for example the statement by Koskenniemi in Summary Record of the 2722nd Meeting, *supra* note 11, p. 73, paras. 38–53, and the reply by Pellet, *ibid*, p. 75, paras. 54–6. See also the comments by Koskenniemi in Summary Record of the 2818th Meeting, UN Doc. A/CN.4/SR.2818, *Yrbk of the* ILC 2004, Vol. I, p. 181, paras. 1–4 and the reply by Pellet, *ibid.*, paras. 5–10.

15 See the comments by Koskenniemi in Summary Record of the 2772nd Meeting, UN Doc. A/CN.4/SR.2772, *Yrbk of the* ILC 2003, Vol. I, pp. 143–4, paras. 1–3.

16 See the statement by Brownlie in Summary Record of the 2772nd Meeting, *ibid.*, para. 4.

17 See for example the statements by Pambou-Tchivounda, Melescanu and Niehaus, *ibid.*, pp. 145–6.

18 Statement by Addo in Summary Record of the 2818th Meeting, *supra* note 14, pp. 183–4, paras. 26–8.

19 *Ibid.*, para. 28.

20 *Ibid.*, para. 54.

disagreements and with no discernible resolution in sight, Candioti proposed that the ILC drop the idea of producing draft articles on unilateral acts.[21] Instead, he argued that the Commission should settle for a set of guidelines that would help States in their every-day practice.[22] Candioti's proposal was accepted by the majority of the ILC members.[23] The following statement made by Kateka was characteristic of the mood prevailing in the Commission at the time; Kateka

> found it puzzling that the Commission was still debating the existence of unilateral acts. Irreconcilable philosophical and ideological differences separated Commission members on the issues of definition and scope of unilateral acts...At that rate it was likely that the Commission would spend the next 10 years on the topic. The Commission would therefore be wise to accept Mr. Candioti's proposal.[24]

Following Candioti's proposal, the Special Rapporteur's ninth report contained "ten guiding principles applicable to unilateral declarations of States capable of creating legal obligations" which were considered and subsequently adopted by the Commission, thus completing the latter's work on the subject.[25]

2.2 *The 2006 Guiding Principles*

The previous section provided a chronological overview of the work of the ILC and its Special Rapporteur on unilateral acts of States. This section aims to briefly sketch out the legal regime provided for under the 2006 Guiding Principles in order to put the discussion in context.

The 2006 Guiding Principles consist of ten general principles applicable to unilateral declarations of States capable of creating legal obligations and each principle is accompanied by a commentary. The ten principles cover a variety of issues, such as definition, interpretation, the capacity of States to formulate

---

21 See the statement by Candioti in Summary Record of the 2854th Meeting, UN Doc. A/CN.4/SR.2854, 4 August 2005, available at http://untreaty.un.org/ilc/guide/9_9.htm, p. 8.

22 *Ibid.*

23 See for example the statement by Xue in Summary Record of the 2854th Meeting, *ibid.*, p. 18, and the statement by Matheson in Summary Record of the 2855th Meeting, UN Doc. A/CN/SR.2855, 15 September 2005, available at http://untreaty.un.org/ilc/guide/9_9.htm, p. 5.

24 See the statement by Kateka in Summary Record of the 2855th Meeting, *ibid.*, p. 13.

25 Report of the ILC on the Work of Its 58th Session, UN Doc. A/61/10, *Yrbk of the ILC* 2006, Vol. II, pp. 362–81.

unilateral acts, form, possible addressees of the act, as well as invalidity and revocability of such acts. As far as definition is concerned, under General Principle 1, unilateral declarations "publicly made and manifesting the will to be bound may have the effect of creating legal obligations."[26] According to the Commission, in order to ascertain that a given unilateral declaration has created obligations for the author State, one must interpret it in accordance with its text and taking into account the context and the circumstances in which it was formulated, as well as the reactions to which it gave rise.[27]

Under the Guiding Principles, the form (oral or written) of a unilateral declaration, does not affect its validity.[28] However, a declaration is void if it conflicts with a peremptory norm of international law.[29] According to Guiding Principle 6, the addressees of a unilateral declaration may be the international community as a whole, one or more several States, or other entities.[30] The Commission specified in Guiding Principle 9 that, while the obligations contained in a unilateral declaration are only incumbent upon the author, the addressees may incur obligations to the extent that they have accepted it.[31] Finally, as far as the issue of revocability is concerned, the Guiding Principles stipulate that a declaration may not be invoked arbitrarily[32] and

26 Guiding Principle 1 of the 2006 Guiding Principles, *supra* note 1.

27 See Guiding Principles 3, 7, *ibid.* According to Guiding Principle 3: "To determine the legal effects of such declarations, it is necessary to take account of their content, of all the factual circumstances in which they were made, and of the reactions to which they gave rise." According to Guiding Principle 7: "A unilateral declaration entails obligations for the formulating State only if it stated in clear and specific terms. In the case of doubt as to the scope of the obligations resulting from such a declaration, such obligations must be interpreted in a restrictive manner. In interpreting the content of such obligations, weight shall be given first and foremost to the text of the declaration, together with the context and the circumstances in which it was formulated."

28 Guiding Principle 5, *ibid.* According to the text of Guiding Principle 5: "Unilateral declarations may be formulated orally or in writing."

29 Guiding Principle 8, *ibid.* According to the text of Guiding Principle 8: "A unilateral declaration which is in conflict with a peremptory norm of general international law is void."

30 Guiding Principle 6, *ibid.*

31 Guiding Principle 9, *ibid.* According to the text of Guiding Principle 9: "No obligation may result for other States from the unilateral declaration of a State. However, the other State or States concerned may incur obligations in relation to such a unilateral declaration to the extent that they clearly accepted such a declaration."

32 Guiding Principle 10, *ibid.* According to the text of Guiding Principle 10: "A unilateral declaration that has created legal obligations for the State making the declaration cannot be revoked arbitrarily. In assessing whether a revocation would be arbitrary, consideration should be given to: (a) Any specific terms of the declaration relating to revocation; (b) The

that, in assessing whether a revocation would be arbitrary, consideration should be given to the terms of the declaration; the extent to which the addressee of the act has relied upon the declaration; and the extent to which there has been a fundamental change of circumstances.[33]

2.3 *Evaluation of the Work of the ILC: Difficulties and Weaknesses*

Having introduced the 2006 General Principles, this section turns to the evaluation of both the work and the final product of the Commission's ten-year struggle with the topic. Such an assessment is a difficult task. On the one hand, the reports prepared by Cedeño, as well as the ensuing debates within the Commission, provide a wealth of information; the importance of this endeavour cannot be underestimated given the scarcity of materials on unilateral acts in modern literature. On the other hand, the final aim of the work needs to be taken into consideration. In the introductory note to the ILC's Guiding Principles, it is stated that: "Clearly, it is important for States to be in a position to judge with reasonable certainty whether and to what extent their unilateral conduct may legally bind them on the international plane."[34] Pellet, as a member of the Commission, had also repeatedly emphasized that: "The aim was to tell States the extent to which they risked becoming trapped by their own declarations, *i.e.* their own commitments. States needed to know, for example, what statements they could make in the international arena without such statements being regarded as legal acts that could be used against them."[35] Thus, the aim of the Commission was to establish the threshold beyond which States became bound by their unilateral behavior. It is in this respect that the work of the ILC fell short of its goal – an argument that the remainder of this section will develop.

At this point, a caveat needs to be entered: naturally, during the course of the Commission's long-standing engagement with unilateral acts, a wide range of issues was discussed. However, it would be impossible to treat all of them here. Therefore, the following discussion of the ILC's work will concentrate on the main difficulties encountered by the Commission and on the main weaknesses of the 2006 Guiding Principles.

---

extent to which those to whom the obligations are owed have relied on such obligations; (c) The extent to which there has been a fundamental change of circumstances."

33 *Ibid.*

34 ILC Report on the Work of Its 58th Session, *supra* note 25, p. 366, para. 173.

35 See the statement by Pellet in Summary Record of the 2853rd Meeting, UN Doc. A/CN.4/SR.2853, 6 September 2005, available at http://untreaty.un.org/ilc/guide/9_9.htm, p. 4.

A The Difficulties Encountered by the ILC

i *Change of Methodological Approach: From a General Approach to a Case-by-case Analysis of Unilateral Acts*

The methodological approach chosen by the Special Rapporteur to tackle the question of unilateral acts of States played a significant role in shaping the debate within the Commission and the overall direction of the project. It is suggested in what follows that the decision of the Special Rapporteur to change his approach and move from an initial all-encompassing approach to a case-by-case analysis contributed to the loss of interest in and the final decision to conclude the project prematurely in 2006.

More specifically, between 1998 and 2002, Cedeño attempted to treat unilateral acts in a holistic fashion; during those first years of getting to grips with the topic, emphasis was placed on the preparation of draft articles that would be applicable to all unilateral acts. Thus, in the first up to the fifth report, one may find, among others, draft articles on the definition of unilateral acts, on the capacity of States to formulate such acts, and on their invalidity.[36] Although certain aspects of the initial approach of the Special Rapporteur are not without criticism, this approach was in accordance with the overall aim of the Commission, *i.e.* to elaborate rules applicable to all unilateral acts.

Disagreements within the Commission and dissatisfaction with the draft articles led the Special Rapporteur to change his approach in 2003. In his sixth report of the same year, Cedeño shifted to a case-by-case analysis of individual acts to be found in State practice, such as recognition.[37] The exposition of relevant practice was not, however, accompanied by an overarching commentary that would sum up the lessons learned and infer general rules applicable to all unilateral acts.

Some members of the Commission expressed doubts about the change of methodological approach by the Special Rapporteur. It was stated that:

> From his prior global approach he had shifted to a case by case study in order to identify general rules applicable to all unilateral acts. It was not clear how his monographic studies would tie in with the ultimate objective of the exercise, namely the elaboration of draft articles enabling states to realize when they ran the risk of being ensnared by the formal expression of their will.[38]

36 Unilateral Acts of States in *Analytical Guide, supra* note 9.

37 V. Rodríguez Cedeño, Sixth Report on Unilateral Acts of States, UN Doc. A/CN.4/534, p. 53.

38 Report of the ILC on the Work on Its 55th Session, UN Doc. A/58/10, *Yrbk of the ILC* 2003, Vol. II, p. 139, para. 278. See also the relevant remarks by Pellet in Summary Record of the

More particularly, Pellet questioned the choice of focusing on recognition of States, which, in his opinion, was a unique institution that produced effects too specific to permit general conclusions to be drawn.[39] Frustrated by the change of direction and the apparent abandonment of the attempt to elaborate draft articles in favour of less rigid guidelines, Pellet's previous remarks were followed by caustic comments:

> He had expressed the fear that Mr. Sreenivasa Rao might become the Garcia Amador of liability, and now Mr. Rodriguez Cedeño seemed to be courting the same danger with regard to unilateral acts. Mr. Garcia Amador, the first, and talented, Special Rapporteur on State responsibility, had never discovered the angle from which to come to grips with the topic. Similarly, Mr. Rodriguez Cedeño produced stimulating reports but failed to provide any proposals for future action. Where was the Commission going with the topic?[40]

Despite harsh criticism, the Special Rapporteur insisted on a case-by-case approach in his seventh and eighth reports – something that was not well-received by the majority of the members of the Commission. Following the presentation of the seventh report in 2004, Gaja remarked that the report was in need of further analysis of the examples cited in order to provide the necessary link between the study of individual acts and general conclusions that would be applicable to all unilateral acts.[41] Similarly, the following year, Escarameia noted that she was disappointed that the Special Rapporteur had not devoted more time to conclusions that would facilitate the deduction of general rules.[42]

The case-by-case approach favoured by the Special Rapporteur in the later years had another drawback. It gave the opportunity and the space to the minority of the members of the ILC who did not believe that unilateral acts can actually produce legal effects on the international plane to argue that no general rules applicable to all unilateral acts may be inferred from State or

2771st Meeting, *supra* note 12, p. 139, paras. 1–10. See also the comments by Melescanu, Economides and Daudi who were in agreement with Pellet, *ibid.*, paras. 11–7.

39 See the statements by Pellet, *ibid.*, p. 140, para. 9.

40 *Ibid.*

41 Report of the ILC on the Work of Its 56th Session, UN Doc. A/59/10, *Yrbk of the ILC* 2004, Vol. II, p. 225, para. 215. See also the comments by Gaja in Summary Record of the 2813th Meeting, UN Doc. A/CN.4/SR.2813, *Yrbk of the ILC* 2004, Vol. I, p. 158, paras. 43–5.

42 See the statements by Escarameia in Summary Record of the 2853rd Meeting, *supra* note 35, p. 3.

judicial practice and thus, the project was futile and should be abandoned. For example, Koskenniemi was one of the few members of the Commission who congratulated the Special Rapporteur on changing his approach in 2003.[43] Koskenniemi relied on the inability of the Special Rapporteur to draw general conclusions from the individual instances of unilateral acts contained in the reports to stage an attack on the viability of the whole project.[44] Although his arguments did not manage to convince the majority of the Commission, the ensuing debates stalled the progress of the Commission's work, as it will be seen in the next section.

ii *Skepticism about the Project*

The Commission's work was also plagued by constant discussions about the feasibility of the project. These doubts took two forms: some members of the Commission, believed that the topic was too difficult to codify, whilst others, notably Koskeniemmi, did not believe in the existence of unilateral acts as a legal institution altogether. The former category was mainly represented by Simma and Brownlie who had repeatedly expressed misgivings about the fitness of the topic for codification.[45] However, it needs to be noted that the above scepticism arose from the difficulties encountered in the task of codification and not from doubts regarding the binding force of unilateral acts. Thus, for example, Brownlie stated that: "It was a little unfair to say that unilateral acts did not exist as a legal institution since they were quite widely accepted as a category of study and as an area of problems. The UK had decided some time ago that the subject was so complex that it was not susceptible to codification."[46]

On the other hand, there were a few members of the Commission, the most vociferous amongst them being Koskenniemi, who persistently objected to the continuation of the project on the ground that unilateral acts did not constitute a legal phenomenon. In 2002, as a newly introduced member to the Commission, Koskenniemi made a forceful attempt to convince the members of the Commission that they had, more or less, wasted their breath on the topic. According to him, unilateral acts only existed as a phenomenon in the

43 See the statements by Koskenniemi in Summary Record of the 2772nd Meeting, *supra* note 15, para. 1.

44 See the statement by Koskenniemi in Summary Record of the 2853rd Meeting, *supra* note 35, p. 5.

45 See for example the statements by Simma in Summary Record of the 2722nd Meeting, *supra* note 11, para. 50, and the statements by Brownlie in Summary Record of the 2772nd Meeting, *supra* note 15, para. 4.

46 See the statements by Brownlie, *ibid.*

social world, and thus, the attempts made by the Commission and its Special Rapporteur to treat them as a unified legal concept were misplaced.[47] In his own words:

> Unilateral acts...did not refer to any particular legal institution. Instead they were a catch-all term to describe ways in which States sometimes were bound other than through the effects of particular institutions, or in which States acted in special ways so as to create legal effects. It was the source of some of the difficulties; the Commission was trying to codify something which did not exist as a legal institution and was at a loss as to how to define it so as to make it a legal institution.[48]

Koskenniemi's comments were met with fierce reactions and the greatest part of the rest of the meetings was spent debating the existence of unilateral acts.

The same pattern governed all subsequent meetings up until the decision to conclude the Commission's work on the subject. The presentation of each of the reports by the Special Rapporteur from 2002 onwards was followed by Koskenniemi's calls to cease all codification efforts on unilateral acts.[49] Such calls invariably sparked long-winded discussions about the project's feasibility. As Pellet stated in 2004:

> Mr. Koskenniemi's statement had brought the Commission back to where it had been in 1997, when it was wondering whether to include the topic of unilateral acts in its agenda. If he had been present at the time, Mr. Koskenniemi, might have persuaded the members, but, now, he had to come around to the idea that the topic was on the agenda. His idea of drafting a preliminary report after seven years of study was rather odd.[50]

Ultimately, both types of arguments against the feasibility of the codification project, *i.e.* both the arguments by Simma and Brownlie on the one hand, and by Koskenniemi on the other, had the same result, namely they led to protracted and unproductive discussions that hindered the chances of significant

47 See the statements by Koskenniemi in Summary Record of the 2722nd Meeting, *supra* note 11, paras. 38–49.

48 *Ibid.*, para. 42.

49 See for example the statements by Koskenniemi in Summary Record of the 2772nd Meeting, *supra* note 15, para. 1; Summary Record of the 2818th Meeting, *supra* note 14, paras. 1–4; Summary Record of the 2853rd Meeting, *supra* note 35, p. 5.

50 Summary Record of the 2818th Meeting, *ibid.*, para. 5.

progress. At the same time, the continuing debate on the viability of the topic forced the Special Rapporteur to spend time justifying the existence of unilateral acts in every report, thus not allowing him to concentrate on other substantial aspects of the topic. Likewise, such discussions distracted the Commission from its focus. Instead of debating substantive issues, the Commission was gripped in a futile dead-lock – constantly reconsidering the very existence of unilateral acts, something accepted by the great majority of members anyway.[51]

iii *Over-reliance on the Model of the Vienna Convention on the Law of Treaties*

Another problem that hampered the work of the Commission was that the Special Rapporteur attempted to follow the model of the Vienna Convention on the Law of Treaties too rigidly. By his own admission in the third report: "In our view, it is very useful to follow the methodology and structure of the 1969 Convention."[52] Indeed, the draft articles contained in Cedeño's first five reports mirror the corresponding articles of the Vienna Convention. His reports included draft articles on the capacity of States to formulate unilateral acts, on persons authorized to formulate unilateral acts on behalf of the State, and on subsequent confirmation of an act formulated by a person not authorized for that purpose among others.[53]

However, by excessively extrapolating from the law of treaties, the Special Rapporteur lost sight of the unique problems that unilateral juridical acts pose in practice. The Commission warned him to that effect in 2000: "It would be inadvisable to follow closely the 1969 Convention since there were essential differences between treaty law and the law on unilateral acts."[54] As it will be

51 See for example the statement by Pambou-Tchivounda in Summary Record of the 2772nd Meeting, *supra* note 15, para 5: "It was impossible not to be shocked by Mr Koskenniemi's questioning of the existence of unilateral acts of States as a legal category and his assertion that such acts reflected the sociological reality of relations between States...Unilateral acts of States had both a theoretical and practical existence, as was evidenced by the numerous references to State practice appearing in the Special Rapporteur's sixth report." See also the statements by Chee and Addo who supported the view that, undoubtedly, unilateral acts existed as a legal institution in international law, *ibid*, paras. 7 and 9.

52 V. Rodríguez Cedeño, Third Report on Unilateral Acts of States, UN Doc. A/CN.4/505, p. 247, at p. 251, para. 21.

53 For an overview of the Special Rapporteur's reports on unilateral acts, see Unilateral Acts of States in *Analytical Guide*, *supra* note 9.

54 Report of the ILC on the Work of Its 52nd Session, UN Doc. A/55/10, *Yrbk of the ILC* 2000, Vol. II, p. 92, para. 537.

shown in the next section, the Commission realized from the very early stages of its engagement with the topic that one of the major problems associated with these acts was how to distinguish between them and acts with no legal effects on the international plane. However, by adhering to the model of the Vienna Convention and by introducing a wide array of issues, Cedeño's reports managed to deflect focus from major issues (such as the distinction between unilateral legal acts and unilateral political acts) to those of rather secondary importance (such as the capacity of States to formulate unilateral acts).

As a result, these major, unresolved issues constantly haunted the debates, frustrating the work of the Special Rapporteur and of the Commission throughout the project. Having failed to produce practical tools for distinguishing between unilateral juridical and political acts in 2004 – after eight years of work on the subject – the Commission acknowledged that: "It would probably have been better not to have made the mistake of choosing the method of dealing with unilateral acts on the same basis as treaties."[55]

B Weaknesses of the 2006 Guiding Principles

Having discussed the difficulties encountered by the Commission in its attempt to codify unilateral acts, the focus will next turn to the Commission's final product, the 2006 Guiding Principles. This section argues that the 2006 Guiding Principles have three main weaknesses: they fail to distinguish between unilateral juridical and unilateral political acts; they fail to define the element of unilateralism; and they fail to establish clear boundaries between unilateral acts and estoppel. In order to provide an accurate account of the reasons underpinning these weaknesses, the following sections will begin by tracing the discussion within the ILC regarding the substantive issues that led to these weaknesses. Then, the focus will turn on how the failure to tackle the aforementioned issues compromised the 2006 Guiding Principles.

i *The Failure to Distinguish between Unilateral Juridical and Unilateral Political Acts*

A review of the debate within the ILC reveals that the members of the Commission acknowledged – from the outset – that the main problem associated with unilateral juridical acts in practice is that of distinguishing between these acts and unilateral political acts, *i.e.* acts with no legal effects. In the debate following the first report, Dugard noted that: "the Commission would have to live with the fact that it was always hard to distinguish between unilateral acts intended to have legal consequences, and those intended to be purely

55 Report of the ILC on the Work of Its 56th Session, *supra* note 41, p. 225, para. 213.

political."[56] As mentioned earlier, it was exactly in that difficulty that the value of the engagement of the ILC with the topic was supposed to lie; the Commission included unilateral acts in its agenda in order to clarify the circumstances under which a unilateral declaration of a State may produce binding obligations on the international plane, thus enhancing certainty in international relations.

According to the Special Rapporteur, the criterion for distinguishing between political and legal acts was that of the intention of the author State to create legal effects,[57] an opinion that was accepted by the majority of the members of the Commission[58] and to which the present author also subscribes. However, neither in the first, nor in the subsequent reports, did the Special Rapporteur elaborate on how the element of intention is to be determined in practice, *i.e.* on how the distinction between legal and political acts of unilateral origin can be practically made.

Individual members of the Commission were more alert to the need to provide States with the necessary tools for determining whether a given unilateral act evidences the intention to create legal effects. As Kolodkin observed in 2004:

> What were the criteria for determining that a given act was juridical? According to the definition given...the main element appeared to be that a unilateral juridical act was one by which a State sought to create obligations or other legal effects under international law...How could one determine whether the State that formulated a unilateral act had or did not have such an intention?[59]

Members of the Commission repeatedly stressed the idea that the context in which the act occurs is of great importance in establishing the intention of the author State to become bound. For example, in the debate following the third report it was stated that:

---

56 See the statement by Dugard in Summary Record of the 2526th Meeting, UN Doc. A/CN.4/SR.2526, *Yrbk of the ILC* 1998, Vol. I, p. 49, para. 3.

57 V. Rodríguez Cedeño, First Report on Unilateral Acts of States, UN Doc. A/CN.4/486, p. 319, at para. 44.

58 See for example the Report of the ILC on the Work of Its 51st session, UN Doc. A/54/10, *Yrbk of the* ILC 1999, Vol. II, p. 134, para. 540. See also the statements by Pellet in Summary Record of the 2525th Meeting, UN Doc. A/CN.4/SR.2525, *Yrbk of the ILC* 1998, Vol. I, p. 46 para. 36.

59 See the statement by Kolodkin in Summary Record of the 2813th Meeting, *supra* note 41, p. 159, para. 47.

> A contextual examination...played a very important role in assessing the intention underlying the act...It was unfortunate that the Special Rapporteur had not sufficiently stressed...the idea of context on which, for example, the ICJ had relied on the case concerning the *Maritime Delimitation and Territorial Questions between Qatar and Bahrain.*[60]

Again in 2004, the Commission reprimanded the Special Rapporteur for not developing the idea of context as a means for determining the binding nature of unilateral acts:

> Even if the report gave examples of several types of declarations...it was not enough simply to cite such declarations: in order to determine whether the intention had been to produce legal effects, the context of the declarations, both ex ante and ex post, had to be taken into account, as the *Nuclear Tests* cases[61] had shown. The report provided next to no information on that subject.[62]

The importance of the context in which a unilateral act occurs was also stressed by a number of States in their replies to a questionnaire prepared by the Special Rapporteur.[63]

The Special Rapporteur's failure to heed the advice of the Commission was a weakness that also compromised the final product. Neither the text of the 2006 Guiding Principles,[64] nor the accompanying commentary offer any concrete interpretative tools for establishing the author's intention to create obligations. At this point, it is worthwhile to revisit the text of Guiding Principle 1:

> Declarations publicly made and manifesting the will to be bound may have the effect of creating legal obligations. When the conditions for this are met, the binding character of such declarations is based on good faith; States concerned may then take them into consideration and rely

---

60 Report of the ILC on the Work of Its 52nd Session, *supra* note 54, p. 93, para. 551.

61 *Nuclear Tests Case*, Australia vs France, *ICJ Reports* 1974, p. 253, New Zealand vs France, ICJ *Reports* 1974, p. 457. The Court's judgments in these two cases are almost identical. Hereinafter, unless otherwise stated, all references made to the *Nuclear Tests Case* will concern the case between Australia and France.

62 Report of the ILC on the Work of Its 56th Session, *supra* note 41, pp. 230–1, para. 234.

63 See the statements by Israel, Austria and Argentina as quoted in V. Rodríguez Cedeño, Fourth Report on Unilateral Acts of States, UN Doc. A/CN.4/419, p. 115, at p. 129, paras. 104–6.

64 2006 Guiding Principles, *supra* note 1.

> on them; such States are entitled to require that such obligations be respected.[65]

The accompanying commentary emphasizes the importance of the intention of the author State in the context of unilateral acts, but offers nothing more:

> The wording of Guiding Principle 1, which seeks both to define unilateral acts in the strict sense and to indicate what they are based on, is very directly inspired by the dicta in the judgments handed down by the International Court of Justice on 20 December 1974 in the *Nuclear Tests Case*. In the case concerning the *Frontier Dispute* (*Burkina Faso v. Republic of Mali*), the Court was careful to point out that 'it all depends on the intention of the State in question.'[66] Most of the cases studied illustrate this principle.[67]

Nevertheless, the relevance of the context in which a unilateral act occurs, for the purpose of ascertaining its legal character, was acknowledged in the Guiding Principles. According to Guiding Principle 3: "To determine the legal effects of such declarations, it is necessary to take account of their content, of all the factual circumstances in which they were made, and of the reactions to which they gave rise."[68] However, despite the importance the third Guiding Principle affords to context, neither its text, nor the accompanying commentary detail any contextual elements that would be of assistance to States when judging the legal status of a unilateral act. The commentary to Guiding Principle 3 simply rehashes the relevant case-law of the ICJ. According to the commentary:

> The wording of Guiding Principle 3 is also inspired by a passage in the ICJ judgments the *Nuclear Tests* cases;[69] allusion is made to this jurisprudence in the Judgments of 22 December 1986 in the *Frontier Dispute* (*Burkina Faso v. Republic of Mali*) case[70] and on 3 February 2006 in the *Armed Activities on the Territory of Congo* case.[71] In the *Military and*

---

65 Guiding Principle 1, *ibid.*

66 *Case concerning the Frontier Dispute*, *ICJ Reports* 1986, p. 554, at p. 573.

67 Commentary to Guiding Principle 1, *supra* note 1, p. 370.

68 Guiding Principle 3, *ibid.*, p. 371.

69 *Nuclear Tests Case*, *supra* note 61.

70 *Frontier Dispute Case*, *supra* note 66.

71 *Case concerning Armed Activities on the Territory of Congo* (*New application: 2002*), *ICJ Reports* 2006, p. 6, at p. 28, para. 49.

> *Paramilitary Activities in and against Nicaragua*[72] and *Frontier Dispute* cases, the Court found nothing in the content of the declarations cited or the circumstances in which they were made 'from which it [could] be inferred that any legal undertaking was intended to exist.'[73] Generally speaking, the cases studied by the Commission confirm the relevance of this principle.[74]

It is submitted that the failure to provide any substantial guidance for ascertaining the element of the intention to create legal effects is the biggest drawback of the Commission's work on the topic. As it was shown above, the Guiding Principles do not add anything new to what the Court had already stated in the *Nuclear Tests Case*. It is undoubtedly the case that the material compiled by the Special Rapporteur did provide a unique opportunity – that was unfortunately missed. It is possible, as will be seen in detail in the sixth chapter, to identify the circumstances under which a State is considered to have crossed the threshold from the political to the legal through the use of some of this material.

ii *The Failure to Define the Element of Unilateralism*

Apart from intention, another issue that elicited strong debates within the Commission was the question of the 'unilateral nature' of unilateral acts, *i.e.* the element of unilateralism. In order to define unilateralism, the Special Rapporteur introduced a distinction between autonomous and non-autonomous acts in his second report. According to Cedeño, autonomous, and thus truly unilateral, acts are: (a) those which are independent of any pre-existing juridical norms and (b) those which do not require either the acceptance of the addressee or any other conduct which may signify acceptance on the addressee's part.[75] Thus, on the basis of this two-pronged concept of autonomy, Cedeño purported to exclude from the ambit of the Commission's work acts that were already regulated by either treaty or customary law as well as acts that required some form of acceptance by the addressee.[76]

---

72 *Case concerning Military and Paramilitary Activities in and against Nicaragua*, Merits, ICJ *Reports* 1986, p. 14.

73 *Ibid.*, p. 132, para. 261.

74 Commentary to Guiding Principle 3, *supra* note 1, p. 371.

75 V. Rodríguez Cedeño, Second Report on Unilateral Acts of States, UN Doc. A/CN.4/500, p. 195, at p. 202, paras. 62–3.

76 *Ibid.*

However, the above concept of autonomy elicited different reactions within the Commission. Some members, such as Pellet, Candioti and Addo, thought that the introduction of the concept of autonomy was too ambiguous[77] and that the autonomous or non-autonomous nature of unilateral acts was of secondary importance.[78] Pellet was particularly apprehensive about the idea of excluding acts that were linked to a pre-existing rule of international law.[79] He asserted that he saw no difference between unilateral acts that had no direct justification in a specific pre-existing rule, such as the French declarations in the context of the *Nuclear Tests* cases, and those which had, such as a unilateral act by which a State delimits its territorial waters to 12 miles.[80]

Other members, such as Rosenstock, Lukashuk and Economides strongly favored the concept of autonomy introduced by the Special Rapporteur. Rosenstock stated that the element of autonomy is implicit in all unilateral acts of States[81] and Lukashuk stressed the importance of this element in the context of unilateral acts.[82] Economides made the most convincing argument in favor of autonomy. According to Economides, what matters is the legal sphere in which the act takes place. Acts that occur within the treaty or customary international law sphere were, in his opinion, "of no concern to the Commission, because the legal regimes were known, whether in the case of... customary acts, or treaty-related acts. What was important for the Commission was an act...[that] was not linked to any other source of law."[83]

Due to the disagreement within the Commission, the question of autonomy was left open and it was suggested that it could be revisited at a later date.[84] However, the question was subsequently buried and never re-surfaced. The result of the failure of the Commission to reach consensus on 'autonomy' was that the 2006 Guiding Principles provide no definition of the element of unilateralism. In fact, the Guiding Principles do not make any reference to the unilateral nature of unilateral declarations at all. Thus, little genuine assistance is given to States in determining whether a given act is truly unilateral or not.

As far as the 'autonomy debate' within the Commission is concerned, it seems that the members of the ILC became entangled in a theoretical battle

77 See the statements by Pellet, Candioti and Addo in Summary Record of the 2603rd Meeting, UN Doc. A/CN.4/SR.2603, *Yrbk of the ILC* 1999, Vol. I, pp. 261–4, paras. 12–35.

78 Statement by Addo, *ibid.*, para. 32.

79 Statements by Pellet, *ibid.*, para. 19.

80 *Ibid.*

81 Statement by Rosenstock, *ibid.*, para. 17.

82 Statement by Lukashuk, *ibid.*, para. 18.

83 Statement by Economides, *ibid.*, para. 23.

84 See the statement by Baena Soares, *ibid*, para. 40.

thereby losing sight of the practical aspects of the topic. The crux of the matter, was not, as Economides correctly pointed out, to provide an abstract definition of the element of unilateralism, but to exclude from the ambit of the Commission's work acts that could be easily explained with reference to customary or treaty law. This would have allowed the Commission to concentrate on and identify the legal regime applicable to the remainder of unilateral acts that pose real problems in practice – *i.e.* to 'voluntary acts' as these were defined in the introduction to this book. As mentioned in the introduction, unilateral acts that are linked to other regimes, such as customary international law and treaty law are not problematic to the extent that their binding force and the rules regulating their formulation can be traced back to these well known legal regimes.

Furthermore, as it will be seen in detail in the fourth chapter, the present author concurs with the definition of unilateralism provided by the Special Rapporteur – one that explains unilateralism in terms of the autonomy of the act to produce legal effects irrespective of acceptance or reliance by the addressee. However, it is submitted that simply providing a definition of the unilateral nature of these acts, as the Special Rapporteur did, is not enough. As with the element of intention, the Special Rapporteur failed to provide any tools that would assist in determining whether a given act is unilateral or not in practice. It is at this point that this work diverges from the approach of the Special Rapporteur: instead of merely defining the element of unilateralism, this study will examine the context in which these acts usually occur in practice and pinpoint a number of factors that indicate the existence of acts of truly unilateral character.

iii *The Failure to Establish Boundaries between Estoppel and Unilateral Acts*

Finally, another major drawback of the ILC's work on the topic is the failure to establish clear boundaries between estoppel and unilateral acts. A detailed analysis of estoppel in international law is reserved for the fourth chapter where the differences between it and unilateral acts are discussed. For the purposes of the present section, it suffices to note that for estoppel to arise in international law, the addressee of the unilateral representation must have relied on it to its own detriment.[85] In his first report on unilateral acts, the Special Rapporteur devoted only a few sentences to the relation between the two phenomena.[86] According to Cedeño, while in cases of estoppel the legal

85 As will be demonstrated in Chapter 4.

86 V. Rodríguez Cedeño, *supra* note 57, para. 131.

effects stem from the expectations that certain unilateral conduct has raised among other subjects of law, in the case of unilateral juridical acts, the legal effects stem from the autonomous intention of the author State to create legal effects on the international plane.[87]

However, the Special Rapporteur's position – which was purely theoretical and not substantiated by reference to practice – failed to convince all members of the Commission. For some, most notably Brownlie, estoppel should have been part of the topic. Thus, in the debate following the first report Brownlie stated that: "In practice, many international lawyers considered that estoppel was indeed part of the field of unilateral acts of States."[88] Others, such as Pellet, did not see any reason to include estoppel in the scope of acts studied by the Commission.[89] In their opinion, unilateral acts could, in some cases, give rise to estoppel, but that was simply a question of legal effects and not of definition.[90]

Disagreement over the inclusion of estoppel continued in subsequent sessions and the Special Rapporteur was repeatedly called to clarify the interplay between the two concepts.[91] However, the Special Rapporteur simply chose to ignore such calls. Cedeño's persistent failure to explain the role of estoppel prompted Brownlie to state in 2004 that "he had been somewhat depressed by the relative absence of reference in the seventh report to the Commission's own previous discussions on the topic...He himself, for example, had made several attempts to get a reasoned explanation why...estoppel [was] excluded from the Special Rapporteur's concept of the subject."[92] Due to the Special Rapporteur's failure to engage with the issue in depth, no agreement was reached on the role of the reliance that unilateral acts may give rise to.

This blurring of lines between estoppel and unilateral acts is also evident in the 2006 Guiding Principles. Already from the preamble it is noted that "in practice, it is often difficult to establish whether the legal effects stemming from the unilateral behaviour of a State are the consequence of the intent that it has expressed or depend on the expectations that its conduct has raised among other subjects of international law."[93] Moreover, Guiding Principle 1

87 *Ibid.*

88 Statement by Brownlie in Summary Record of the 2525th Meeting, *supra* note 58, para. 25.

89 Statement by Pellet, *ibid.*, para. 38.

90 *Ibid.*

91 See for example the Report of the ILC on the Work of Its 53rd Session, UN Doc. A/56/10, *Yrbk of the ILC* 2001, Vol. II, p. 204, para. 234, where it was stated that: "Hope was expressed that the issues of estoppel...could be elaborated upon further."

92 Statement by Brownlie in Summary Record of the 2813th Meeting, *supra* note 41, para. 53.

93 2006 Guiding Principles, *supra* note 1.

oscillates between the intention of the author State and the reliance placed upon the act by other States as the decisive factor in attributing legal effects to a unilateral act: "Declarations publicly made and manifesting the will to be bound may have the effect of creating legal obligations...*States concerned may then take them into consideration and rely on them*; such States are entitled to require that such obligations be respected."[94]

The result is once again disappointing; instead of clearly distinguishing between the two phenomena, the Guiding Principles seem to (at least partially) conflate them. Is a unilateral act binding when it evidences the will of the author State to create legal effects or is it binding only if the addressee relies on it? This question cannot be answered on the basis of the Guiding Principles.

3 Conclusion: The Differences between the Work of the ILC on Unilateral Acts and the Present Study

The previous section introduced and analysed the most problematic aspects of the ILC's work on unilateral acts of States. This section will summarise the arguments made in this chapter and highlight the differences between the work of the ILC and the present study. It was shown earlier that two of the main difficulties faced by the Commission in its effort to codify unilateral acts resulted from the reports drawn up by Cedeño. These are that: (a) the reports employed a case-by-case exposition of individual instances of State practice involving unilateral acts without arriving at any general conclusions applicable to all of them, and that (b) they too closely followed the model of the Vienna Convention on the Law of Treaties, thereby diverting the focus of the Commission from the main problems pertaining to unilateral acts in practice.

By way of contrast, the present work has adopted a more practical approach. Rather than being confined to purely theoretical analysis, this book is premised on the idea that it is necessary to tackle the practical problems pertaining to unilateral acts, *i.e.* the problem of defining the threshold beyond which a State may become bound by its unilateral behavior; and the problem of establishing whether a given act is of truly unilateral character. The structure of the book reflects this idea, and thus Chapter 4 focuses on the unilateral nature of unilateral acts, whereas Chapters 5 and 6 concentrate on forming a solid distinction between unilateral juridical and unilateral political acts.

As far as the substantive weaknesses of the work of the ILC and its final product, the 2006 Guiding Principles, are concerned, it was shown earlier that these are threefold: (a) the lack of any tools for ascertaining whether the author

94 Guiding Principle 1, *ibid.* (Emph. added.).

State intended to become bound by means of its unilateral act; (b) the absence of a definition of the element of unilateralism; and (c) the failure to establish clear boundaries between unilateral acts and estoppel. In contrast, Chapter 6 examines the context, both legal and factual, in which unilateral acts usually occur in practice and pinpoints a number of factors to be taken into consideration in ascertaining the binding nature of a given act. Moreover, Chapter 4 not only defines the element of unilateralism with reference to relevant State and judicial practice but also provides a list of factors – derived again from the legal and factual context in which such acts usually take place in practice – that indicate the existence of an act of truly unilateral character. Finally, this study makes a clear distinction between unilateral acts and estoppel. Chapter 4 argues that while, under international law, the former needs some form of detrimental reliance on behalf of the addressee, the emphasis on the latter is purely on the intention of the author State. By doing so, this book builds upon the work of the ILC and, hopefully, remedies some of the gaps of the 2006 Guiding Principles.

CHAPTER 4

The Unilateral Nature of Unilateral Juridical Acts

1 Introduction

The first chapter of this book dealt with the problematics of conceptualising unilateral acts in the context of the sources of international law. It was argued therein that the problem of the relation of unilateral acts to the recognised sources of international law may not be answered without first establishing the legal nature of such acts. The second chapter focused on the questions of definition and classification of unilateral acts. It was argued that a definition of unilateral acts, rather than attempting to cover all situations in which such acts may occur, should concentrate on the essentials of their legal nature, namely on the element of unilateralism and on the element of the intention to create legal effects. Furthermore, it was claimed that a typology of unilateral acts based on the criterion of context would be preferable, since this criterion best reflects the variety of circumstances in which such acts occur in practice. The third chapter focused on the work of the International Law Commission on unilateral acts. It was established therein that, despite the commendable efforts of the Commission's Special Rapporteur and members, the final product (the 2006 Guiding Principles)[1] falls short of providing any real assistance to the problem of ascertaining the legal character of a unilateral act in practice.

Against this backdrop, this chapter aims to explore the first element of the legal nature of unilateral acts, namely the element of unilateralism. The question of the unilateral nature of acts commonly designated as unilateral has been a fiercely debated one. As it will be explained below, a number of international lawyers have questioned the extent to which legal effects may arise from acts of strictly unilateral origin. For them, the binding force of an act of seemingly unilateral origin does not stem from the act *per se*, but from the reciprocal relationship of which the act forms part. In this vein, opponents of the concept of unilateral juridical acts in international law have treated all instances of such acts in State and judicial practice as borderline examples of international agreements or estoppel.

1 Guiding Principles applicable to unilateral declarations of States capable of creating legal obligations with commentaries thereto, in Report of the ILC on the Work of Its 58th Session, UN Doc. A/61/10, *Yrbk of the ILC* 2006, Vol. II, p. 369.

 | DOI 10.1163/9789004300767_006

On this basis, this chapter aims to answer two main questions: First, are unilateral acts, or some of them, of strictly unilateral origin, or could such acts be considered as resulting in the formation of international agreements, or as instances of estoppel? Secondly, if it is proven that some unilateral juridical acts may not be convincingly brought under the umbrella of international treaties or estoppel, then what is the legal definition of unilateralism? With respect to these questions, the chapter argues the following: it will be argued that by way of contrast to international agreements and estoppel where a degree of mutuality, consent or reliance is needed for the legal effects to arise, international law does not prescribe any such requirements in the case of some unilateral acts. Therefore, this chapter claims that a number of unilateral acts with legal effects on the international plane are of strictly unilateral origin.

Furthermore, it is argued that, while in the case of acts of a contractual nature the emphasis is on the interlocking of intentions, in the case of unilateral acts, the intention of the author State is, subject to certain conditions, autonomous in the production of the ensuing effects. Thus, this chapter defines unilateralism in terms of the autonomy of the act to produce legal effects in international law irrespective of any kind of acceptance or reliance on behalf of the addressee. Finally, while this chapter puts primary emphasis on the element of autonomy as the determinant factor in establishing the truly unilateral nature of an act, it is also supported here that the context in which the act occurs, *i.e.* the factual circumstances and the legal environment surrounding the making of the act, plays an important role in ascertaining the existence of the element of autonomy in practice.

The structure of this chapter is based on the idea that a clear distinction must be drawn between unilateral juridical acts and other phenomena in international law before defining the element of unilateralism. Thus, this chapter is conceptually divided in two parts. The first part aims to prove that unilateral acts constitute a legal institution distinct from international agreements or estoppel and the second part aims to establish a legal definition of unilateralism.

Finally, a note on the terms used in this chapter needs to be made. The terms 'unilateralism' and 'unilateral nature of unilateral juridical acts' are used interchangeably throughout the chapter. Although unilateralism, as mentioned in the introduction, is a broad concept that encapsulates a whole array of actions, political, philosophical and legal choices,[2] it is used here to refer to the unilateral nature of unilateral acts.

---

2 See generally P.M. Dupuy, The Place and Role of Unilateralism in Contemporary International Law, in "Unilateralism in International Law: A United States-European Symposium" held by

2 Unilateral Acts as a Legal Phenomenon Distinct from International Agreements or Estoppel

The first part of this chapter starts with a review of the literature regarding the element of unilateralism. In this part, the arguments of lawyers opposed to the idea that legal effects may arise from a unilateral act will be discussed. For reasons of convenience, these lawyers will be henceforth collectively referred to as 'deniers of the unilateral nature of unilateral juridical acts' or simply as 'deniers.' The deniers are divided in two categories: the first category is comprised of international lawyers such as J.L. Brierly and H. Lauterpacht who considered unilateral acts as leading to the creation of international agreements, while the second one includes international lawyers, such as A. Giganti, who viewed unilateral acts as instances of estoppel. This part of the chapter also sheds light on the position of the 'believers in the unilateral nature of unilateral juridical acts', namely on the position of international lawyers, such as Spender, Fitzmaurice, Ammoun and Verzijl, who accepted the possibility of legal effects arising from acts of purely unilateral origin.

Against this backdrop, the chapter continues by examining two possible scenarios: the possibility of viewing unilateral acts as culminating into the establishment of international agreements (the treaty scenario) and the possibility of viewing such acts as instances of estoppel (the estoppel scenario). To this end, the chapter briefly enquires into the concepts of agreement and estoppel in international law. Next, the unilateral statements made by France in the context of the *Nuclear Tests Case*[3] are used to test the applicability of the treaty and estoppel scenarios. The chapter concludes by asserting that the concept of unilateral acts, at least as this was propounded by the ICJ, is fundamentally irreconcilable with both that of international agreements and with that of estoppel.

The example of the French statements in the *Nuclear Tests Case* is used here for two reasons: first, the judgment of the International Court of Justice in this case remains the most important pronouncement of the Court in the field of unilateral juridical acts till this day. Secondly, all international lawyers belonging to the category of the deniers wrote in an era when judicial practice pertaining to unilateral acts was quite limited. The only significant pronouncement

the University of Michigan's Centre for International Law, 11 *EJIL* 19 (2000); P. Sands, 'Unilateralism', Values, and International Law, *ibid.*, p. 291.

3 *Nuclear Tests Case*, Australia vs France, ICJ *Reports* 1974, p. 253, New Zealand vs France, *ICJ Reports* 1974, p. 457. The Court's judgments in these two cases are almost identical. Hereinafter, unless otherwise stated, all references made to the *Nuclear Tests Case* will concern the case between Australia and France.

regarding unilateral acts at the time concerned the Ihlen Declaration in the context of the *Eastern Greenland Case*.[4] However, as it was briefly discussed in the first chapter, the context of negotiations within which the Declaration was made casts doubts on whether the Declaration is of truly unilateral character. It is submitted that by applying the deniers' arguments to the *Nuclear Tests Case*, where no such context exists, the inadequacies of these arguments are best exemplified.

2.1 *Literature Review*

A Deniers of the Unilateral Nature of Unilateral Acts

i) *Brierly, Lauterpacht: The Treaty Scenario*

As seen in the first chapter, scholarly opinion has been quite hesitant towards accepting the concept of unilateral legal acts. What seems particularly hard for academics to accept is the idea that legal relations may be borne out of acts of unilateral character.[5] Thus, a number of international lawyers have attempted to impart an element of acceptance or reliance to the legal relationship brought about by a unilateral act in order to disprove that legal effects may arise from an act of purely unilateral origin.

More particularly, some lawyers have employed the theory of the presumed consent of the addressee, *i.e.* they have presupposed the existence of some form of tacit acceptance on the part of the addressee, in order to bring such acts within the concept of international treaties. Thus, for example, Brierly, in his first report on the Law of Treaties, stressed that

> [I]nternational legal rights and obligations may of course arise otherwise than by agreement between a plurality of persons. They may thus arise by unilateral act, or as a result of an act to which the beneficiary of rights created by such act is a stranger. But there is a considerable division of opinion as to the extent to which international legal rights arising otherwise than ex delicto may be created by a truly unilateral act. A possible explanation of the binding force of so-called unilateral declaration creative of rights against the declarant may be found in the theory of presumed consent of the beneficiary.[6]

4 *Legal Status of Eastern Greenland Case*, PCIJ *Series A/B* 1933, No. 53, p. 22.

5 W. Fiedler, Unilateral Acts in International Law, in Berhardt R. (ed.), *Encyclopaedia of Public International Law*, Vol. IV, (Amsterdam, Oxford, North-Holland, 1984), p. 1018 at p. 1020.

6 J.L. Brierly, Report on the Law of Treaties, *Yrbk of the ILC* 1950, Vol. II, p. 227.

In the same vein, Lauterpacht, in his 1953 Report on the Law of Treaties, viewed unilateral acts from a contractual perspective.[7] In his report, Lauterpacht was primarily concerned with the creation of treaty obligations by means of a unilateral instrument. More particularly, the point that he was attempting to demonstrate was that an international instrument regardless of its form or designation may constitute an international agreement if the elements that pervade instruments of a contractual character under international law, (the consensual element and the intention to create rights and obligations) are present.[8] Thus, in his opinion, unilateral declarations following the pattern of offer and acceptance (such as unilateral declarations accepting an offer or accepting the terms of an already existing instrument, as well as unilateral declarations that have been accepted by the State to which they are addressed) constitute in essence treaty undertakings.[9] In support of his argument, Lauterpacht adduced instances of acts, such as declarations made under Art.36.2 of the Statute of the International Court of Justice,[10] which, although unilateral in form, are more akin to international treaties, since they are made within a more general contractual context.[11] On this basis, Lauterpacht regarded a number of unilateral acts with legal effects in international law as partaking of the character of an international agreement.[12]

It must be noted here that the reference made by Lauterpacht to the phenomenon of unilateral juridical acts was necessarily restricted in its scope, since it was made in the context of his report to the ILC regarding the Law of Treaties. He did not attempt to exhaust the sphere of unilateral acts. Rather, the examples used were confined to those unilateral acts which were relevant to his topic, namely to unilateral acts which could be validly regarded as treaties, since they required a degree of reciprocity in order to create legal effects on the international plane. Lauterpacht himself admitted in his report that "there may indeed be border line cases in which the character of a unilateral act conceived as a treaty is less apparent and therefore controversial."[13]

---

7 H. Lauterpacht, Report on the Law of Treaties, *Yrbk of the ILC* 1953, Vol. II, p. 101.

8 *Ibid.*, p. 93 *et seq.*

9 *Ibid.*, p. 102.

10 *Statute of the International Court of Justice*, 26 June 1945, San Francisco, available at http://www.icj-cij.org/documents/index.php?p1=4&p2=2&p3=0. Hereinafter also referred to as the 'ICJ Statute.'

11 A detailed discussion of the nature of Art. 36.2 of the ICJ Statute is reserved for a later part of this chapter.

12 H. Lauterpacht, Report on the Law of Treaties, *supra* note 7, p. 101.

13 *Ibid.*, p.103.

The example he cited was the *Free Zones Case*[14] in which a declaration made before the Court by the Swiss agent was held to be binding.[15] Lauterpacht conceded that viewing the Swiss declaration as anything but unilateral was problematic.[16] However, instead of exploring whether a legal basis for the binding force of such acts may exist outside the framework of the law of treaties, he simply reiterated the principle that, when a unilateral declaration follows the pattern of offer and acceptance, then it is quite safe to assume that a treaty has been created.[17] On this basis, Lauterpacht's position regarding unilateral acts is ambiguous. While he attempted to conceptualise these acts within the framework of international agreements, he simultaneously admitted the existence of some unilateral acts that may not be explained with recourse to patterns of offer and acceptance.[18]

ii) *Giganti: The Estoppel Scenario*

Other lawyers, such as Giganti,[19] dismissed the idea that unilateral acts may be interpreted as constituting international agreements. In their opinion, the theory of the presumed consent of the addressee (an important element in the line of argumentation adopted by Brierly and Lauterpacht) failed to satisfactorily explain the bindingness of all unilateral acts since it presupposed an element of acceptance even in cases where acceptance was patently absent. These lawyers have treated the theory of the presumed consent of the addressee as a result of misconceived attempts to deal with the binding force of unilateral acts at a very early stage of development of the phenomenon in question. In the words of Giganti: "It appears, rather, that presumed consent is a legal

14 *Case of the Free Zones of Upper Savoy and the District of Gex*, PCIJ *Series* A/B 46, (1932), p. 96.

15 *Ibid.*, p. 170.

16 The French agent regarded the declaration made by Switzerland as an offer to conclude a Special Agreement and as such he had no power to accept it. Notwithstanding this, the Court held that, taking into account the circumstances under which the declaration was made, the declaration was binding upon Switzerland. *Ibid.* The case will be discussed in more detail later in the chapter.

17 H. Lauterpacht, *supra* note 7, p. 103.

18 It needs to be noted that, later in his career, Lauterpacht changed his view on the issue and considered that binding effects may be borne out of acts of a stricty unilateral nature. This view will be explored in detail in the next chapter.

19 A. Giganti, The Effect of Unilateral State Acts in International Law, 2 NYUJ *Int'l L.& Pol.* 333 (1962).

fiction that was created at a time when the justification for the binding character of unilateral acts was unclear."[20]

However, such lawyers, while disassociating unilateral acts from the law of treaties, preferred to bring unilateral acts under other institutions of international law rather than looking into the possibility of such acts constituting a legal institution of their own. For example, Giganti rejected the idea that the binding character to be attributed to unilateral acts is the result of a contractual relation established between the author of the act and the addressee and maintained that unilateral acts are in reality instances of estoppel.[21] Although Giganti's argument about the relation between unilateral acts and estoppel will be examined in detail in the relevant section of this chapter, it is worthwhile to mention that the scholar came to this conclusion by arguing that both estoppel and unilateral acts were based upon the principle of good faith. In his view, the main ground for developing the concept of estoppel in international law was to maintain good faith in international relations. Similarly, Giganti opined that good faith also serves as the equitable ground for unilateral acts in international law and therefore, unilateral acts should be seen as a special application of the more general concept of estoppel.[22]

B Believers in the Unilateral Nature of Unilateral Acts: Spender, Fitzmaurice, Ammoun and Verzijl

Particularly pertinent in this section is the discussion of the Joint Dissenting Opinion of Judges Spender and Fitzmaurice in the *South West Africa Cases.*[23] In the preliminary objections phase of the case, the International Court was faced with the question as to whether the Mandate for South West Africa was an international agreement still in force for the purpose of establishing the jurisdiction of the Court.[24] The majority of the judges decided in the affirmative. However, Judges Spender and Fitzmaurice disagreed with the findings of the majority on this point. Their particular point of disagreement was that the Court identified the Mandate as an international agreement merely on the ground that it gave rise to international rights and obligations.[25]

20 *Ibid.*, p. 344.

21 *Ibid.*, p. 351.

22 *Ibid.*

23 Joint Dissenting Opinion of Judge Spender and Judge Fitzmaurice in the *South West Africa Cases*, *ICJ Reports* 1962, p. 319, at p. 465.

24 *South West Africa Cases*, *ibid.*, p. 329.

25 See *supra* note 23, p. 476.

According to Spender and Fitzmaurice, the test for determining the treaty status of an international instrument is not whether the instrument creates legal effects on the international plane or not, but whether it partakes of the nature of an international agreement, *i.e.* whether it is of a contractual nature. The Judges noted that:

> [N]o one has ever contested that the Mandate gave (and as so long as it continues in force as an institution gives) rise to international obligations. But that does not of itself make it a treaty, convention or other form of international agreement. It cannot be too strongly emphasised that the test is not, or is not merely, the creation of international obligations, *but the character of the act or instrument that gives those obligations their legal force.*[26]

The two Judges argued that, on the basis of the judgment, it was implied that all acts embodying an international engagement must necessarily be of a contractual nature.[27] However, according to Spender and Fitzmaurice, this conclusion was erroneous in light of the existence of acts of a unilateral nature that may also embody international rights and obligations. In their own words: "Unilateral declarations may contain undertakings, and can certainly create valid international obligations; but…they do not come within the category of treaties, conventions or other forms of international agreements, since they have no bilateral character."[28] Thus, the Judges unequivocally accepted the possibility of legal effects arising from acts of strictly unilateral origin.

Before rendering the above Joint Dissenting Opinion in the *South West Africa Case*, Fitzmaurice had already dealt to some extent with the question of the unilateral nature of acts commonly designated as such in State practice. In his seminal articles on the Law and Procedure of the International Court of Justice,[29] Fitzmaurice considered the question of the interpretation of unilateral declarations alongside questions of interpretation of international agreements. In his view, unilateral declarations are of two kinds: declarations that are unilateral in form, but not in substance; and declarations that are unilateral both in form and in substance.[30] It is clear that he accepted the possibility of

26 *Ibid.*

27 *Ibid.*

28 *Ibid.*, p. 477.

29 G. Fitzmaurice, The Law and Procedure of the International Court of Justice 1951–4: Treaty Interpretation and Other Treaty Points, 33 *BYIL* 203 (1957).

30 *Ibid.*, p. 230.

legal effects arising from an act of purely unilateral nature subject to the conditions that the element of intent is present and that due consideration has been given to the substance of the declaration as well as to the circumstances surrounding the making of the declaration: "Such a Declaration may or may not create binding legal obligations for the declaring party, according to its wording and intent, and the circumstances of its making..."[31]

The same view, namely that legal effects may arise from a purely unilateral act, was shared by Judge Ammoun in his Separate Opinion in the *North Sea Continental Shelf Cases*.[32] Here the Court was confronted with the question as to whether the Federal Republic of Germany, which had not ratified the Geneva Convention on the Continental Shelf, was bound by the provisions of Art.6 of the Convention. Denmark and the Netherlands argued *inter alia* that, although Germany was not contractually bound by the Convention, it had nonetheless unilaterally assumed the obligations of the Convention by means of a series of public statements and proclamations.[33] The Court rejected this argument and stated that "only the existence of a situation of estoppel could suffice to lend substance to this contention."[34] Judge Ammoun, in his Separate Opinion, rejected the overly restrictive approach taken by the majority. In his view, the Court should have also taken into account the "well-settled doctrine that a State may be bound by a unilateral act"[35] in order to clinch the conclusion that Germany was not bound by the Convention. Finally, it should be noted that, apart from Fitzmaurice, Spender and Ammoun, Verzijl also expressly acknowledged the existence of juridical acts of a purely unilateral character. In his study on international juridical acts, Verzijl argued that the most important distinction between international juridical acts is that between unilateral and bi/multilateral juridical acts.[36]

The picture that emerges upon review of the relevant literature is perplexing. This section showed that the question of the unilateral nature of unilateral acts is far from settled. Although some international lawyers, such as Fitzmaurice, Spender, Ammoun and Verzijl, had, from very early on, contemplated and accepted the possibility of legal effects arising out of unilateral acts,

31 *Ibid.*

32 Separate Opinion of Judge Ammoun in the *North Sea Continental Shelf Cases, ICJ Reports* 1969, p. 3, at p. 101.

33 *North Sea Continental Shelf Cases, ibid.*, p. 25, para. 27.

34 *Ibid.*, para. 30.

35 See *supra* note 32, para. 21.

36 J.W.H. Verzijl, *International Law in Historical Perspective, Vol. VI: Juridical Facts as Sources of International Rights and Obligations*, (Leiden: Sijthoff, 1973), pp. 48 *et seq.*

the same idea has been opposed by others, such as Lauterpacht, Brierly and Giganti, who attempted to bring unilateral acts within the framework of other phenomena such as international agreements, or estoppel.

Against this background, the next part of the chapter will inquire into the legal nature of international agreements. It will be shown that the element of agreement or reciprocity is central to the concept of treaty in international law. Next, the validity of the treaty-scenario (as this was discussed here) will be tested against the French statements in the *Nuclear Tests Case*. It will be argued that the statements in question may not be validly considered as culminating into the establishment of a treaty between the disputing parties since the element of agreement/reciprocity was absent in that case.

2.2 *Unilateral Acts as a Legal Phenomenon Distinct from International Agreements*

A The Concept of Agreement in International Law: Agreement as Concurrence of Wills in the Production of Legal Effects

A review of the relevant State and judicial practice regarding the concept of treaty or agreement in international law shows that, although international law adopts a liberal approach to this concept (in the sense that no particular requirements of form need to be met for an instrument to qualify as a treaty)[37] the presence of the element of *agreement* between two or more subjects of international law is imperative in order for an instrument to qualify as an international treaty.[38] Therefore, international law dictates that, rather than a mere record of the parallel intentions of its parties, an international treaty proper must reflect *consensus ad idem, i.e.* it must embody the concurrence of wills between a plurality of subjects of law to create specific legal effects on the international plane.[39]

The need for the presence of the element of agreement, in the sense of concurrence of wills or meeting of minds for the production of specific legal effects, has also been a standard feature of the definition of international treaties in the various attempts to codify the international law of treaties. Thus,

37 A. Aust, *Modern Treaty Law and Practice*, 3rd ed., (Cambridge: Cambridge University Press, 2013), pp. 15–6.

38 See the Dissenting Opinion of Judge Weeramantry in the *Land and Maritime Boundary between Cameroon and Nigeria Case, ICJ Reports* 1998, p. 275, at pp. 368 *et seq.*; See also the Joint Dissenting Opinion of Judge Spender and Judge Fitzmaurice in the *South West Africa Cases, supra* note 23, p. 476.

39 K. Widdows, What is an Agreement in International Law, 50 *BYIL* 117 (1978), p. 118; G. Fitzmaurice, *The Law and Procedure of the International Court of Justice*, Vol. I, (Cambridge: Grotius, 1986), p. 67.

according to Art.1 of the Harvard Draft Convention on the Law of Treaties, the term 'treaty', as used in the text of the Convention, referred to "a formal instrument of *agreement* by which two or more States establish or seek to establish a relation under international law."[40] Similarly, according to Art.2.1 of the Vienna Convention on the Law of Treaties, 'treaty' means "an international *agreement* concluded between States in written form and governed by international law, whether embodied in a single instrument or in two or more related instruments and whatever its particular designation."[41]

The element of concurrence of wills or agreement has also featured in the literature as one of the two main elements of the legal nature of international agreements (the other being the intention of the author States to become bound). Thus, for example, in the first chapter of his 1961 book on the international law of treaties, McNair explained that, in his view, the term 'international agreement' denotes a "written agreement by which two or more States or international organisations create or intend to create a relation between themselves operating within the sphere of international law."[42] In the same vein, Reuter described an international treaty as "an expression of concurring wills attributable to two or more subjects of international law and intended to have legal effects under the rules of international law."[43] Furthermore, Brierly viewed treaties as "contractual engagements between states"[44] and Lauterpacht, in his edition of *Oppenheim's International Law*, defined treaties as "agreements of a contractual nature, between States, or organisations of States, creating legal rights and obligations between the Parties."[45] Finally, Kelsen defined treaties as agreements "normally entered into by two or more States under general international law."[46]

B Absence of the Element of Agreement in the *Nuclear Tests Cases*

The above section demonstrated that, in international law, the element of agreement (as concurrence of wills or as meeting of minds to produce specific

---

40 See Art. 1 of the Harvard Draft Convention on the Law of Treaties, 29 *AJIL* 657 (Suppl.) 1935 (Emph. added).

41 See Art. 2.1 of the *Vienna Convention on the Law of Treaties*, 22 May 1969, Vienna, 1155 UNTS 331, 8 ILM 679 (1969) (Emph. added).

42 A. McNair, *The Law of Treaties*, (Oxford: Clarendon Press, 1961), p. 4.

43 P. Reuter, *Introduction to the Law of Treaties*, 2nd ed., (London: Kegan Paul, 1996), p. 30.

44 J.L. Brierly, *The Law of Nations: An Introduction to the Law of Peace*, 6th ed., (Oxford: Oxford University Press, 1963), p. 317.

45 H. Lauterpacht (ed.), *Oppenheim's International Law*, 8th ed., (London: Longmans, Green & Co.,1955), Vol. 1, p. 877.

46 H. Kelsen, R.W. Tucker (ed), *Principles of International Law*, 2nd rev. ed., (New York: Holt, Rinehart & Winston, 1966), p. 317.

legal effects on the international plane) is an indispensable part of the concept of international agreements. This part argues that the statements made by France in the context of the *Nuclear Tests Cases* may not be reasonably held to have culminated in the establishment of a treaty, in any form, between France on the one hand and Australia and New Zealand on the other because the element of agreement between the disputing parties was absent.

First, the International Court of Justice, when upholding the binding character of the French statements, made it tolerably clear that these undertaking were of a strictly unilateral nature.[47] According to the Court: "The unilateral statements of the French authorities were made outside the Court, publicly and *erga omnes*...As was observed above, to have legal effect, there was no need for these statements to be addressed to a particular State, nor was acceptance by any other State required."[48] Furthermore, even if one postulates the French statements as an offer for the conclusion of an international agreement, the response of the applicants may not, by any stretch of the imagination, be construed as acceptance thereof. Far from accepting that the French statements had rendered the object of the dispute moot, neither Australia nor New Zealand considered the statements as unequivocal assurances that nuclear testing would cease. In the course of the oral proceedings, the Attorney-General of Australia stated that: "The recent French Presidential statement cannot be read as a firm, explicit and binding undertaking to refrain from further atmospheric tests. It follows that the Government of France is still reserving to itself the right to carry out atmospheric nuclear tests."[49] In the same vein, New Zealand observed that it "has not been given anything in the nature of an unqualified assurance that 1974 will see the end of atmospheric nuclear testing in the South Pacific."[50] On this basis, it becomes apparent that the attempt to bring all unilateral acts in State and judicial practice within a treaty concept is not successful to the extent that some of them lack the requisite element of agreement, as the example of the *Nuclear Tests Cases* shows.

2.3 *Unilateral Acts as a Legal Phenomenon Distinct from Estoppel*

This part of the chapter examines the validity of the estoppel-scenario, *i.e.* the possibility of viewing all unilateral acts as instances of estoppel. To this end, it begins by discussing the doctrine of estoppel in international law. It will be

47 *Nuclear Tests Case*, Australia vs France, *supra* note 3, p. 253, at p. 269, para. 50; *Nuclear Tests* Case, New Zealand vs France, ICJ *Reports* 1974, p. 457, at p. 474, para. 52.

48 *Ibid.*

49 *Nuclear Tests Case*, Australia vs France, *ibid.*, p. 261, paras. 27–28, and p. 268, para. 47.

50 *Nuclear Tests Case*, New Zealand vs France, *supra* note 47, p. 465, para. 27.

argued here that one of the essential requirements of estoppel in international law is the existence of the element of detrimental reliance on the part of the addressee. As with the treaty-law scenario, this part will investigate whether the binding nature of the statements made by the French authorities in the context of the *Nuclear Tests Case* may be attributed to the application of the principle of estoppel. This part will argue that the legal effects arising from the French statements may not be explained on the basis of estoppel since the element of detrimental reliance was absent in that case.

A Detrimental Reliance as an Essential Element of Estoppel in International Law

Estoppel originates from the general principle of good faith.[51] Its essential aim is to promote stability and predictability in international relations by securing that a representation of fact is, under certain circumstances, binding upon the State that made it. According to the Dissenting Opinion of Judge Spender in the *Case concerning the Temple of Preah Vihear:*

> The principle operates to prevent a State from contesting before the Court a situation contrary to a clear and unequivocal representation previously made by it to another State, either expressly or impliedly, on which representation the other State was, in the circumstances, entitled to rely and in fact did rely, and as a result, that other State has been prejudiced or the State making it has secured some benefit or advantage for itself.[52]

In other words, estoppel is the equivalent at the international level of the simple principle "that a man is not allowed to blow hot and cold- to affirm at one time and deny at another."[53]

As far as judicial practice is concerned, both the Permanent Court and the International Court of Justice have on various occasions applied, either expressly or implicitly, the principle of estoppel.[54] On all these occasions, the

51 B. Cheng, *General Principles of Law as Applied by International Courts and Tribunals*, (Cambridge: Grotius, 1987), pp. 141–9.

52 Dissenting Opinion of Judge Spender in the *Case Concerning the Temple of Preah Vihear, ICJ Reports* 1962, p. 6, at pp. 143–4.

53 *Cave vs. Mills*, 7 *Hurlstone & Norman* 913 (1862), p. 927, as cited in B. Cheng, *supra* note 51, p. 141.

54 See the case-law mentioned in I. Sinclair, *Estoppel and Acquiescence*, in V. Lowe, M. Fitzmaurice (eds.), *Fifty Years of the International Court of Justice: Essays in honor of Sir R. Jennings*, (Cambridge: Cambridge University Press, 1996), p. 104, at p. 105 *et seq.*

rule of estoppel was neither interpreted nor applied broadly. On the contrary, throughout the case-law some essential conditions for the application of the principle have arisen. Bowett in his article on estoppel[55] has enumerated them: (a) The meaning of the statement must be clear and unambiguous; (b) The statement or representation must be voluntary, unconditional and authorized and (c) Reliance in good faith upon the representation of one party by the other party to his detriment (or to the advantage of the party making the representation).

In order to substantiate the view that unilateral acts owe their binding force to the principle of estoppel, Giganti tried to downplay the role of detrimental reliance in international-law estoppel. He maintained that, although detrimental reliance is an important element of estoppel in domestic legal systems, it has not been stressed as such by international judicial practice.[56] Giganti relied on the application of estoppel in the *Temple of Preah Vihear case*[57] to substantiate this argument.

The case concerned a territorial dispute between Cambodia and Thailand over the Temple of Preah Vihear. In 1904, the boundary between Cambodia and Thailand was established by a treaty that determined that it was to follow the watershed line and provided *inter alia* for a Mixed Commission to draw a more detailed map. The map placed the Temple of Preah Vihear within the territory of Cambodia, but the Mixed Commission never officially endorsed it. However, Cambodia relied on the map and Thailand, although having left Cambodia's sovereignty over the Temple unchallenged at the time, proceeded at a later stage to argue that the map contained a material error. However, the Court dismissed this argument on the ground that there was no reaction on behalf of Thailand's authorities for over fifty years and that Cambodia had been relying on this course of conduct for the same period of time.[58] Thus, Thailand was estopped from challenging Cambodia's sovereignty over the Temple. In this case, it seems that the Court applied the doctrine of estoppel despite the fact that the representation in question was clearly not to the detriment of the addressee. On this basis, Giganti concludes, detrimental reliance is not a characteristic element of estoppel in international law.[59]

55 D.W. Bowett, Estoppel before International Tribunals and its relation to Acquiescence, 33 BYIL 176 (1957), pp. 188–94.

56 *Ibid.*

57 *Case concerning the Temple of Preah Vihear, supra* note 52, p. 6.

58 *Ibid.*, p. 26.

59 A. Giganti, *supra* note 19, p. 351.

However, this argument seems to be unfounded both in theory and in international jurisprudence. At first, there are some theoretical considerations underpinning the requirement of detrimental reliance in international-law estoppel. In the *Gulf of Maine Case*, the ICJ indicated that estoppel is premised on the general principle of good faith.[60] Scholarship has backed this proposition. According to the jurisprudential analysis of Cheng, good faith forms the conceptual basis of the rule in municipal legal systems[61] and McGibbon observes that estoppel has been widely invoked before international tribunals "with the emphasis…upon an insistence of good faith and equitable conduct."[62] Thus, estoppel is grounded on the need to preserve good faith in international relations and to prevent States from taking advantage of their own inconsistency to the prejudice of other States.[63] However, a change in position by States does not necessarily imply lack of good faith. In the context of international relations, States frequently change their asserted foreign policy for a variety of reasons without this always resulting in harm to other States. It would be absurd to maintain that States should stick to outmoded policies even when no other State has put faith in the existence of these policies. Thus, to argue that detrimental reliance is not a precondition for estoppel would be to accept the possibility of applying estoppel even in cases when the complaining party has not relied upon the statement made and consequently, it has not changed its position.[64]

Furthermore, it would be wrong to draw any general inferences from the decision of the ICJ in the *Temple of Preah Vihear Case*, since this decision has been a rather isolated instance of the Court applying the doctrine of estoppel in the absence of any proof of detrimental reliance. In fact, the panel of the judges in that very case was divided over the applicability of estoppel. Judge Alfaro insisted that detrimental reliance is a prerequisite of estoppel; Judges Wellington Koo and Spencer took the view that estoppel was applied without any evidence of such reliance; and Judge Fitzmaurice considered the possibility that detrimental reliance might not be essential for estoppel to operate.[65]

60 *Delimitation of the Maritime Boundary on the Gulf of Maine Area, ICJ Reports* 1984, p. 246, at p. 305.

61 B. Cheng, *supra* note 51, pp. 141–9.

62 I.C. McGibbon, Estoppel in International Law, 7 *ICLQ* 468 (1958), at p. 487.

63 Separate Opinion of Judge Alfaro in the *Case concerning the Temple of Preah Vihear, supra* note 52, p. 40, at p. 42.

64 M. Wagner, Jurisdiction by Estoppel in the International Court of Justice, 74 *Cal. L. Rev.* 1777 (1986), at p. 1781.

65 R. Higgins, *Problems and Process: International Law and How We Use It*, (Oxford: Clarendon Press, 1994), p. 36.

However, the discord surrounding the role of detrimental reliance did not last for long, since subsequent judgments of the ICJ have indicated that estoppel requires detrimental reliance.[66]

B Absence of Detrimental Reliance in the *Nuclear Tests Cases*

In the *Nuclear Tests Case* the element of detrimental reliance was absent. As mentioned above, far from relying on the French statements, both New Zealand and Australia expressly declared them to have fallen short of the firm and unequivocal assurances they hoped to receive.[67] Thus, the legal effects attributed to the French statements may not be explained on the basis of estoppel.

C The Importance of the Time-element in Distinguishing between Unilateral Juridical Acts and Estoppel

Speaking more broadly, there is an additional element that differentiates estoppel from unilateral legal acts. This element relates to the time that obligations arise under the two legal concepts. In unilateral legal acts, the emphasis is on the intention of the declarant State; thus, the unilateral act becomes binding upon the declarant State immediately upon communication to the addressee. The autonomy of the unilateral legal act in producing binding effects the moment that it is formulated was stressed by the ICJ in the *Nuclear Tests Case*: "When it is the intention of the State making the declaration that it should become bound according to its terms, that intention confers on the declaration the character of a legal undertaking, the State being *thenceforth* legally required to follow a course of conduct consistent with the declaration."[68] On the contrary, in estoppel the emphasis is on the reliance given by the addressee to the declaration, rather than on the intention of its maker.[69] Logic dictates that reliance involves an element of duration; a period of time, short as it may be, must run for the addressee of the declaration to act or adopt a conduct to its own detriment upon which the element of reliance will be established. Thus, in the case of estoppel, the binding effects of the statement do not arise automatically, *i.e.* at the moment that the representation is made. For all of these reasons, the argument that estoppel may serve as the legal basis of unilateral legal acts is, in the opinion of the author, unfounded.

---

66 See for example the *North Sea Continental Shelf Cases, supra* note 33, para. 30.

67 See *supra* notes 49, 50.

68 *Nuclear Tests Case, supra* note 3, para. 43 (Emph. added).

69 H. Thirlway, The Law and Procedure of the International Court of Justice, 60 *BYIL* 4 (1989), at p. 11.

2.4 *Interim Conclusions*

The above section examined whether and to what extent unilateral acts may be considered as a legal phenomenon distinct from other phenomena in international law. It was shown that a number of international lawyers have denied the truly unilateral nature of such acts and they have more conveniently treated them either as acts leading to the conclusion of an international agreement or as instances of estoppel. However, it was argued that not all instances of unilateral acts in State and judicial practice may be explained by having recourse to the treaty and estoppel scenarios. More particularly, it was demonstrated that the treaty and estoppel scenarios are not applicable to the statements made by the French authorities in the context of the *Nuclear Tests Case*. On the basis of these statements, the above section concluded that some acts exist in international law, the nature of which may not be perceived as other than unilateral. The next part of this chapter will focus on elucidating the concept of the unilateral nature of unilateral acts (unilateralism).

3 The Unilateral Nature of Unilateral Juridical Acts

This section defines unilateralism in terms of the autonomy of the author's intention to produce legal effects irrespective of the existence of any corresponding acceptance or reliance on behalf of the addressee/s. It is also supported here that a theoretical definition of the element of unilateralism only partly resolves the questions pertaining to the unilateral nature of unilateral acts in international law. More particularly, it is argued that the above definition, while accurately describing the essence of unilateralism at an abstract, theoretical level, is not helpful in establishing whether a given act is truly unilateral in practice.

Therefore, while putting primary emphasis on the autonomy of the author's intention as the legal criterion for determining the unilateral nature of a given act, it is asserted that it is also necessary to provide means for ascertaining that the element of autonomy is present or absent in any given case. For this purpose, this section will examine the relevant case-law and provide a number of indicators of unilateralism. It is envisaged that these indicators would assist in determining whether an act is truly autonomous in practice.

3.1 *The Definition of the Unilateral Nature of Unilateral Juridical Acts in Judicial Practice*

A The Element of Unilateralism in the *Nuclear Tests Case*

From an etymological point of view, the word 'unilateral' derives its origin from Latin and it is a combination of the words 'unus', which means one and 'latus', which means side.[70] According to the Oxford English Dictionary, a unilateral act is an act "performed or undertaken by or on the part of one side; made, enjoyed, shared in, felt, *etc.*, by only one person or party",[71] while in legal terminology, it denotes an act "made or entered upon by one party, esp. without reciprocal obligation on the part of another or others; binding or imposed upon one party only."[72] The term 'unilateral' is commonly used to emphasize the fact that a certain course of action or conduct emanates from a single side, *e.g.* a 'unilateral decision' or a 'unilateral approach', as opposed to conduct that involves two, or more, sides; for example a 'bi/multilateral decision' or a 'bi/multilateral approach.'

As far as the international law meaning of the concept of unilateralism is concerned, international jurisprudence is of limited assistance. With the exception of the *Nuclear Tests Case*, the International Court of Justice – or indeed any international judicial body – has not discussed the element of unilateralism in detail. Even in the context of the *Nuclear Tests Case*, the Court was laconic in its reference to the unilateral character of unilateral juridical acts. The relevant dictum reads:

> An undertaking of this kind, if given publicly, and with an intent to be bound, *even though not made within the context of international negotiations*, is binding. In these circumstances, *nothing in the nature of a quid pro quo nor any subsequent acceptance of the declaration, nor even any reply or reaction from other States*, is required for the declaration to take effect, since such a requirement would be *inconsistent with the strictly unilateral nature of the juridical act* by which the pronouncement by the State was made.[73]

There are two observations to be made in relation to the above dictum. First, by expressly denying the need for a negotiating framework to exist in order for a unilateral act to produce legal effects, the Court ended the longstanding debate that had started with Permanent Court's pronouncement in the *Eastern Greenland Case*.[74] As mentioned earlier in the book, prior to the Court's judgment in the *Nuclear Tests Cases*, the only other significant example of judicial

70 D. Harper, *Online Etymology Dictionary*, available at http://dictionary.reference.com.

71 J.A. Simpson, E.S.C. Weiner (eds.), *The Oxford English Dictionary*, 2nd ed., (Oxford: Clarendon Press, 1989, online version June 2011), available at http://www.oed.com.

72 *Ibid.*

73 *Nuclear Tests Case*, *supra* note 3, para. 43 (Emph. added).

74 *Eastern Greenland Case*, *supra* note 4.

practice involving unilateral acts was the Ihlen Declaration in the context of the *Eastern Greenland Case*. The fact that the Ihlen Declaration was made in the context of negotiations between Norway and Denmark led a number of international lawyers to treat the Declaration as having culminated into the conclusion of an international agreement rather than as a unilateral juridical act. However, in the *Nuclear Tests Cases*, the Court made it abundantly clear that legal effects may be borne out of acts of strictly unilateral origin.

Secondly, as far as the element of unilateralism *per se* is concerned, the Court stated that, in the case of unilateral juridical acts, no form of reciprocity or mutuality is needed for the act to produce the intended legal effects. Therefore, according to the Court, the concept of the unilateral nature of a unilateral act is akin to a concept of autonomy of the act to create legal effects irrespective of any kind of acceptance, reliance or even reaction on the part of the addressee. Apart from describing unilateral acts as autonomous juridical acts, the ICJ did not clarify the element of unilateralism any further.

Nevertheless, the pronouncement of the Court regarding the unilateral nature of unilateral juridical acts leaves many questions unanswered. What does it really mean that a juridical act must be autonomous in the production of legal effects in order to be of strictly unilateral origin according to the above dictum? Is autonomy to be understood as a factual or as a legal element qualifying the relation borne out of an act of unilateral character? Furthermore, is the criterion of autonomy, as propounded by the Court, a formal criterion, *i.e.* are all acts emanating from one State to be considered as truly unilateral, such as acts that ratify an international treaty, or is it one relating to the content of the act, *i.e.* are all acts of recognition to be considered as truly unilateral? In view of all the questions arising out of the Court's pronouncement in the *Nuclear Tests Cases*, it is submitted that the element of unilateralism needs to be further explored. Thus, the next part of this section attempts to clarify the Court's definition of the element of unilateralism.

B Unilateralism as Autonomy of the Author's Intention to Produce Legal Effects

In order to understand the Court's position on unilateralism and thus, to answer the question as to whether this element was treated as a fact or as a legal characteristic pertaining to unilateral acts, attention must be paid not only to the wording of the relevant dictum, but also to the context within which it was uttered. The Court referred to unilateralism in the part of the judgment in which the legal status of unilateral declarations in international law was determined. In upholding the binding force of unilateral acts, the ICJ put primary emphasis on the intention of the author State to create legal effects on the international plane. In the text of the judgment directly preceding the dictum on unilateralism the Court stated:

> It is well recognised that declarations made by way of unilateral acts... may have the effect of creating legal obligations...When it is *the intention* of the State making the declaration that it should become bound according to its terms, *that intention confers on the declaration the character of a legal undertaking,* the State being thenceforth legally required to follow a course of conduct consistent with the declaration.[75]

It was in the context of stressing the significance of intention in relation to the binding force of unilateral acts on the international plane that the Court's reference to unilateralism was made. It is worthwhile reiterating the relevant dictum: "*In these circumstances,* nothing in the nature of a *quid pro quo* nor any subsequent acceptance of the declaration, nor even any reply or reaction from other States, is required for the declaration to take effect..."[76] The use of the phrase "in these circumstances" indicates that the reference to unilateralism was not made in a vacuum; rather, it was directly linked to the previous discussion regarding the element of intention. Thus, when the Court alluded to the concept of unilateralism being akin to a concept of autonomy, it essentially referred to the autonomy of the intention of the author State to produce legal effects irrespective of any kind of reciprocity on behalf of the addressee. In other words, unilateralism was construed by the ICJ to refer to the intention of the author State that, in the case of unilateral juridical acts, is autonomous in generating the purported legal effects irrespective of the existence of any corresponding intention on behalf of the addressee, or of any other State.[77]

On this basis, it is submitted that the Court in its judgment in the *Nuclear Tests Case* did not perceive unilateralism as a mere factual statement to the effect that only one State is involved in the production of legal effects. On the contrary, unilateralism was envisaged as an essential of the legal nature of unilateral juridical acts, since it specifies the type of intention required under international law for legal effects to arise by means of such acts. According to

75 *Nuclear Tests Case, supra* note 3, para. 43 (Emph. added).

76 *Ibid.*

77 The same view, namely that unilateralism refers to the autonomy of the act to produce legal effects irrespective of acceptance or reliance on behalf of the adreseee was also adopted by the Special Rapporteur of the ILC on Unilateral Acts of States, as discussed in Chapter 3. See V. Rodríguez Cedeño, Second Report on Unilateral Acts of States, UN Doc. A/CN.4/500, p. 195, at p. 200.

the Court, an expression of intention that emanates from a single side and is not linked to a corresponding intention by any other subject of law may create legal effects on the international plane.

C Autonomy and Its Discontents

The above definition of the element of unilateralism is not without problems. The main flaw of this definition is that it does not help one to establish whether a particular act is of truly unilateral origin or not. It was argued above that unilateralism means autonomy of the act to produce legal effects irrespective of any kind of acceptance or reliance on behalf of the addressee of the act. A corollary to this argument is that, in the case of a strictly unilateral act, the fact that the addressee has accepted or relied on the act in question is immaterial since the legal effects of the act are produced *ipso facto*. However, how is one to determine whether a particular act needs to be accepted or relied upon in order to create legal effects, or whether acceptance is immaterial?

In this light, it is submitted that the task of defining unilateralism is not complete without providing some means of ascertaining whether a particular act does in fact enjoy the requisite degree of autonomy to be characterised as truly unilateral. Thus, the next part of this chapter provides a set of interpretative tools (indicators of unilateralism) that would facilitate the determination of the unilateral nature of a given act in practice. These include the absence of a treaty law context; the absence of a rule that requires reciprocity; the absence of a context of negotiations; the existence of circumstances that preclude the conclusion of an agreement and the absence of a pattern of offer and acceptance.

3.2 *Indicators of Unilateralism*

A The Absence of a Treaty Law Context

The fact that an act of seemingly unilateral origin pertains to the conclusion, entry into force, modification and termination of an international agreement, such as reservations, interpretative declarations as well as acts of ratification, accession and amendment of an international agreement, is highly indicative of its bi/multilateral, rather than unilateral, nature. Although seemingly unilateral, such acts may not be considered to be autonomous to the extent that they operate under a condition of reciprocity and are governed by the regime of the Vienna Convention on the Law of Treaties.[78]

78 For a discussion of unilateral acts that pertain to international agreements see generally A. Aust, *supra* note 37.

B The Absence of a Rule that Requires Reciprocity

Similar to the existence of a treaty context, the fact that an act derives its validity from a rule that commands some form of reciprocity in order for the act to produce its purported legal effects may indicate that the act in question is not of truly unilateral character. Declarations made under Art. 36.2 of the ICJ Statute are a pertinent example.[79] According to Art. 36.2:

> The states parties to the present Statute may at any time declare that they recognise as compulsory *ipso facto* and without special agreement, in relation to any other states accepting the same obligation, the jurisdiction of the Court in all legal disputes concerning: a. the interpretation of a treaty; b. any question of law; c. the existence of any fact which, if established, would constitute a breach of an international obligation; d. the nature and extent of the reparation to be made for the breach of an international obligation.

The ICJ has repeatedly upheld that although unilateral in form, declarations under Art. 36.2 of its Statute are essentially of contractual character. For example, in the *Nicaragua Case*,[80] the Court pointed out that:

> Declarations of acceptance of the compulsory jurisdiction of Court are facultative, unilateral engagements, that States are absolutely free to make or not to make...However, the unilateral nature of declarations does not signify that the State making the declaration is free to amend the scope and the contents of its solemn commitments as it pleases... In fact, the declarations, even though they are unilateral acts, establish a series of bilateral engagements with other States accepting the same obligation of compulsory jurisdiction, in which the conditions, reservations and time-limit clauses are taken into consideration.

Similarly, in the *Anglo-Iranian Oil Co. Case*, the Court stated that: "In the present case the jurisdiction of the Court depends on the Declarations made by the Parties under Article 36, paragraph 2, on condition of reciprocity.... By these Declarations, jurisdiction is conferred on the Court only to the extent to which the two Declarations coincide in conferring it."[81]

---

79 ICJ Statute, *supra* note 10.

80 *Case Concerning Military and Paramilitary Activities In and Against Nicaragua*, *ICJ Reports* 1984, p. 392 at p. 418.

81 *Anglo-Iranian Oil Co. Case*, ICJ *Reports* 1952, p. 93, at p. 103. See also what the Court stated in the *Land and Maritime Boundary between Cameroon and Nigeria Case*: "Any State party

C The Absence of a Context of Negotiations

The fact that an act is made within a context of negotiations may also indicate that the act in question is part of a contractual relationship, rather than an autonomous, unilateral act. Particularly relevant here is the discussion surrounding the Ihlen Declaration in the *Eastern Greenland Case*. Although the facts of the case have been briefly mentioned earlier in the book, it is worthwhile reiterating them here. The *Eastern Greenland Case* concerned a dispute between Denmark and Norway over the sovereignty of Eastern Greenland.[82] More specifically, the initiation of proceedings before the Permanent Court of Justice was triggered by a declaration of occupation of Eastern Greenland issued by the Norwegian government on July the 10th, 1931. Two days later, Denmark filed an application against the Norwegian Government claiming that the territory in question was subject to its own sovereignty and thereby asked the Court to declare the invalidity of Norway's declaration of occupation.[83] One of the main arguments adduced by the applicant was that the Norwegian Government had, in the past, recognized the applicant's sovereignty over the disputed territory through a series of engagements, including *inter alia* a Declaration made by the Norwegian Minister of Foreign Affairs, Mr. Ihlen, in the context of negotiations with his Danish counterpart.[84]

According to the Minutes of the discussion between the two Ministers, the Danish Minister indicated the willingness of his government to refrain from raising any objection regarding Spitzbergen at the then forthcoming Paris Peace Conference and, at the same time, requested assurances to the effect that Norway would not oppose the Danish claim over the whole of Greenland at the same Conference.[85] After a few days, Mr. Ihlen replied that "the plans of

to the Statute, in adhering to the jurisdiction of the Court in accordance with Article 36, paragraph 2, accepts jurisdiction in its relations with States previously having adhered to that clause. At the same time, it makes a standing offer to the other States party to the Statute that have not yet deposited a declaration of acceptance. The day one of those States accepts that offer by depositing in its turn its declaration of acceptance, the consensual bond is established and no further condition needs to be fulfilled." *Land and Maritime Boundary between Cameroon and Nigeria Case*, *ICJ Reports* 1998, p. 275, at p. 291. See also G. Fitzmaurice, *supra* note 29, p. 232.

82 For a detailed account of the history of the dispute between Denmark and Norway over Greenland as well as of the claims advanced by the parties, see generally L. Preuss, The Dispute Between Norway and Denmark Over the Sovereignty of Eastern Greenland, 26 *AJIL* 469 (1932).

83 *Eastern Greenland Case*, *supra* note 4, p. 25.

84 *Ibid.*, p. 69.

85 *Ibid.*, p. 36.

the Royal [Danish] Government respecting the Danish sovereignty over the whole of Greenland…would meet no difficulties on the part of Norway."[86] This Declaration, the content of which had not been contested by either party, was interpreted by Denmark as constituting definitive recognition of its sovereignty over the whole of Greenland.

However, the Court did not uphold the Danish contention. In the light of both the wording of the declaration as well as of subsequent events, the Court was of the opinion that the Ihlen Declaration could not be interpreted as a definitive recognition of Danish sovereignty. More particularly, the Court, based on the French version of the Declaration, found that Mr. Ihlen's assurances regarding Greenland were formulated in the future tense.[87] In other words, instead of recognizing any already existing legal situation between the two States, as Denmark argued, the Declaration was merely setting out the future Norwegian position regarding the Danish claims of sovereignty.

Furthermore, the Court gave due weight to the subsequent attitude of the Danish government. If Denmark considered Ihlen's Declaration as having finally and unconditionally settled the question of Danish sovereignty over the whole of Greenland, then it would be expected that no further assurances would be requested. However, it was established that two years after the Declaration was made, the Danish Government made a further request to Norway in an attempt to gain the desired recognition.[88] In this light, the Court concluded that "Mr. Ihlen cannot have meant to be giving then and there a definitive recognition of Danish sovereignty over Greenland, and…also that he cannot have been understood by the Danish Government at the time as having done so."[89]

Having rejected the Danish position regarding the legal effects of Ihlen's declaration, the Court proceeded to establish whether the Declaration had any other legal effects beyond those proclaimed by Denmark. More particularly, the Court attempted to establish whether the Declaration *per se* could be interpreted as having created an obligation on behalf of Norway to refrain from occupying the whole of Greenland.[90] In other words, having excluded the possibility that the Declaration was an admission of an already existing legal situation, the Court endeavoured to establish whether the statement itself created an obligation of future conduct for Norway. Indeed, the majority of the judges

86 *Ibid.*

87 *Ibid.*, p. 69.

88 *Ibid.*

89 *Ibid.*

90 *Ibid.*

found that this was the case. In the words of the Court: " The Court considers it beyond all dispute that a reply of this nature given by the Minister of Foreign Affairs on behalf of his Government in response to a request by the diplomatic representative of a foreign Power, in regard to a question falling within his province, is binding upon the country to which the Minister belongs."[91] Thus, the Court concluded that, on the basis of this oral undertaking, Norway was obliged to refrain from contesting Danish sovereignty over the whole of Greenland.[92]

Although the Court did not mention the formal source of Norway's obligation, the emphasis given to the contextual framework within which the statement took place (negotiations), to the fact that the declaration was made as a response to a request by the agent of another State, as well as to the interdependence between the Danish claim over Greenland and the Norwegian claim over Spitzbergen demonstrate that the Court viewed the Declaration from a contractual perspective.[93]

This opinion is also shared by the majority of international lawyers and the *Eastern Greenland Case* features in most textbooks of international law as the standard example confirming the validity of informal agreements.[94] More particularly, McNair was of the opinion that the assurances given by Mr. Ihlen on behalf of Norway, in conjunction with the same kind of assurances given earlier by Denmark, resulted into the creation of a contractual relationship between the two States, in which "the one promise was the consideration or quid pro quod for the other."[95] On this basis, the learned author argued that the conversation between the two Ministers led to the conclusion of an international agreement, "though one which would be wrongly described as a treaty",[96] a term which McNair reserved only for a specific type of international agreements, namely those concluded in written form.[97]

91 *Ibid.*, p.70.

92 *Ibid.*

93 See for example J.W. Garner, The International Binding Force of Unilateral Oral Declarations, 27 *AJIL* 493, 1933; Joint Dissenting Opinion of Judge Spender and Judge Fitzmaurice in the *South West Africa Cases, supra* note 23, at pp. 475–6.

94 See for example the literature cited in D.J. Harris, *Cases and Materials on International Law*, 7th ed., (London: Sweet & Maxwell, 2010), p. 47, fn. 147.

95 A. McNair, *supra* note 42, p. 10.

96 *Ibid.*

97 According to McNair a treaty is "a written agreement by which two or more States or international organisations create or intend to create a relation between themselves operating within the sphere of international law." See *ibid.*, p. 4.

In the same vein, Pellet, considered that, in the light of the similar type of assurances given earlier by Denmark regarding Spitzbergen, the reply given by Mr. Ihlen constituted in essence an acceptance of an offer, and thus, led to the establishment of an oral agreement.[98] Finally, the *Eastern Greenland Case* has been consistently referred to by the successive Special Rapporteurs of the ILC on the Law of Treaties as judicial practice in support of the view that the form, written or otherwise, of an agreement does not affect its binding force in international law.[99]

---

98 A. Pellet, *Article 38*, in A. Zimmermann, C. Tomuschat, K. Oelles-Frahm (eds.), *The Statute of The International Court of Justice: A Commentary*, 2nd ed., (Oxford: Oxford University Press, 2012), p. 731, at p. 764.

99 In his Report on the Law of Treaties, Special Rapporteur J.L. Brierley remarked that "the binding nature of oral agreements has been recognised by the Permanent Court of International Justice" and cited *inter alia* the *Eastern Greenland Case* as proof thereof. See J.L. Brierley, Report on the Law of Treaties, *Yrbk of the ILC* 1950, Vol. II, p. 222, at p. 227. His successor, H. Lauterpacht, was more sceptical about the value of the judgment in question. In his own words: "There is slight – and occasionally exotic- authority in support of the view that a treaty may be the result of an oral agreement. It is not certain to what extent certain passages in the judgment of the Permanent Court of International Justice in the case of Eastern Greenland...can be regarded as supporting this view. It is probable that, as the fact and the contents of the oral declaration made, in that case, by the Norwegian Minister for Foreign Affairs were not disputed, the Court did not address itself to that question at all." See H. Lauterpacht, Report on the Law of Treaties, *Yrbk of the ILC* 1953, Vol. II, p. 90 at p. 159. However, this point was not picked upon by the next Special Rapporteur of the ILC on the same subject, G. Fitzmaurice, who concurred with Brierley on the question of the validity of oral agreements and also referred to the relevant passages of Brierley's Report, including the case-law mentioned therein, in support of his position. See G. Fitzmaurice, Report on the Law of Treaties, *Yrbk of the ILC* 1956, Vol. II, p. 104, at p. 117. The next Special Rapporteur, H. Waldock, was of the same persuasion and mentioned the *Eastern Greenland Case* as an instance of State-practice confirming the validity and enforceability of oral agreements. He stated: "In short, without going further into the matter, paragraph 2 acknowledges the existence of oral agreements such as that resulting from the Ihlen Declaration in the Eastern Greenland Case...and it puts on record that their omission from the draft articles is not to be understood as in any way affecting the legal position to them." H. Waldock, First Report on the Law of Treaties, *Yrbk of the ILC* 1962, Vol. II, p. 27 at p. 35. Although any further exploration of the question of the general validity of oral agreements in international law would be beyond the ambit of the present chapter, it suffices here to mention that in its final draft on the Law of Treaties, the ILC endorsed the view of the majority of its Special Rapporteurs and confirmed the validity of oral agreements. As a result, Art. 3 of the Vienna Convention on the Law of Treaties specifically provides that although the Convention itself is only applicable to written international agreements, this does not affect the legal force of other types of agreements

The previous exposition showed that a careful appreciation of the context within which a unilateral act occurs is necessary for the determination of the unilateral nature of a given act. The example of the *Eastern Greenland Case* demonstrates that a seemingly unilateral act, made within a context of negotiations, may in fact form part of a reciprocal relationship.

D The Existence of Circumstances that Preclude the Conclusion of an International Agreement

International lawyers have traditionally been quite reluctant to consider elements extraneous to the legal sphere in their analysis. However, in the real world, extra-legal considerations often play an important role in shaping the actions of States in the international arena. More often than not, governments are faced with the difficult task of having to make concessions at the international level while keeping an uncompromising profile at home. Thus, the path of 'doing business' by concluding an international agreement is not always available for States on the grounds of domestic policy. Thus, it is submitted that unilateral acts can, and have been, used by States as an alternative to treaties in cases where the normal path of concluding an international agreement is unavailable for reasons of political expediency. It is further argued that taking into account whether any circumstances exist that preclude a State from entering into an international agreement is helpful in establishing whether an act is of truly unilateral origin. The statement made by the Head of State of Mali in the context of the *Frontier Dispute Case*[100] and the 2010 non-use of force promise made by Georgia are pertinent examples.

In the *Frontier Dispute Case* the Court was confronted with a statement made by the Head of State of Mali in the course of an interview with a French news agency. During the interview, the Head of State of Mali stated that his government would comply with any decision reached by the Organisation of African Unity Commission regarding the frontier dispute between Mali and Burkina Faso.[101] In assessing the legal character of the statement, the Court quoted the relevant dictum of the *Nuclear Tests* Judgment to the effect that "when it is the intention of the State making the declaration…that intention confers on the declaration the character of a legal undertaking" and added that "thus it all depends on the intention of the State in question."[102]

including agreements concluded orally. See the text of Art. 3 of the Vienna Convention on the Law of Treaties, *supra* note 41.

100 *Case concerning the Frontier Dispute*, *ICJ Reports* 1986, p. 554.

101 *Ibid.*, p. 573.

102 *Ibid.*

However, the Court distinguished the case before it from the *Nuclear Tests Case*. According to the Court, in the latter case, there were policy considerations that prevented France from terminating the dispute by concluding an international agreement. More particularly, it was noted that "the French Government could not express an intention to be bound otherwise than by unilateral declarations. It is difficult to see how it could have accepted the terms of a negotiated agreement without thereby jeopardizing its contention that its conduct was lawful."[103] The Court went on to state that in the present circumstances "there was nothing to hinder the parties from manifesting an intention to accept the binding character of the conclusions of the Mediation Committee by the normal method: A formal agreement."[104] Such a line of reasoning clearly demonstrates that the Court will take into account policy considerations in ascertaining the unilateral nature of a given act.

The 2010 non-use of force pledge made by the President of Georgia to European Parliament members[105] is a telling example of how unilateral acts may be used in lieu of international agreements to break political impasse. In his November 2010 address before the European Parliament, President Saakashvili stated that his country would not resort to force to settle the dispute with Russia over the breakaway regions of South Ossetia and Abkhazia. The Georgian President declared that:

> But – in order to prove that Georgia is definitely committed to a peaceful resolution of its conflict with the Russian Federation – we take today the unilateral initiative to declare that Georgia will never use force to restore its territorial integrity and sovereignty, that it will only resort to peaceful means in its quest for de-occupation and reunification… *My pledge here, in front of you, constitutes a unilateral declaration of a state under international law.*[106]

Georgia has reiterated on a number of occasions that its 2010 statement constitutes a binding unilateral undertaking.[107]

103 *Ibid.*

104 *Ibid.*

105 President of Georgia's Address to European Parliament Members: Georgia Makes 'Unilateral Pledge' of Non-Use of Force, 23 November 2010, available at http://www.usa.mfa.gov.ge/index.php?lang_id=ENG&sec_id=595&info_id=8979.

106 *Ibid.* (Emph. in the original).

107 See for example the Resolution on Basic Directions of Georgia's Foreign Policy, 7 March 2013, available at http://www.civil.ge/eng/article.php?id=25828 and the Statement by the Ministry of Foreign Affairs of Georgia Regarding the Unscheduled Large-scale Military

The reason for making a commitment in the form of a unilateral act, instead of a treaty, was without a doubt political. During the Geneva discussions, Russia urged Georgia to conclude agreements on the non-use of force with the breakaway regions.[108] However, signing such agreements could be interpreted as implicit recognition of the entities in question – something that Georgia was not prepared to accept.[109] Thus, the only other viable alternative – from a political point of view – was the formulation of a unilateral act. The 2010 Georgian pledge illustrates the point made by the Court in the *Frontier Dispute Case*: the political context within which an act is made may adduce evidence about the act's unilateral nature.

E The Absence of a Pattern of Offer/Acceptance

A (seemingly) unilateral act that forms part of a bilateral exchange would not normally enjoy the requisite degree of autonomy to be characterised as truly unilateral. An example of this type of pseudo-unilateral acts is the declaration made by the Swiss agent during the oral proceedings in the *Free Zones Case*.[110] In that case the Permanent Court was faced with the question whether the Treaty of Versailles had in effect abolished the customs-free zones south of Geneva. During oral argument, the Swiss representative declared that if the zones were maintained, Switzerland would agree to the appointment of a committee of experts in order to settle the terms of the exchange of goods between the zones and Switzerland.[111] The French representative questioned the binding character of the declaration. However, the Court stated that "having regard to the circumstances in which this declaration was made, the Court must however regard it as binding on Switzerland."[112]

Taken at face value, the Swiss declaration seems to be autonomous. However, a careful examination of its terms, as well as of the text of the judgment, reveals

---

Drills by the Russian Armed Forces in the Black Sea Region, 29 March 2013, available at http://uk.mfa.gov.ge/index.php?lang_id=ENG&sec_id=595&info_id=18005.

108 N. Mikhelidze, The Geneva Talks Over Georgia's Territorial Conflicts: Achievements and Challenges, prepared for the Istituto Affari Internazionali (IAI) in the Framework of the Observatory on the Caucasus, November 2010, available at http://www.iai.it/pdf/DocIAI/iai1025.pdf, p. 4.

109 *Ibid.* See also the interview given by the three co-chairs of the Geneva discussions, P. Morel (EU), A, Turunen (UN), B. Nurgaliyev (OSCE) in Q&A: 'New Context' for Geneva Talks after Non-Use of Force Pledges, *Civil Georgia*, 15 December 2010, available at http://www.civil.ge/eng/article.php?id=22960.

110 *Case of the Free Zones of Upper Savoy and the District of Gex, supra* note 14.

111 *Ibid.*, p. 169.

112 *Ibid.*, p. 170.

that it was formulated by Switzerland as an offer for the conclusion of an agreement. According to the text of the judgment:

> In the course of the oral arguments before the Court, the Swiss Agent declared, on behalf of his Government, that if the zones were maintained, the Federal Government would, *if France so desired*, agree to the terms of the exchange of goods between the zones and Switzerland being settled by experts, failing agreement with regard to them by the Parties.[113]

The Court also treated the Swiss declaration as an offer by stressing that "if the French Government chooses to avail itself of this *offer*, it will be able to obtain in favour of the inhabitants of the zones an arrangement for the admission of their produce into Switzerland, which will not depend exclusively on the will of the Swiss Government."[114] Subsequent practice verifies this view. In 1933 France accepted the Swiss proposal made during the proceedings before the Court and, subsequently, a panel of experts was called upon to establish a new regime for the importation of goods from the zones into Switzerland.[115]

Similarly, unilateral declarations concerning the protection of minorities made to the Council of the League of Nations in the 1920s are best viewed as bilateral undertakings, rather than unilateral acts, due to the existence of a pattern of offer and acceptance. Although a number of States made such declarations, including Finland, Lithuania, Latvia and Estonia,[116] the most well-known declaration of this type is the one made by Albania in 1921 since it became the subject of an advisory opinion by the Permanent Court. The factual background to the Albanian declaration is the following. In December 1920 the Assembly of the League of Nations adopted a recommendation according to which: "in the event of Albania, the Baltic and Caucasian States being admitted into the League, the Assembly requests that they should take the necessary measures to enforce the principles of the Minorities Treaties, and that they should arrange with the Council the details required to carry this object into effect."[117] Subsequently, Albania was admitted to the League of

113 *Ibid.*, p. 169 (Emph. added).

114 *Ibid.*, p. 170 (Emph. added).

115 M.O. Hudson, The Aftermath of the Permanent Court's Judgment in the Free Zones Case, 28 *AJIL* 322 (1934), p. 324.

116 For an overview, see C. Broelmann, *The PCIJ and International Rights of Groups and Individuals*, in C. Tams, M. Fitzmaurice (eds.), *Legacies of the Permanent Court of International Justice*, (Leiden: M. Nijhoff, 2013), pp. 123–143.

117 *Minority Schools in Albania*, Advisory Opinion, *PCIJ Series A/B*, 1935, No. 64, p. 5.

Nations on December 17th, 1920. On October 2nd, 1921, Albania made a declaration before the Council of the League of Nations concerning the protection of racial, religious and linguistic minorities in its territory.[118] The Council took note of the declaration in a resolution. In 1933 Albania amended its Constitution and provided for the abolition of all private schools – including those used by the Greek minority. This amendment triggered a request for an advisory opinion by the Permanent Court as to whether the decision to abolish private schools was in conformity with the 1921 declaration.[119]

Although the Court did not question the binding force of the Albanian declaration, it carefully avoided pronouncing on its exact legal nature. Nowhere in the judgment does it become abundantly clear whether the Court considered it as a bilateral or a unilateral undertaking. According to the Court: "The declaration of 2 October 1921 belongs to the numerous category of *international acts* designed for the protection of minorities."[120] The use of the generic term 'international act' has generated much doctrinal controversy over the precise legal character of the Albanian declaration. While some international lawyers, such as Suy, consider the declaration as part of an international agreement, others, such as Jacque, view it as an autonomous unilateral undertaking.[121]

Upon closer scrutiny, the claim that the Albanian declaration forms part of a reciprocal relationship seems more convincing. First, the text of the 1920 recommendation by the Assembly of the League of Nations was drafted in such a way as to indicate that the declaration was a precondition for the admission of Albania to the League of Nations. More particularly, a close reading of the 1920 recommendation shows that it was construed as an offer to Albania and to other States: if they accepted to issue declarations concerning the protection of minorities in their respective territories, they would be admitted to the League. The proposition that the Albanian declaration fits into the pattern of offer and acceptance is also supported by the text of the advisory opinion: "what the Council of the League of Nations *asked Albania to accept*, and what *Albania did accept*, was a regime of minority protection substantially the same as that which had been already agreed upon with other States…"[122] Secondly, the context within which the declaration was made warrants the

118 *Ibid.*

119 *Ibid.*

120 *Ibid.*, p. 15.

121 For an overview of the debate see C. Eckart, *Promises of States under International Law*, (Oxford: Hart Publishing, 2012), p. 90.

122 *Minority Schools in Albania*, *supra* note 117, p. 16.

conclusion that it was part of a bilateral exchange. Before the declaration was made, negotiations had taken place between Albania and a representative of the Council of the League and it was only after agreement had been reached, that the declaration was made by Albania.[123] Finally, the UN Secretary-General also endorsed the position that the Albanian declaration constituted in essence the acceptance of an offer made by the League of Nations in his 1950 Study of the Legal validity of the Undertakings concerning Minorities.[124] The example of the 1921 Albanian declaration shows that a careful assessment of the context within which the act is made is needed before any conclusions regarding the autonomous character of an act are drawn.

4 Conclusion

This chapter explored the element of the unilateral nature of unilateral acts (unilateralism). It was shown that a number of lawyers (deniers) have denied that legal effects may be borne out of acts of purely unilateral origin and that these lawyers have treated such acts either as leading to the formation of international agreements or as instances of estoppel. Thus, the first part of this chapter was focused on proving that some unilateral acts exist, the legal force of which may not be explained with recourse to the concepts of international agreement or estoppel. For this purpose the chapter analysed the relevant concepts and it was asserted that the element of agreement or meeting of minds is central to the concept of agreement in international law, while the element of detrimental reliance is central to that of estoppel. The chapter continued by testing the validity of the deniers' claims against the French statements in the *Nuclear Tests Case*. It was argued that the binding force attributed to the statements in question by the ICJ may not be explained by having recourse to the concepts of international agreement or estoppel insofar as no evidence of agreement or detrimental reliance exists. Against this background the chapter continued by exploring the element of unilateralism in international law. Upon analysis of the relevant judicial practice, unilateralism was defined as the autonomy of an act to produce legal effects irrespective of acceptance or reliance on behalf of the addressee. The chapter went on to identify a number of indicators of unilateralism that would assist in ascertaining the purely

123 ECOSOC, Study of the Legal Validity of the Undertakings concerning Minorities, UN Doc. E/CN.4/367 (1950), p. 13.

124 *Ibid.*

unilateral nature of an act in practice. In this respect it was supported that the absence of a treaty law context, the absence of a rule requiring reciprocity, the absence of a context of negotiations, the existence of circumstances that preclude the conclusion of an international agreement and the absence of a pattern of offer and acceptance may indicate that a given act is of unilateral nature.

CHAPTER 5

The Concept of Juridical Acts in International Law

1 Introduction

Having examined the question of the unilateral nature of unilateral acts, the next two chapters will explore the vexed question of their juridical nature, namely the question as to whether and to what extent unilateral acts may produce binding effects on the international plane. From the outset, one might have expected that a study on the phenomenon of unilateral acts would mainly focus on exploring the element of unilateralism rather than on determining the legal character of such acts, since the former task has been rarely undertaken, and thus it seems more 'exotic' from an international lawyer's point of view. Indeed, one might suggest that such a task is superfluous, especially in light of the ongoing debate in theory regarding the extent to which unilateral acts constitute a new source of law. Surely, if, as seen in the first chapter, there is such a debate, then *ex hypothesi* such acts must be legally relevant?

The answer to this question is not as straightforward as it may seem. The concept of unilateral acts in international law has elicited such a wide spectrum of reactions that no aspect of it may be considered as a given. As discussed in the first chapter, for some lawyers the discourse on unilateral acts mainly pertains to the challenges that such acts pose to traditional conceptions of international law-making. At the other end of the spectrum, some lawyers deny that international law comprises such a concept as unilateral acts.[1] In this vein, it has been asserted that "unilateral acts only describe a sociological reality of informal interaction between States"[2] and thus, they may not create enforceable duties, or more generally have any legal effects in international law. According to this line of argumentation, unilateral acts operate in a context of actions and expectations, within which compliance is based more on rules of international comity rather than hard law. Thus, for example, Judge De Castro in his Dissenting Opinion in the *Nuclear Tests Case*[3] questioned the decision reached by the majority of the Court regarding the binding character

1 M. Koskenniemi, *From Apology to Utopia: The Structure of International Legal Argument*, re-issued with new epilogue, (Cambridge: Cambridge University Press, 2005), pp. 345 *et seq.*

2 Report of the ILC on its 55th Session, UN Doc. A/58/10, *Yrbk of the ILC* 2003, Vol. II, para. 273.

3 *Nuclear Tests Case*, Australia vs France, *ICJ Reports* 1974, p. 253, New Zealand vs France, *ICJ Reports* 1974, p. 457. The Court's judgments in these two cases are almost identical. Hereinafter,

 | DOI 10.1163/9789004300767_007

of the French statements. Judge De Castro argued that France did not purport to give any assurances of a legal nature at the time; in his view, "the attitude of the French Government warrants rather the inference that it considers its statements to belong to the political domain."[4]

More radically, Rubin, in his commentary on the same case, criticised the Court for applying a concept of unilateral acts with binding force in international law, which, according to his opinion, was not supported either by State practice, or by legal theory.[5] Similarly, Koskenniemi argued in relation to unilateral acts in the form of declarations that "the doctrine of unilateral declarations cannot provide the law with the kind of objectivity, which is taken to distinguish it from political argument."[6] Simply put, for some international lawyers, unilateral acts may not create any legal effects on the international plane. In light of the objections to the existence of unilateral acts as a legal institution, this and the following chapters purport to examine whether and under which circumstances unilateral acts may be justifiably considered as 'legal' or 'juridical acts', a term which, as will be explained shortly, is used to connote acts with legal effects on the international plane.

This chapter begins by addressing the preliminary question of the distinction between 'law' and 'non-law' and argues that this distinction is of cardinal importance in international law due to the changing nature of modern State interaction. The chapter continues by exploring the concept of juridical acts in

---

unless otherwise stated, all references made to the *Nuclear Tests Case* will concern the case between Australia and France.

4 Dissenting Opinion of Judge De Castro in the *Nuclear Tests Case*, *ibid.*, p. 372 at 375. Note, however, that Judge De Castro, in contrast to Koskenniemi, does not seem to question the bindingness of unilateral acts when uttered publicly and with the intention to be bound. Fron his dissenting opinion, it may be deduced that the Judge agreed with the majority regarding the existence of such a rule but disputed that France, in the case at hand, had shown the requisite degree of intention to become bound by its statements.

5 See generally A. Rubin, The International Legal Effects of Unilateral Declarations, 71 *AJIL* 1 (1977).

6 M. Koskenniemi, *supra* note 1, p. 354. Similarly, D.J. Harris argued that: "There seems to be little evidence to support the rule stated by the Court whereby a state may be bound by a unilateral public pronouncement inetnded by it to be binding without more. If there is such a rule, it is submitted that further by way of evidence of intent should be required than was present on the facts of the *Nuclear Tests* cases." D.J. Harris, *Cases and Materials on International Law*, 6th ed., (London: Sweet & Maxwell, 2004), p. 798. See, however, the comments made in the latest edition of the same book: "Although there was at the time little evidence to support it, the rule stated by the Court whereby a state may be bound by a unilateral public pronouncement intended by it to be binding without more has now taken root." D.J. Harris, *Cases and Materials on International Law*, 7th ed., (London: Sweet & Maxwell, 2010), p. 49.

national and in international law for the purpose of ascertaining whether that theory offers any criteria for distinguishing between unilateral juridical acts and unilateral political acts. It will be shown that the doctrine in question is prevalent in countries following the civil law tradition, but it has largely remained underdeveloped in international law. In light of the lack of an overarching theory of international juridical acts, the chapter continues its enquiry in the law of treaties since this is the closest area of law to unilateral acts in which the problem of distinguishing between legal and non-legal acts has been fully addressed. It will be demonstrated that there is consensus both in doctrine and in judicial practice that the main criterion for distinguishing between legally binding agreements and mere political pledges is the objective or manifest intention of the author States to be bound by their acts.[7] Against this background, the next chapter will then concentrate on unilateral acts with a view to establish whether and under which circumstances international law attaches legal consequences to these acts.

A final note on the use of the term 'juridical/legal acts' throughout this chapter must be made here. The idea of developing a coherent and systematic theory of legally relevant acts in international law did not find much ground amongst English-speaking authors, in comparison to their French[8] and German[9] colleagues. Indeed, if one takes a look at the index of most standard textbooks on international law written in English, the term 'juridical acts' is conspicuously absent. The only notable exception is Verzijl's *International Law in a Historical Perspective*,[10] in which the Dutch scholar wrote extensively on the subject of international juridical acts. In his writings, Verzijl referred to State acts that produce legal effects in international law as international 'juridical acts' or 'acts in law.'[11] In the same vein, both terms are used here to connote acts that are recognised by international law to be of legal significance.

7 See J.E.S. Fawcett, The Legal Character of International Agreements, 30 *BYIL* 381 (1953), p. 385.

8 See for example the discussion about 'actes juridiques' in J-P. Jacque, *Elements Pour une Theorie de l'Acte Juridique en Droit International*, (Paris: LGDJ, 1972) and J. Carpentier, *Engagements Unilatéraux et Engagements Conventionnels: Différences et Convergences*, in J. Makarczyk (ed.), *Theory of International Law at the Threshold of the 21st Century: Essays in Honour of K. Skubiszewski*, (The Hague: Kluwer Law International, 1996), p. 357.

9 See for example the discussion about 'Rechtsgeschäfte' or 'Rechtsakte' in A. Verdross, B. Simma, *Universelles Völkerrecht: Theorie und Praxis*, 3rd Aufl., (Berlin: Duncker & Humblot, 1984), pp. 424 *et seq.*

10 J.H.W. Verzijl, *International Law in a Historical Perspective, Vol. VI: Juridical Facts as Sources of International Rights and Obligations*, (Leiden: Sijtoff, 1973).

11 *Ibid.*, p. 48.

'Juridical' or 'legal' acts are juxtaposed here to 'political acts', a term employed to signify acts of a non-juridical nature, *i.e.* acts of no legal consequence in international relations.

2 The Distinction between Law and Non-law

2.1 *The Distinction between "Law" and "Non-law" as a Key Feature of All Legal Systems*

The main focus of this chapter is on the distinction between legal and non-legal acts in international law. However, before embarking upon any further discussion, it is worthwhile at this point to briefly assess the importance of drawing a clear line between 'legal' and 'non-legal' more generally. In other words, as Bothe queried,[12] is it meaningful to distinguish between law and non-law in international relations?

The distinction between 'legal' and 'non-legal' acts, or more generally the distinction between 'law' and 'non-law', has been a perennial problem in international law since its early days.[13] Nevertheless, it would be wrong to assume that this problem is endemic to the international legal order. On the contrary, retaining a clear distinction between legal and non-legal is central to all legal systems irrespective of the level, municipal or international, at which they operate, since blurring this distinction would entail blurring the boundaries between law and other disciplines. At this point, one may question whether such boundaries exist and if so, which purpose they may serve. Answering such questions involves, alongside traditional legal analysis, a brief, albeit necessary, excursion to a domain frequently avoided by international lawyers: sociology. However, as it is often the case, "if we are to understand the significance of international law and how it works and evolves, it is essential to look outside of the law itself."[14]

---

12 See generally M. Bothe, Legal and Non-Legal Norms – A Meaningful Distinction in International Relations? 11 *Netherlands YIL* 65 (1980). Although Bothe's article is about the distinction between legal and non-legal norms, the same questions are applicable *mutatis mutandis* to legal and non-legal acts, or more generally to 'law' and 'non-law.'

13 See generally H. Kelsen, B. Litschewski Paulson and S.L. Paulson (trs.), *Introduction to the Problems of Legal Theory: A Translation of the First Edition of the Reine Rechtslere or Pure Theory of Law*, (Oxford: Clarendon Press, 1992); H. Lauterpacht, *The Function of Law in the International Community*, new ed., (Oxford: Oxford University Press, 2011).

14 O. Schachter, *International Law in Theory and Practice*, (London: M. Nijhoff Publishers, 1991), p. 3.

From a sociological point of view, law is but one of the many choices aimed at co-ordinating different, and often conflicting, interests including politics, social science or even theology.[15] However, it is often asserted that, in achieving its social function, the legal order is fundamentally different to all other rival solutions.[16] In the words of the International Court of Justice: "Law exists, it is said, to serve a social need; but precisely for that reason it can do so only through and within the limits of its own discipline. Otherwise, it is not a legal service that would be rendered."[17] Therefore, one may ask which unique qualities law has that differentiate it from other available problem-solving candidates, and thus, make the distinction between them meaningful.

Modern international lawyers, such as Schachter and Koskenniemi, have convincingly argued that law, in comparison to all other disciplines is an autonomous system that enjoys two unique features, *i.e.* normativity and concreteness.[18] The claim that the legal order is 'normative' means that law is, at least to some degree, binding. Thus, while acknowledging the role of power and politics in the formation of law, Koskenniemi and Schachter argue that a legal system operates, or at least must operate in order to be called 'legal', independently of politics and restrains the action of its subjects irrespectively of their will.[19] In the words of Schachter, a legal system "lacks the character of law if it is not in some degree 'binding', that is, it must be a means of independent

15 In this respect, see the famous dictum by M. Huber as arbitrator in the *Island of Palmas Case*: "International law, like law in general, has the object of assuring the co-existence of different interests which are worthy of legal protection." *Island of Palmas Case*, 2 *Rep. of Int'l. Arbitral Awards* 829 (1928), at p. 870. On the function of international law, see also P. Allott, The Concept of International Law, 10 *EJIL* 31 (1999).

16 J. Raz, *Practical Reason and Norms*, (Oxford: Oxford University Press, 1975), p. 149 *et seq*. See also the comments made by Judges Spender and Fitzmaurice in their Joint dissenting Opinion on the *South West Africa Cases*: "We are not unmindful of, nor are we insensible to, the various considerations of a non-juridical character, social, humanitarian and other, which underlie this case; but these are matters for the political rather for the legal arena. They cannot be allowed to deflect us from our duty of reaching a conclusion on the basis of what we believe to be the correct legal view." Joint Dissenting Opinion of Sir Percy Spender and Sir Gerald Fitzmaurice to the *South West Africa Cases*, *ICJ Reports* 1962, p. 465, at p. 466.

17 *South West Africa Cases*, *ICJ Reports* 1966, p. 6, at p. 34, para. 49.

18 O. Schachter, *The Nature and Process of Legal Development in International Society*, in R. MacDonald, D. Johnston (eds.), *The Structure and Process of International Law: Essays in Legal Philosophy, Doctrine and Theory*, (The Hague: M. Nijhoff, 1983), p. 745 at p. 747; M. Koskenniemi, *supra* note 1, pp. 17–24.

19 O. Schachter, *ibid.*; M. Koskenniemi, *ibid.* See also, H. Kelsen, M. Knight (tr.) *Pure Theory of Law*, 2nd rev. and enlarged ed., (Clark: Lawbook Exchange, 2005), p. 33 *et seq*.

control that effectively limits the acts of entities subject to it. To that degree, law must be independent of politics. Nor is it law if decisions are wholly arbitrary or capricious."[20] Thus, normativity, as a feature of any given legal order, relates to the fact that the subjects of such an order are not free to ignore or disobey the rules imposed thereby in pursuit of their own interests.

While normativity provides the law with the necessary degree of independence to fulfil its social function irrespectively of the individual interests and wills of its subjects, concreteness keeps it in touch with the ever-fluctuating realities of the social environment in which law is called to operate. In other words, the element of concreteness of legal rules means that the content of such rules derives from and represents the actual pattern of the behaviour of legal subjects and not from an abstract theory or ideology of how this behaviour ought to be. In this respect, Koskenniemi argues that, by way of contrast to religion or morality, where a pre-determined set of rules is supposed to govern the conduct of affairs between individuals or States without taking into consideration their own wishes or the changing structure of the society, legal rules are created and developed in accordance with the actual behaviour of the subjects of law.[21]

2.2 *The Distinction between Law and Non-law in the International Legal System*

From the outset, it needs to be noted that in determining the legal character of a given instrument the international judge is in a far worse situation than his national counterpart. In the early 1980s, Jennings voiced concern over the increasing difficulty of distinguishing between legal and non-legal norms at the international level.[22] The situation has not improved much over the years. The declining importance of form and formalities in international law, as well as the recent proliferation of soft-law instruments (a term that will be used here to denote instruments of dubious binding nature)[23] has made the line between law and non-law very hard to discern on the international plane.

---

20 O. Schachter, *ibid.*

21 M. Koskenniemi, *supra* note 1, p. 17.

22 R.Y. Jennings, What Is International Law and How Do We Tell When We See It? 37 *Schweizeriches Jahrbuch für Internationales Recht* 59 (1981), p. 60.

23 It needs to be noted at the outset that the term 'soft-law' has a number of different meanings and that there is little agreement amongst international lawyers on what exactly it means. See J. Murphy, *The Evolving Dimensions of International Law: Hard Choices for the World Community*, (Cambridge: Cambridge University Press, 2010), p. 20. From a law-ascertaining perspective, the term is used to describe "a variety of legally non-binding instruments used in international relations." A. Boyle, C. Chinkin, *The Making of*

In municipal legal systems, the law often stipulates specific requirements regarding the form of legal transactions, the non-observance of which may result in rendering the transaction in question invalid. As the Court noted in the *Case concerning the Temple of Preah Vihear*:

> As regards the question of forms and formalities, as distinct from intentions, the Court considers that, to cite examples drawn from the field of private law, there are cases where, for the protection of the interested parties, or for reasons of public policy, or on other grounds, the law prescribes as mandatory certain formalities which, hence, become essential for the validity of certain transactions, such as for instance testamentary dispositions; and another example, amongst many possible ones, would be that of a marriage ceremony.[24]

However, this is not the case with international law where the form in which a legal transaction is clothed does not affect its legal character or validity, but is rather of evidentiary value.[25] As the Court added in its judgment in the aforementioned case:

> But the position in the cases just mentioned (wills, marriage, *etc.*) arises because of the existence in those cases of mandatory requirements of law as to forms and formalities. Where, on the other hand, as is generally the case in international law, which places the principal emphasis on the intentions of the parties, the law prescribes no particular form, parties are free to choose what form they please provided their intention clearly results from it.[26]

The lack of strict requirements relating to form means that the distinction between legal and non-legal transactions is more difficult to observe in international law.

Secondly, recent changes in international relations have obscured the distinction between law and non-law at the international level even further. In

International Law, (Oxford: Oxford University Press, 2007), p. 212. See also A. Boyle, Some Reflections on the Relationship of Treaties and Soft Law, 48 *ICLQ* 901 (1999), at pp. 901–2.

24 *Case concerning the Temple of Preah Vihear*, *ICJ Reports* 1961, p. 17 at p. 31.

25 See generally M. Lachs, *Some Reflections on Substance and Form in International Law*, in W. Friedmann, L. Henkin, O. Lissitzyn (eds.), *Transnational Law in a Changing Society: Essays in Honor of Philip C. Jessup*, (New York: Columbia University Press, 1972), p. 99 *et seq.*

26 *Case concerning the Temple of Preah Vihear*, *supra* note 24, p. 31.

recent years, international law has witnessed a growing tension between the need for flexibility, simplicity and speed in the conclusion of agreements on the one hand, and the need for stability and predictability on the other. The aforementioned need for flexibility, simplicity and speed in modern international relations has generated a large number of international instruments, the normative effect of which is unclear, *i.e.* of soft-law instruments.[27] Modern State-practice is anything but unfamiliar with 'Memoranda of Understanding' or 'Common positions', terms that are employed in practice to denote instruments that embody some sort of common understanding but fall short of international agreements proper.[28] However, the widespread use of such instruments entails that the distinction between legal and political acts has become blurry.[29] In light of these difficulties, questioning the meaningfulness of this distinction becomes more relevant than ever. Do the declining importance of form and the proliferation of soft-law instruments signify that there is now no point in keeping clear boundaries between law and non-law?

This question has been at the epicentre of modern scholarly debate.[30] Supporters of the soft law concept have argued that the positivist, binary approach to international law, *i.e.* understanding and describing international law in terms of 'legal' and 'non-legal', is not well suited to reflect the increasing complexity of modern international relations.[31] According to this line of argumentation, soft law instruments have proven to be as – or, in some instances, even more – effective than their 'hard' counterparts, thereby rendering the distinction between law and non-law redundant.[32] From this point of view, modern international law is conceptualised as a continuum, rather than as a dichotomy between binding and non-binding norms.[33]

27 There is a vast amount of literature on the topic of 'soft – law instruments.' See indicatively H. Hillgenberg, A Fresh Look at Soft Law, 10 *EJIL* 499 (1999); A. Boyle, *Soft Law in International Law-Making*, in M. Evans (ed.), *International Law*, 4th ed., (Oxford: Oxford University Press, 2014), at p. 118; C. Chinkin, The Challenge Of Soft Law: Development and Change in International Law, 38 *ICLQ* 850 (1989).

28 R. Baxter, International Law in "Her Infinite Variety", 29 *ICLQ* 549 (1980).

29 J. Klabbers, *Law-Making and Constitutionalism*, in J. Klabbers, A. Peters, G. Ulfstein (eds.), *The Constitutionalization of International Law*, (Oxford: Oxford University Press, 2009), p. 80 at p. 83.

30 See for example the recent Symposium on Soft Law, 25 *LJIL* 309 (2012).

31 See for example, L. Blutman, In the Trap of a Legal Metaphor: International Soft Law, 59 *ICLQ* 605 (2010), pp. 613–4; M. Goldmann, We need to cut off the head of the King: Past, Present and Future Approaches to International Soft Law, 25 *LJIL* 335 (2012).

32 U. Fastenrath, Relative Normativity in International Law, 4 *EJIL* 305 (1993), pp. 330 *et seq.*

33 L. Blutman, *supra* note 31.

Although the idea that graduated normativity is an inescapable fact of modern international affairs has found its way into mainstream legal scholarship,[34] it is submitted that the arguments in favour of keeping distinct boundaries between legal and political acts still hold more sway. At first, the need to maintain stability, reliability and predictability in international relations dictates that States should be in a position to know whether a certain act has or does not have legal repercussions.[35] Furthermore, as Klabbers correctly observes, the muddying of waters between law and non-law is problematic from a rule of law perspective.[36] According to Klabbers, international law as it stands now is – to a large extent at least – the result of "democratically reached agreement between interested actors."[37] However, making away with the distinction between 'hard' and 'soft' instruments would mean that we also make away with the democratic guarantees normally associated with formal law-making processes.

More importantly, although it is true that the use of soft-law instruments has increased in recent years, States still find the distinction between legal and political acts relevant. This is evidenced by the fact that States often explicitly proclaim the non-binding character of particular instruments they conclude in order to disperse doubts regarding their non-legal nature. For instance, the signatories to the Helsinki Final Act,[38] not only included specific references to its political nature in the text of the Act itself,[39] but they also made a number of subsequent statements underscoring its non-binding character.[40] The same practice was followed in relation to the 2007 Declaration on the Rights of Indigenous Peoples, a 'soft-law' declaration adopted under the auspices of the United Nations.[41] Although the USA and Canada initially rejected the UN Declaration, they have recently changed their position and issued statements to support it. In these statements, however, the non-binding character of the

34 See generally J. D'Aspremont, Softness in International Law: A Self-Serving Quest for New Legal Materials, 19 *EJIL* 1075 (2008).

35 P. Weil, Towards Relative Normativity in International Law? 77 *AJIL* 413 (1983), pp. 418–9; J. Klabbers, The Undesirability of Soft Law, 67 *Nordic JIL* 381 (1998), pp. 387–91.

36 J. Klabbers, Informal Agreements in International Law: Towards a Theoretical Framework, 5 *Finnish YIL* 267 (1994), pp. 361–2.

37 J. Klabbers, *supra* note 29, p. 105.

38 OSCE, Final Act of the Conference on Security and Co-operation in Europe, adopted in Helsinki on 1 August 1975, also known as the Helsinki Final Act, available at http://www.osce.org/mc/39501.

39 H.S. Russel, The Helsinki Declaration: Brobdingnag or Lilliput? 70 *AJIL* 242 (1976), p. 247.

40 *Ibid.*, fn. 21.

41 See GA, Declaration on the Rights of Indigenous Peoples, UN Doc. A/RES/61/295 (2007).

duties enshrined in the 2007 UN Declaration was highlighted.[42] These two examples show that, far from rendering the distinction between legal and political acts obsolete in their every-day practice, States are often quite careful to emphasize the non-binding character of obligations undertaken by means of so-called 'soft-law' instruments.

Finally, the distinction between legal and political acts is still pertinent when it comes to questions of State Responsibility. According to the law of State Responsibility, the breach of obligations of a legal nature entails certain consequences for the offending State[43] – such as the obligation to make reparation.[44] However, the breach of obligations of a non-legal nature does not engage the responsibility of a State in the same way. If legal and non-legal obligations were conflated, the regime of sanctions for breaches of obligations of a legal nature under international law would be impossible to apply. This would mean that international law would lose its normativity – as this term was described above – and therefore, would no longer be 'law' proper. As Klabbers noted "by creating uncertainty at the edges of legal thinking, the concept of soft-law contributes to the crumbling of the entire legal system."[45]

3 The Lack of a Developed Theory on Juridical Acts in International Law

The previous section showed that the distinction between legal and non-legal acts in international law is not only quite difficult to make due to the special characteristics of the international legal order, but also of paramount significance in the light of the increased use of soft-law instruments in modern State interaction. Therefore it is perhaps surprising that a fully-fledged theory of international juridical acts (*i.e.* of legal acts of both bi/multi and unilateral

42 For the Canadian Statement of Support see Canada's Statement of Support on the United Nations Declaration on the Rights of Indigenous Peoples, available at http://www.aadnc-aandc.gc.ca/eng/1309374239861/1309374546142. For the US Statement of Support see Announcement of US Support for the United Nations Declaration on the Rights of Indigenous Peoples: Initiatives to Promote the Government-to-Government Relationship & Improve the Lives of Indigenous Peoples, available at http://www.state.gov/documents/organization/153223.pdf.

43 See Art. 12 of the ILC's Articles on State Responsibility: Draft Articles on Responsibility of States for Internationally Wrongful Acts, with Commentaries, UN Doc. A/56/10, *Yrbk of the ILC* 2001, Vol. II, p. 59.

44 See Art. 1, *ibid.*

45 J. Klabbers, *supra* note 35, p. 391.

origin) has not yet emerged. Although the question of the legal nature of international agreements has attracted much scholarly attention, only a few international lawyers, such as Verzijl, Lauterpacht and D'Aspremont, have addressed the more general problem of ascertaining the legal character of international juridical acts. In order to provide some background to the concept of juridical acts, this part of the chapter will first briefly explore the concept in question from a comparative law perspective. It will be shown that juridical acts are a predominantly civil law concept that places primary emphasis on the intention of the author in determining the binding force of acts, of either contractual or unilateral origin. Next, the focus will turn to the attempts that have been made so far in theory to develop a doctrine of juridical acts in international law and it will be argued that – in a similar fashion to the civil law understanding of these acts – the intention of the author State has featured in the writings of the aforementioned lawyers as the primary criterion for differentiating between juridical and political acts.

3.1 *A Brief Excursus to the Concept of Juridical Acts in National Law: Juridical Acts as a Predominantly Civil Law Concept*

According to the 2008 study conducted by the Joint Network on European Private Law, juridical acts are a concept rooted in countries with a civil law tradition.[46] The concept originates in the French legal system, where it plays a key role in the classification of the sources of obligation. Under French law, the sources of obligations are systematised on the basis of a distinction between juridical acts and juridical facts. More particularly, according to the Proposals for Reform of the Law of Obligations and the Law of Prescription published by the French Ministry in 2006,[47] obligations may arise either from juridical acts or from juridically significant facts.[48] While juridical acts are described as "exercises of will which are intended to produce legal effects" and expressly

46 B. Fauvarque-Cosson, D. Mazeud (eds.), *European Contract Law, Materials for a Common Frame of Reference: Terminology, Guiding Principles, Model Rules* (Munich: Sellier, European Law Publishers, 2008) p. 66. See also J.H. Merryman, R. Perez-Perdomo, *The Civil Law Tradition: An Introduction to the Legal Systems of Europe and Latin America*, (Stanford: Stanford University Press, 2007), p. 75, in which juridical acts are described as "the proudest achievement of the civil law doctrine."

47 J. Cartwright, S. Whittaker, *Proposals for Reform of the Law of Obligations and the Law of Prescription; English Translation of Avant-projet de Réforme du Droit des Obligations et de la Prescription* (2005), 2007, available at http://www.justice.gouv.fr/art_pix/rapportcatatla0905-anglais.pdf.

48 *Ibid.*, Art. 1101.

include both contracts and unilateral acts,[49] juridical facts consist of "conduct and or events to which the law attaches legal consequences."[50] Principal examples of the former category would include contracts and unilateral promises, whereas of the latter, the birth or death of an individual.[51]

While not all civil law countries have adopted the refined dichotomy of the sources of obligations the French system has, juridical acts are a common topos in the civilian tradition. Despite terminological differences, the term is used throughout the civil law world to connote acts that create legal effects based upon the manifestation of intention by their author/s.[52] Indeed, the element of intention lies at the very core of the concept: according to the Italian definition, juridical acts are "declarations of will setting out the intended legal effects and to which the legal system attaches legal effects in accordance with the intended result,"[53] while under the Dutch Civil Code, juridical acts are declarations of will, to which the law gives binding effect to the extent that they manifest their authors' intention to become bound thereby.[54] Similar definitions that emphasise the element of intention are to be found in the civil codes of Germany, Greece, Belgium, Austria, Portugal, Slovenia, Slovakia, Bulgaria, Hungary and other civil law countries.[55] It is also important to note that the

---

49 *Ibid.*, Art. 1101–1.

50 *Ibid.*, Art. 1101–2.

51 B. Fauvarque-Cosson, D. Mazeud, *supra* note 46, pp. 66–86.

52 C. von Bar, E. Clive, H. Schulte-Nölke, *Principles, Definitions and Model Rules of European Private Law, Draft Common Frame of Reference* (DCFR), prepared by the Study Group on a European Civil Code and the Research Group on EC Private Law (*Acquis* Group), 2009, available at http://ec.europa.eu/justice/contract/files/european-private-law_en.pdf, pp. 173–4.

53 B. Fauvarque-Cosson, D. Mazeud, *supra* note 46, p. 84. The concept of juridical acts, or '*atti giuridici*', is the creation of doctrine and is not to be found in the Italian Civil Code (*Codice Civile*) or in any special legislation. However, *atti giuridici* are of paramount importance in the Italian theory of classification of obligations. See M. Cappelletti, J.H. Merryman, J.M. Perillo, *The Italian Legal system: An Introduction*, (Stanford: Stanford University Press, 1967), pp. 177–9.

54 Art. 3:33 of the Dutch Civil Code (*Burgerlijk Wetboek*). See also J.M.J. Chorus, P.H.M. Gerver, E.H. Hondius, *Introduction to Dutch Law*, 4th rev. ed., (Deventer: Kluwer, 2006), pp. 151–3.

55 B. Fauvarque-Cosson, D. Mazeud, *supra* note 46, p. 76–86. For instance, according to the German Civil Code (*Bürgerliches Gesetzbuch*), juridical acts (*Rechtsgeschäfte*), namely acts that express the intention to be bound, include both contracts and unilateral acts (*Einseitige Rechtsgeschäfte*). See Arts. 104–11 of the German Civil Code. The Greek Civil Code (*Αστικός Κώδικας*), which was modeled after the German Civil Code, also embodies the concept of juridical acts and puts primary emphasis on the intention of the parties to create legal

2009 Model Rules on European Private Law,[56] prepared by the Study Group on a European Civil Code and the Research Group on EC Private law under the auspices of the European Commission, expressly refer to juridical acts as a core common concept of EU private law. Model rule II.1:101 (2) provides that a juridical act is "any statement or agreement, whether express, or implied from conduct, which is intended to have legal effects as such. It may be unilateral, bilateral or multilateral."[57] By way of contrast, legal systems based on the common law tradition have not adopted the concept of juridical acts – with the exception of the 'hybrid' Scottish system.[58]

A perusal of the relevant legislation, case-law and literature reveals that, although juridical acts of a bi/multilateral origin, *i.e.* contracts, are more commonly used, the civil law tradition has long accepted that juridical acts may also encompass acts of unilateral origin.[59] Indeed, the majority of States that have incorporated the concept of juridical acts into their legal systems have also expressly acknowledged the binding force of unilateral undertakings – without the need for any form of acceptance or reliance by the addressee.[60] Thus, the civil law tradition accepts the enforceability of gratuitous promises, *i.e.* promises under which the promisor undertakes to do or refrain from doing something without receiving anything in exchange, such as public promises of rewards, gift promises or unilateral undertakings made in the context of

---

effects thereby (Art. 130 of the Greek Civil Code). See generally, M. Stathopoulos, *Contract Law in Greece*, 2nd rev. ed., (The Hague: Kluwer Law International, 2009), pp. 83–4. The concept of juridical acts, as manifestations of the intention of their author/s to be bound, is also prevalent in Belgian legal theory. See P. Van Ommeslaghe, *L'engagement Par Volonté* Unilatérale en Droit Belge, 1982 *Journal des Tribunaux* 144 (1982), pp. 144–9. Under Art. 34 of the Slovak Civil Code (*Občiansky Zakonník*), acts in law, or juridical acts, are manifestations of will aimed at the creation, modification or termination of rights and obligations. In a similar vein, Art. 67, para. 1 of the Estonian Civil Code (*Tsiviilseadustiku Üldosa Seadus*) defines juridical acts as declarations of intention directed at bringing about a certain legal consequence. Scottish law also recognises that intention is central to the formation of voluntary obligations. The latter are divided in two categories, namely contracts and unilateral promises. See Scottish Law Commission, Memorandum No. 35, Constitution and Proof of Voluntary Obligations: Unilateral Promises, 10 March 1977, available at http://www.scotlawcom.gov.uk/publications/discussion-papers-and-consultative-memoranda/1970-1979/.

56 C. von Bar, E. Clive, H. Schulte-Nölke, *supra* note 52, p. 170.

57 *Ibid.*

58 M.A. Hogg, Promise: The Neglected Obligation in European Private Law, 59 *ICLQ* 461 (2010), p. 464.

59 B. Fauvarque-Cosson, D. Mazeud, *supra* note 46, pp. 73–4, 82–4.

60 P. Lenner, Promises of Rewards in a Comparative Perspective, 10 *Ann. Surv. Int'l & Comp. L.* 53 (2004), pp. 61–5; M.A. Hogg, *supra* note 58, pp. 463–4.

business.[61] The binding effects of such gratuitous promises are expressly recognised in German, Austrian, Bulgarian, Slovenian, Estonian, Italian, Portuguese, Dutch, Belgian, Finnish, Swedish and Scottish law.[62]

On the other hand, short of deeds under seal, purely unilateral promises that have not been accepted or relied upon by the promisee are not enforceable against the promisor in common law legal systems.[63] This is not to say that the concept of unilateral undertakings is entirely foreign to the common law tradition. However, for such promises to create binding effects, some form of *quid pro quod* or reliance on behalf of the addressee is needed. As Judge Jessup noted in his Separate Opinion to the *South West Africa* cases: "it is also generally recognised that there may be *unilateral agreements*, meaning agreements arising out of unilateral acts in which only one party is promisor and may well be the only party bound."[64]

The main reason underpinning the difficulty of the common law tradition to recognise the binding force of gratuitous promises lies in the importance attached to the doctrine of consideration within that legal tradition. Although English law and American law adopt slightly different definitions, the doctrine of consideration insists on the existence of an element of exchange, or reciprocity, in the formation of contracts.[65] Thus, purely gratuitous promises are not considered enforceable in the absence of an element of reciprocity, *i.e.* in the absence of consideration. As Justice Parker stated in *Mills v. Wyman*:

> General rules of law established for the protection and security of honest and fair-minded men, who may inconsiderately make promises without any equivalent, will sometimes screen men of a different character from engagements which they are bound in *foro conscientae* to perform…The

---

61 P. Lenner, *ibid.*, pp. 61–2.

62 C. von Bar, E. Clive, H. Schulte-Nölke, *supra* note 52, pp. 180–1. See, for example, Art. 111 of the German Civil Code (*Bürgerliches Gesetzbuch*); Art. 3:32 of the Dutch Civil Code (*Burgerlijk Wetboek*); Art. 44 of the Bulgarian Obligations and Contracts Act of 1950; Art. 1989 of the Italian Civil Code (*Codice Civile*); Art. 67, para. 2 of the Estonian Civil Code (*Tsiviilseadustiku Üldosa Seadus*); Section 1 of the Scottish Requirements of Writing (Scotland) Act of 1995.

63 J. Beatson, A. Burrows, J. Cartwright, *Anson's Law of Contracts*, 29th ed., (Oxford: Oxford University Press, 2010), p. 91; J. Cooke, D. Oughton, *The Common Law of Obligations*, 3rd ed., (Oxford: Oxford University Press, 2000), pp. 66–7.

64 Separate Opinion of Judge Jessup to the *South West Africa Cases*, ICJ *Reports* 1962, p. 387, at p. 402. (Emph. added).

65 C. Larroumet, Detrimental Reliance and Promissory Estoppel as the Cause of Contracts in Louisiana and Comparative Law, 60 *Tul. L. Rev.* 1209 (1986), pp. 1210–11.

> rule that a mere verbal promise, *without any consideration*, cannot be enforced by action, is universal in its application, and cannot be departed from to suit particular cases in which a refusal to perform such a promise may be disgraceful.[66]

On the other hand, the civil law counterpart of consideration, cause or *causa*, is a much broader concept that examines the aims motivating each party to create obligations by means of a juridical act – rather than merely the existence of an element of reciprocity of obligations.[67] Thus, in civil law jurisdictions, a juridical act without a cause, *i.e.* without an achievable aim, or with an unlawful cause is invalid.[68] The main rationale underpinning the concept of cause is the protection of individuals. Under normal circumstances, individuals do not enter into contractual or other obligations, unless they wish to pursue an aim. For example, in entering into a contract for sale, the buyer promises to pay the agreed amount of money *because* the seller promises to deliver the item and similarly, the seller promises to deliver the item *because* the buyer promises to pay the agreed amount of money. In this sense, "for bilateral contracts, the *cause* of the obligation of each of the parties lies in the obligation of the other."[69] The function of the concept of cause is to protect a party in cases where the pursued aim cannot be realized by allowing the party in question to be released from their own obligations. Thus, in the abovementioned example, if the item for sale is destroyed and thus, the seller is unable to deliver it, the buyer is released from their obligation to pay the agreed amount of money: the existence of the buyer's *cause* of obligation has ceased to exist. However, as far as unilateral undertakings are concerned, the civil law tradition has accepted that the intention of the author to give something solely for the "pleasure of doing something good" is a valid cause for the creation of legally binding effects.[70]

---

66 *Mills v. Wyman*, 20 *Mass.* (3 *Pick.*) 207 (1825), pp. 209–10, available at http://grammar.ucsd.edu/courses/lign105/student-court-cases/mills.pdf. (Emph. added).

67 C. Calleros, Cause, Consideration, Promissory Estoppel, and Promises under Deed: What Our Students Should Know about Enforcement of Promises in a Historical and International Context, *13 Chi. – Kent J. Int'l & Comp. L.* 83 (2013), p. 96.

68 See for example Art. 1131 of the French Civil Code (*Code Civil*): "An obligation without cause or with a false cause, or with an unlawful cause, may not have any effect." See also Art. 1261 of the Spanish Civil Code (*Código Civil*): "There is no contract unless the following requirements are met: 1. Consent of the contracting parties. 2. A certain object that is the subject matter of the contract. 3. Cause of the obligation established."

69 T. Kadner Graziano, *Comparative Contract Law: Cases, Materials and Exercises*, (Basingstoke: Palgrave MacMillan, 2009), para. 338.

70 *Ibid.*, paras. 338–49; C. Larroumet, *supra* note 65, p. 1220.

3.2 *The Concept of Juridical Acts in International Law: An Underdeveloped Idea*

As remarked earlier, Verzijl's *International Law in a Historical Perspective* is one of the rare English-language works in which the question of international juridical acts is treated at length. More particularly, in the sixth volume of the aforementioned treatise, Verzijl attempted to provide a systematic exposition of all legally relevant facts, *i.e.* of all events or actions from which juridical relations may originate.[71] In his view, all juridical relations, namely the totality of rights and obligations between international legal persons, may be traced back to three main legally relevant, or juridical, facts.[72] These include the simple fact of the co-existence of States which entails compliance to and respect of certain fundamental obligations and rights;[73] natural events which may give rise to new international rights and obligations (such as the emergence of an island in the territorial sea); and actions undertaken by subjects of international law.[74]

As far as the latter category is concerned, Verzijl attempted to bring all the manifestations of a State's action at the international level into two broad categories, namely to lawful acts (international juridical acts) and to unlawful acts (international delicts.)[75] According to Verzijl, State acts that are "intended to produce specific legal effects on the inter-state level and in fact producing them under normal circumstances"[76] belong to the category of juridical acts or "acts in law." Regarding the typology of acts that make up the category of juridical acts, Verzijl argued that the main distinction to be found in practice is between unilateral and plurilateral acts.[77] Thus, Verzijl propounded a concept of international juridical acts in which the element of the intention to create legal effects was central. In his view, these acts, which may be of either unilateral or plurilateral origin, produce legal effects because they evidence the intention of their author State, or States, to become bound on the international plane.[78] Therefore, according to Verzijl's definition of international juridical acts, the intention to create legal effects is the key criterion for determining the legal status of an international act.

---

71 J.H.W. Verzijl, *supra* note 10. Note that the sixth volume is entitled "Juridical Facts as Sources of International Rights and Obligations."

72 *Ibid.*, p. 2.

73 *Ibid.*, p. 4 *et seq.*

74 *Ibid.*

75 *Ibid.*

76 *Ibid.*, p. 48.

77 *Ibid.*

78 *Ibid.*

The same view, namely that intention is the main determinant of international rights and obligations, has also been shared by Lauterpacht.[79] As Fitzmaurice observed in his commentary on Lauterpacht's judicial pronouncements, although the latter did not develop a theory on international juridical acts as such, he emphasized the role of intention in establishing the juridical nature of instruments of either unilateral or treaty character.[80] One of the many examples offered by Fitzmaurice is Lauterpacht's Separate Opinion in the *Norwegian Loans Case*,[81] in which the latter noted that "whether it is a treaty or a unilateral declaration, it is – if it is to be treated as a legal text... – a manifestation of intention to create reciprocal rights and obligations."[82] Furthermore, Lauterpacht argued that, since both treaties and unilateral undertakings constitute legal acts, in the sense that both kinds of acts manifest the intention of States to create legal effects, the same rules of interpretation and invalidity applicable to treaties are also applicable *mutatis mutandis* to unilateral undertakings. More specifically, in his Separate Opinion in the aforementioned case, Lauterpacht examined the effects of the French Declaration made under Art. 36. 2 of the ICJ Statute that contained a reservation excluding issues of national jurisdiction – as understood by the French Government – from the compulsory jurisdiction of the Court.[83] In Lauterpacht's opinion,

79 Note however that Lauterpacht, as a Special Rapporteur of the ILC, was more reluctant to pronounce upon the binding nature of unilateral acts as such. More specifically, in discussing the creation of obligations by means of unilateral declarations, Lauterpacht supported that unilateral declarations following the pattern of offer and acceptance, such as unilateral declarations accepting an offer or accepting the terms of an already existing instrument, as well as unilateral declarations that have been accepted by the State to which they are addressed, constitute in essence treaty undertakings. Although not addressing the question directly, Lauterpacht admitted the possibility of binding unilateral acts which do not follow the abovementioned pattern of offer and acceptance. While Lauterpacht admitted the limitations of adopting a contractual perspective towards all unilateral acts, he did not go as far as accepting unilateral acts as a separate genus of juridiacal acts. However, as it will be shown below, by 1957 Lauterpacht seems to have accepted the view that purely unilateral acts, in the sense of acts that by no stretch of interpretation may be brought within a contractual frame, are binding as such. See H. Lauterpacht, Report on the Law of Treaties, UN Doc. A/CN.4/63, *Yrbk of the ILC* 1953, Vol. II, p. 90, at p. 101.

80 G. Fitzmaurice, *The Law and Procedure of the International Court of Justice*, Vol. II, (Cambridge: Grotius, 1986), pp. 822–9.

81 *Certain Norwegian Loans Case*, *ICJ Reports* 1957, p. 9.

82 Separate Opinion of Judge Sir Hersch Lauterpacht in the *Certain Norwegian Loans Case*, *ibid.*, p. 34 at p. 49.

83 *Certain Norwegian Loans Case*, *ibid.*, p. 21.

instruments purporting to create obligations but which, at the same time, contain an "automatic" reservation, *i.e.* a reservation to the effect that the extent of the obligation contained therein shall be reserved for the exclusive determination of the author State, are not legal instruments at all.[84] In support of his argument, he adduced evidence to the effect that the rule regarding the invalidity of such instruments is common to all major legal systems and thus, constitutes a general principle of law.[85]

Most importantly for the present purposes, Lauterpacht argued that this rule is applicable not only to treaties, but also to instruments of unilateral character.[86] This point, namely that both treaties and unilateral acts, in which a reservation of the 'automatic' type has been inserted, should be considered invalid was later reiterated in Lauterpacht's Dissenting Opinion in the *Interhandel Case*.[87] In that case, Lauterpacht repeated his opinion in the *Norwegian Loans Case* and added: "…it is not therefore necessary to repeat here the views there expressed, in particular those derived from general principles of law applicable to all legal instruments, whether bilateral or unilateral, *intended* to create legal rights and obligations."[88]

Juridical acts have remained at the margins of contemporary international legal scholarship. One of the few modern international lawyers to engage with the topic is Jean D'Aspremont.[89] In a similar vein to Verzijl, D'Aspremont classified all legal obligations into two main categories: juridical acts and juridical facts. Juridical acts allow subjects of international law to create new rules to the extent that they manifest the intention of their author/s to be bound. In his own words: "to enable it to qualify as legal act, the legal effect of the act in question must *directly* originate in the will of the legal subject to whom the behaviour is attributed and not to any pre-existing rule in the system."[90] On the other hand, juridical facts are acts the legal basis of which may be found in a pre-existing rule in the system. Thus, the legal effects of juridical facts "originate in the legal system itself, which provides for such an effect prior to the adoption of the act."[91] The theory of juridical acts has been central to D'Aspremont's

84 Separate Opinion of Judge Sir Hersch Lauterpacht in the *Certain Norwegian Loans Case*, *ibid.*, p. 39.

85 *Ibid.*

86 *Ibid.*

87 Dissenting Opinion of Judge Sir Hersch Lauterpacht in the *Interhandel Case*, *ICJ Reports* 1959, p. 6 at p. 95.

88 *Ibid.*, p. 106. (Emph. added).

89 J. D'Aspremont, *supra* note 34.

90 *Ibid.*, p. 1078.

91 *Ibid.*, p. 1079.

attack against soft law theorists. He argues that the problem of distinguishing between legal and non-legal obligations, namely the problem of 'soft law' vs. 'hard law', only arises in relation to obligations that stem from the will of the author State/s, *i.e.* from juridical acts, and not from any other pre-existing rule. Thus, according to him, the *problèmatique* of soft law cannot be properly understood "short of a sound theory of the legal act."[92] It is unnecessary to discuss in detail D'Aspremont's arguments against soft law. It has been clarified from the outset that the present author subscribes to the view that the distinction between legal and non-legal acts needs to be preserved if international law is to retain its distinctiveness and effectiveness. Irrespective of where one's sympathies might lie, the point made by D'Aspremont is still valid. In practice, the question of the binding force of an act does not normally arise in relation to acts that are based upon an established rule of customary law, or a general principle of law. It does, however, arise in relation to international agreements and unilateral acts.

On the basis of the above, it is evident that the concept of international juridical acts is far from adequately developed in theory. However, the few international lawyers who have touched upon the topic concluded that the criterion for establishing that acts of either unilateral, or bi/multilateral origin are to be considered as juridical acts – in contrast to mere political pledges – is the intention of their author to be bound.

4 Intention as the Criterion for Distinguishing between Legal and Non-legal Acts: The View from the Law of Treaties

As seen above, with few exceptions, legal literature is of limited assistance to the question of ascertaining the legal nature of international acts. Nevertheless, an area in which the problem of distinguishing between legal and non-legal acts is of utmost practical significance is that of the law of the treaties. In this field of international law, States, lawyers and international judicial bodies are commonly faced with instruments of controversial legal nature. At this point, an excursion to the law of treaties is considered essential since it will provide the necessary foundation upon which the argument of the next part of this chapter will be built, namely that both types of legal acts share intention as the determinant of their legal character and that the same methodology can be applied to both in order to establish the presence of the requisite element of intention.

92 *Ibid.*, p. 1078.

4.1 *Intention and the 1969 Vienna Convention on the Law of Treaties*

Although it does not cover the whole spectrum of agreements under international law,[93] it is customary to make a reference to the 1969 Vienna Convention on the Law of Treaties[94] as a starting point in every discussion relating to international agreements. According to the definition inserted in the Vienna Convention, an international treaty is "an international agreement concluded between States in written form and governed by international law, whether embodied in a single instrument or in two or more related instruments and whatever its particular designation."[95] Although the above definition does not make any direct reference to intention, the requirement that a treaty is "governed by international law" is generally interpreted as encompassing the element of the intention to create legal effects. More particularly, an examination of the reports produced by the successive Special Rapporteurs of the International Law Commission on the Law of Treaties shows that the intention to create legal effects was consistently cited as the key criterion for ascertaining the legal character of an international agreement.

In his first report on the law of treaties, Lauterpacht defined international treaties as agreements concluded "between States, including organisations of States, intended to create legal rights and obligations of the parties."[96] In a similar vein, Lauterpacht's successor, Fitzmaurice inserted the requirement of the intention to create rights, obligations or, more generally, to establish relationships in international law in his definition of international treaties.[97]

93 See Art. 3 of the *Vienna Convention on the Law of Treaties*, 22 May 1969, Vienna, 1155 UNTS 331, 8 ILM 679 (1969).

94 *Ibid.*

95 Art. 2.1 (a) of the Vienna Convention.

96 H. Lauterpacht, *supra* note 79, p. 93. In the commentary following the definition of international agreements, Lauterpacht highlighted the problem of distinguishing between instruments of a legal character and mere declarations of policy in the field of international law. As examples of the latter category, he cited, *inter alia*, the 1941 Atlantic Charter and the Universal Declaration of Human Rights adopted by the GA in 1948. The difference between such non-binding instruments and international agreements properly so called lied, in his opinion, in the fact that the latter instruments evidence the intention of their author States to create rights and obligations on the international plane. Thus, Lauterpacht concluded that "in the event of a dispute on the subject it must properly be a question for judicial determination whether an instrument, whatever its description, is in fact intended to create legal rights and obligations between the parties and as such coming within the category of treaties." *Ibid.*, pp. 96–8.

97 G. Fitzmaurice, Report on the Law of Treaties, UN Doc. A/CN.4/101, *Yrbk of the ILC* 1956, Vol. II, p. 104, at p. 107. The relevant part of his 1956 Report on the Law of Treaties reads: "For the purposes of the application of the present Code, a treaty is an international

Despite the persistent references to intention by both Lauterpacht and Fitzmaurice, the International Law Commission decided to omit any express reference to the intention of the author States from the definition of an international treaty. However, this decision did not imply any disagreement with the Special Rapporteurs' position regarding the paramount significance of the element of intention;[98] rather the ILC considered that the element of intention was already encompassed within the phrase "governed by international law."[99] Against this background, Waldock in succeeding Fitzmaurice as the fourth Special Rapporteur of the ILC on the law of treaties omitted a direct reference to intention in his definition of an international treaty.[100]

At the Vienna Conference, the question of clarifying the circumstances under which an international agreement becomes binding under international law was raised again. More specifically, the representative of the Chilean Government, Rodriguez, proposed an amendment to expressly include the element of intention to create legal effects into the Convention's definition.[101]

---

agreement embodied in a single formal instrument (whatever its name, title or designation) made between entities both or all of which are subjects of international law possessed of international personality and treaty-making capacity, and intended to create rights and obligations, or to establish relationships, governed by international law."

98 More specifically, it was pointed out that: "However informal or unusual in character an instrument might be, and even if not expressed in normal treaty language, it would nevertheless rank as a treaty or international agreement if it was intended to create legal effects." See Report of the ILC on the Work of Its 11th Session, UN Doc. A/CN.4/122, *Yrbk of the ILC* 1959, Vol. II., p. 87, at p. 96.

99 *Ibid.*, pp. 96–7.

100 H. Waldock, First Report on the Law of Treaties, UN Doc. A/CN.4/144, *Yrbk of the ILC* 1962, Vol. II, p. 27. However, a number of States, including Australia, Luxembourg and the United Kingdom, expressed some reservations about the lack of any reference to the element of intention in the proposed definition of an international treaty. More specifically, it was feared that "without any reference to intent, the definition would embrace a great quantity of informal understandings reached by exchange of notes which are not intended to give rise to legal rights." However, it was finally decided that no specific reference was needed since it was concluded that the phrase "governed by international law" embraced the element of the intention to create legal effects. See H. Waldock, Fourth Report on the Law of Treaties, UN Doc. A/CN.4/177, *Yrbk of the ILC* 1965, Vol. II, p. 3.

101 Rodriguez stated that "it often happened that declarations made on the international plane represented, like treaties, a concurrence of wills, but did not produce legal effects. Such declarations were often the preliminaries to a real agreement, which was concluded later when circumstances permitted. It would be dangerous to confuse them with treaties and make both of them subject to the rules of the convention, thereby gravely restricting freedom of expression in international affairs." As quoted in J. Klabbers, *The Concept of Treaty in International Law*, (The Hague: Kluwer Law International, 1996), p. 58.

Nevertheless, such an amendment was not finally accepted, since, once again, the phrase "governed by international law" was regarded as encompassing the element of intention.[102]

4.2 *The Criterion of Intention in the Jurisprudence of International Courts*

Apart from the 1969 Vienna Convention on the Law of Treaties, the intention to create legal effects on the international plane also features in the judgments of international judicial bodies as the main criterion for differentiating between international agreements and political undertakings.[103] In this regard, the *Aegean Sea Continental Shelf Case*[104] and the Separate Opinion of Judge Read in the *Advisory Opinion on the International Status of South West Africa*[105] will be briefly discussed.

The first case concerned a dispute between Turkey and Greece over the issue of delimitation of the continental shelf of the Aegean Sea. More particularly, one of the questions put forward to the International Court of Justice concerned the legal status of the so-called Brussels Communiqué, a communiqué issued jointly by Greece and Turkey on the 31st of May 1974.[106] According to the Court, the nature of the Brussels Communiqué as an international agreement "depends on the nature of the act or transaction to which the Communiqué gives expression."[107] Having regard to the terms of the Communiqué as well as to the context in which it was issued, the Court concluded that it did not amount to a legal undertaking since "it was not *intended*

102 See for example the statement made by Yassen, Chairman of the Drafting Committee, *ibid.*, p. 62.

103 See for example the case-law mentioned in J. Klabbers, *supra*, note 101, pp. 164 *et seq.*

104 *Aegean Sea Continental Shelf Case*, *ICJ Reports* 1978, p. 3.

105 Separate Opinion of Judge Read in the *International Status of South West Africa Advisory Opinion*, *ICJ Reports* 1950, p. 128 at p. 164.

106 In the Communiqué it was stated that: "In the course of their meeting, the two Prime Ministers had an opportunity to give consideration to the problems which led to the existing situation as regards relations between their countries. They decided [ont decide] that those problems should be resolved [doivent etre resolus] peacefully by means of negotiations and as regards the continental shelf of the Aegean Sea by the International Court at the Hague. They defined the general lines on the basis of which the forthcoming meetings of the representatives of the two Governments would take place. In that connection they decided to bring forward the date of the meeting of experts concerning the question of the continental shelf of the Aegean Sea and that of the experts on the question of air space." See *supra* note 104, pp. 39–40.

107 *Ibid.*

to, and did not, constitute an immediate commitment by the Greek and the Turkish Prime Ministers, on behalf of their respective governments, to accept unconditionally the unilateral submission of the present dispute to the Court."[108]

Similarly, Judge Read in his Separate Opinion in the *Advisory Opinion on the International Status of South West Africa*[109] identified the intention to create legal obligations as one of the essentials of the juridical nature of international agreements. In his own words: "It is unnecessary to discuss the juridical nature of an international agreement. It is sufficient, for present purposes, to state that an 'arrangement agreed between' between the United Nations and the Union necessarily included two elements: a meeting of minds; and an intention to constitute a legal obligation."[110]

4.3 *The Problem of Establishing the Element of Intention in the Law of Treaties*

The above sections demonstrated that intention is the determinant factor in attributing legal effects to an international agreement. However, as Klabbers phrased it, intention is an "awkward concept."[111] This is so because intention, in the common sense of the term, refers to a psychological element – to the state of mind that an individual may have at a given moment in time. Undoubtedly, it is very hard to discern the intentions of individuals – as Cicero once said: "There is nothing more obscure than human intentions."[112] And if one considers that the task at hand is discerning not the intentions of individuals but that of abstract entities, such as States, then the difficulties are only multiplied. How is one to determine whether a particular instrument expresses the intention of its authors to become bound according to its terms?

The difficulties that are borne from the concept of intention have been addressed in theory by differentiating between the subjective and the objective intention of a State or, in other words, between the real and the manifest

108 *Ibid.*, p. 44 (Emph. added). For a commentary of the judgment see H. Thirlway, The Law and Procedure of the International Court of Justice 1960–1989, part III, 62 *BYIL* 1 (1991), at pp. 14–5.

109 Separate Opinion of Judge Read in the *International Status of South West Africa Advisory Opinion*, *supra* note 105.

110 *Ibid*, p. 170.

111 J. Klabbers, *supra* note 101, p. 65.

112 M.T. Cicero, *Pro Murena: Speech in Defense of Lucius Licinius Murena*, 63 BC, available at http://www.perseus.tufts.edu/hopper/text?doc=Cic.+Mur.+36&fromdoc=Perseus%3Atext%3A1999.02.0019, para. 36.

will of a State.[113] International lawyers, like Klabbers[114] and Fitzmaurice,[115] have argued that, in the context of the law of treaties, the task of establishing the intention to be bound, is not an investigation into the motives and reasons, *i.e.* into the subjective or real intention of a particular State/s, but one of establishing the objective or manifest intention of the State/s in question. In other words, it has been suggested that what one is looking for in ascertaining whether a certain instrument is an international agreement or not is not the what the States really had in mind when they produced a particular instrument – something that would be impossible to fathom – but what was manifested to the outside world.

This objective reading of the criterion of intention is supported by the judgment of the Court in the *Maritime delimitation and territorial questions between Qatar and Bahrain Case*.[116] In this case, the International Court of Justice was faced, amongst others, with the question of the legal status of the agreed minutes of a discussion between the Foreign Ministers of Qatar and Bahrain that took place in Doha in December 1990.[117] According to Qatar, the 1990 Minutes amounted to an international agreement that enabled the ICJ to exercise jurisdiction over the dispute. Bahrain disagreed and argued that the minutes were a simple record of negotiations and did not rank as an international agreement.[118] Bahrain based its argument on a subjective interpretation of the element of intention claiming that, at the time that the discussion between the two Ministers took place, there was no intention on its behalf to create a binding instrument. In support thereof, Bahrain cited a statement made by its Minister for Foreign Affairs in 1992, in which he stated that: "At no time did I consider that in signing the Minutes I was committing Bahrain to a legally binding agreement."[119]

However, the Court did not accept Bahrain's contention. In the opinion of the Court, the 1990 Minutes "do not merely give an account of discussions and summarize points of agreement and disagreement. They enumerate the commitments to which the Parties have consented. They thus create rights and

113 J. Klabbers, *supra* note 101, p. 65.

114 *Ibid.*

115 M. Fitzmaurice, The Identification and Character of Treaties and Treaty Obligations between States in International Law, 73 *BYIL* 141 (2002), pp. 165–8.

116 *Maritime Delimitation and Territorial Questions between Qatar and Bahrain Case*, *ICJ Reports* 1994, p. 112.

117 *Ibid.*, pp. 118–9. The agreed minutes concluded between the disputing parties will be henceforth referred to as "the Doha Minutes" or as the "1990 Minutes."

118 *Ibid.*, p. 120.

119 *Ibid.*, p. 121.

obligations in international law for the parties. They constitute an international agreement."[120] Thus, by rejecting Bahrain's argument and by focusing on the actual content of the Minutes, the Court clearly favoured an objective interpretation of the element of intention.

Nevertheless, simply stating that what one is looking for in determining the legal character of an international instrument is the objective or manifest intention of its authors is not enough. The next question that naturally arises is whether there are any indicators of the manifest intention of a State/s to become bound by an international agreement. A review of the relevant case-law of international judicial bodies reveals that when confronted with the question of determining the legal status of an international instrument, these bodies have recourse to a number of indicators of the manifest intention of its authors.[121] These indicators relate to the actual terms used in the instrument and to the context surrounding it. Thus, on the basis of the pertinent case-law, Klabbers compiled a list of indicators of manifest intention including: whether the instrument in question specifically expresses consent to be bound, whether it contains provisions regarding entry into force and judicial settlement, whether it is registered under Art.102 of the UN Charter,[122] and whether any statements were made during the stage of negotiations that evidence the manifest intention of the authors of the instrument to become bound by it.[123]

Finally, it is worth commenting on the approach employed by the ICJ with regard to determining the legal nature of an international agreement on the basis of the above indicators of manifest intention. A close examination of the line of argumentation of the Court in the *Aegean Sea Continental Self Case* and in the *Qatar vs. Bahrain Case* shows that the Court, in establishing the existence of the requisite element of intention, will first examine the actual terms of the agreement and, if no objective evidence of an intention to be bound can be inferred therefrom, then it will continue its investigation by scrutinizing the context surrounding the agreement.[124] As it was stated in the *Aegean Sea Continental Self Case*: "In determining what was indeed the nature of the act or transaction embodied in the Brussels Communiqué, the Court must have regard above all to its actual terms and to the particular circumstances in which it was drawn up."[125]

120 *Ibid.*
121 J. Klabbers, *supra* note 101, p. 72; M. Fitzmaurice, *supra* note 115, p. 168.
122 *Charter of the United Nations*, 26 June 1945, San Francisco, 1 UNTS XVI (1945).
123 J. Klabbers, *supra* note 101, pp. 75–89.
124 *Ibid.*, p. 200, M. Fitzmaurice, *supra* note 115, p. 168.
125 *The Aegean Sea Continental Self Case*, *supra* note 104, p. 39, para. 96.

In that case, the Court, having examined the actual terms of the Communiqué, decided that the text of the agreement gave rise to a "divergence of views"[126] and continued by investigating the context in which the Communiqué was drawn up[127] – only to conclude that the instrument in question was not intended to create any binding commitment.[128] By way of contrast, in the *Qatar v. Bahrain Case*, the Court considered that the 1990 Minutes clearly expressed the intention of the parties to become bound[129] and thus, there was no need to have recourse to the context surrounding their making. According to the judgment:

> The Court does not find it necessary to consider what might have been the intentions of the Foreign Minister of Bahrain, or, for that matter, those of the Foreign Minister of Qatar. The two Ministers signed a text recording commitments accepted by their Governments, some of which were to be given immediate application. Having signed such a text, the Foreign Minister of Bahrain is not in a position subsequently to say that he intended to subscribe to a "statement recording a political understanding", and not to an international agreement.[130]

4.4 *Intention and Its Discontents: Calls to Move Away from Intention*

The previous section showed that the element of manifest intention is the criterion for identifying the binding nature of acts of a contractual origin and that the ICJ has established its own methodology for deciding whether the requisite element of intention has been met. However, some international lawyers, such as D'Aspremont, have argued that, due to the hurdles associated with ascertaining intention, international law should do away with the criterion of intention altogether and replace it with a more tangible one.[131] Since intention lies at the core of the theory of international juridical acts, it would be worthwhile to assess at this point the merits of such criticisms. In his monograph, D'Aspremont laments the formidable difficulties of identifying the legal character of international agreements and unilateral acts. According to him, the

126 *Ibid.*, p. 41, para. 100.

127 *Ibid.*, pp. 41–4, paras. 100–6.

128 *Ibid.*, p. 44, para. 107.

129 *Maritime Delimitation and Territorial Questions between Qatar and Bahrain Case, supra* note 116, para. 25.

130 *Ibid.*, para. 27.

131 J. D'Aspremont, *Formalism and the Sources of International Law: A Theory of the Ascertainment of Legal Rules*, (Oxford: Oxford University Press, 2011), p. 180.

problem lies in the very criterion upon which law-ascertainment is based on the international plane, *i.e.* the criterion of intention: "Indeed, such a criterion ultimately bases the identification of international legal acts on a fickle and psychological element."[132] D'Aspremont argues that although the Court has made some attempts to provide a clear methodology for establishing intention in the context of law-ascertainment, these attempts have been rather inconsistent and in its more recent case-law, the Court seems to have abandoned these efforts.[133] In his view, the difficulties inherent in determining the existence of an element as intangible as intention necessitate the replacement of this criterion with another one that would provide much needed clarity and consistency. D'Aspremont then moves on to suggest that intention should be replaced with what he calls 'written linguistics indicators', namely with words or phrases contained in the instrument itself that would clearly indicate the binding nature of the instrument in question.[134] Such indicators "should be as simple as possible to contain the indeterminacy inherent in ordinary language and leave as little doubt as possible as to the instrument of the nature concerned."[135] As an example, D'Aspremont cites the practice of the Security Council when adopting legally binding decisions under Chapter VII of the UN Charter.[136] Indeed, when the Security Council seeks to impose legally binding obligations on the basis of Chapter VII, it uses very clear and consistent terminology adding the words 'decides' in the text of the resolution itself in order to demonstrate its binding character.[137]

Although D'Aspremont's arguments may be appealing in their mathematical simplicity, upon further consideration, it seems – in the opinion of the present author at least – that they are not convincing. First, D'Aspremont argues that the ICJ seems to have abandoned its efforts to provide for a clear methodology in establishing intention in its later case-law. The two examples mentioned are the 1975 Maroua Declaration in the context of the *Cameroon v. Nigeria Case*[138] and the press release of 31 May 2005 creating GTAN in the context of the *Pulp Mills Case*.[139] However, a close examination of these two instances does not lend support to the view propounded by D'Aspremont.

132 *Ibid.*

133 *Ibid.*, pp. 182–4.

134 *Ibid.*, p. 188.

135 *Ibid.*

136 *Ibid.*, p. 190.

137 *Ibid.*

138 *Case concerning the Land and Maritime Boundary between Cameroon and Nigeria*, ICJ *Reports* 2002, p. 303.

139 *Case concerning Pulp Mills on the River Uruguay*, ICJ *Reports* 2010, p. 14.

In the *Cameroon v. Nigeria Case*, the Court was confronted *inter alia* with the question of the legal nature of the 1975 Maroua Declaration, a joint communiqué issued by the parties in which it was stated that "the two Heads of state of Cameroon and Nigeria *agreed* to extend the delineation of the maritime boundary between the two countries from Point 12 to Point G on the Admiralty Chart No. 3443 annexed to this Declaration."[140] Cameroon claimed before the Court that the Declaration constituted a binding agreement between the two States to the extent that its wording clearly "*manifested their intention* to be bound by the instrument they signed."[141] Nigeria counter-argued that the Declaration was not an international agreement to the extent that it had not been approved by Nigeria's Supreme Military Council after having been signed by the Head of State.[142] Contrary to D'Aspremont's assertions, the Court followed its established methodology in examining the juridical nature of the instrument in question. It first scrutinised the actual content of the Declaration in order to determine whether it evidenced the manifest intention of the two States to be bound thereby. Having quoted the abovementioned part of the Declaration where it was expressly mentioned that the two States "agreed" on a specific maritime boundary between them, the Court concluded that, in its view, the Declaration "entered into force immediately upon its signature."[143] The fact that the Court quoted the actual content of the Declaration before coming to a conclusion as to its juridical nature, verifies the Court's adherence to its previous methodology: where the actual terms of an instrument evidence the manifest intention of its authors to become bound, the Court has no need to have recourse to contextual indicators. This point is also supported by the arguments put forward by the parties in the case at hand. In their submissions, both Cameroon and Nigeria built their argumentation around the existence or validity of the intention to be bound by the 1975 Declaration – thereby confirming that, in their view as well, the element of intention was critical for the Court's determination of the juridical character of the Declaration.[144]

The second example given by D'Aspremont relates to the joint press release of 31 May 2005 by Uruguay and Argentina creating the GTAN, a joint commission for the study of the effects that the construction of paper factories would

140 *Case concerning the Land and Maritime Boundary between Cameroon and Nigeria, supra* note 138, para. 264. (Emph. added).

141 *Ibid.*, para. 253.

142 *Ibid.*, para. 258.

143 *Ibid.*, para. 264.

144 *Ibid.*, paras. 253–8.

have on the ecosystem of the Uruguayan River.[145] In its submissions, Uruguay argued that, on the basis of the joint press release, the two States "decided to make the GTAN the body within which the direct negotiations between the Parties...would take place."[146] On the other hand, Argentina considered that in creating the GTAN, the two States did not wish to substitute it for CARU – another joint commission that had been established earlier for the management of the shared river resources.[147] Having accepted that the press release in question "sets out an agreement between the two States", the Court found in favour of Argentina and concluded that by establishing GTAN, the two States did not agree to derogate from obligations undertaken under earlier treaties.[148] However, this example does not support D'Aspremont's thesis to the extent that it does not relate to law-ascertainment at all. As the submissions of both parties evidence, the question put forward to the Court did not concern the juridical status of the joint press release of 31 May 2005; neither Uruguay, nor Argentina disputed that the instrument in question constituted an international agreement. Rather, what was in dispute was the scope of obligations undertaken thereby. If it is accepted that the identification of the juridical character of an instrument and its interpretation are two distinct operations – and D'Aspremont makes this distinction with some forcefulness[149] – then it stands to reason that an example of the latter may not be used to refute the validity of the Court's approach to the former.

Furthermore, D'Aspremont's thesis seems to suffer from a degree of internal inconsistency. In his critique of the Court's current approach to ascertaining the element of intention, he argues that the authors of an instrument may deliberately use ambiguous terms in its drafting – in order to benefit from that ambiguity later on and, possibly, deny that they ever intended to create legal effects thereby.[150] However, how would resort to 'written linguistics' assuage this particular problem? Even if we postulate that the threshold of law-identification changes from intention to written linguistics, the residual problem of deliberate ambiguity would still persist: if States consciously use ambiguous terms, having recourse exclusively to the language of the instrument itself would not yield much clarity either. Finally, it needs to be noted that the only example used by D'Aspremont to illustrate the benefits of 'written linguistics', *i.e.* the

145 *Case concerning Pulp Mills on the River Uruguay*, *supra* note 139, para. 132.

146 *Ibid.*, para. 133.

147 *Ibid.*, para. 90.

148 *Ibid.*, paras. 138–50.

149 J. D'Aspremont, *supra* note 131, p. 180.

150 *Ibid.*, pp. 183–4.

resolutions of the UN Security Council when acting under Chapter VII, is not truly representative of the types of instruments that raise problems in practice. Arguably, the framework within which the UN Security Council makes a decision to impose obligations upon Member States is fundamentally different to the one within which States undertake obligations by means of a treaty or a unilateral act. While the Security Council has a vested interest in making it abundantly clear to Member States that specific obligations are bestowed upon them, the same does not always hold true for States when they negotiate treaties or decide, for their own reasons, to commit themselves through unilateral acts.

All in all, it seems that criticism about the Court's inconsistent approach to intention is unwarranted. In its recent case-law, the Court has re-affirmed its previously established methodology of determining intention by having recourse both to the content of the act and to the context within which it was adopted. Furthermore, calls to move away from intention as a law-identification criterion fall short of convincing to the extent that alternative criteria, such as D'Aspremont's 'written linguistics' theory, suffer – when put to the test – from a greater degree of indeterminacy than intention.

5 Conclusion

This chapter examined the distinction between legal and non-legal acts with a view to establishing a criterion for distinguishing between unilateral acts with legal effects on the international plane and unilateral political acts. At the beginning of the chapter, it was argued that the distinction between law and non-law is central to all legal systems and that keeping clear boundaries between the two at the international level is of cardinal importance due to the recent proliferation of soft law instruments and the declining importance of form and formalities in international law. Subsequently, the chapter examined the theory of juridical acts in order to establish whether that theory provides an answer to the problem of ascertaining the legal character of an act. It was shown that, although international law lacks a fully developed theory of international juridical acts, the handful of international lawyers who have dealt with the topic concur that the intention to be bound is the criterion for distinguishing between legal and non-legal acts.

The chapter continued by focusing on the law of international agreements since this is the field of law nearest to that of unilateral acts in which the problem of distinguishing between binding and non-binding instruments has arisen and resolved. It was demonstrated that, according to both doctrine and judicial practice, the manifest or objective intention of the author States to be bound is the criterion for distinguishing between binding agreements and mere political understandings. Furthermore, it was shown that, in the law of treaties, ascertaining the existence of the manifest intention to be bound involves interpretation of the agreement in accordance with its actual text and with the context surrounding it. It was demonstrated that, in practice, a number of indicators of the manifest intent to be bound are used to facilitate the task of interpretation including, amongst others, registration under Art.102 of the UN Charter and the existence of provisions regarding entry into force and judicial settlement. Finally, the discussion turned to D'Aspremont's critique against the element of intention as the principal law-identification criterion and to current theorizing on law-identification. It was shown that his criticism is, to a large extent, unfounded since alternative law-ascertainment criteria fail to offer more clarity. Against this background, the next chapter will examine the distinction between legal and non-legal acts in the field of unilateral acts.

CHAPTER 6

Unilateral Acts as Juridical Acts

1 Introduction

The previous chapter established that, according to the thus far underdeveloped theory of international juridical acts, intention is the criterion for distinguishing between legal and non-legal acts in international law. The criterion was tested against the background of international agreements and it was concluded that, at least as far as these instruments are concerned, the theory of international juridical acts holds true. According to both practice and the literature, the intention to be bound is the criterion for distinguishing between legally binding treaties and political agreements. This chapter turns to unilateral acts and argues that, as with international agreements, the element of the objective or manifest intention of the author State to be bound is the determinant factor in attributing legal effects to them.

Having ascertained this, the chapter goes on to deal with the question of determining the intent to be bound in practice; a question that has been overlooked in the work of the ILC on the topic. This chapter will demonstrate that an analysis of the pertinent case-law can produce a number of indicators of the manifest intent to be bound that refer both to the content of the act and to the context in which the act was made. In doing so, this chapter will empirically validate the theory of international juridical acts. By establishing that international adjudicative bodies use (a) the same criterion for determining the legal character of acts of both bi/multilateral and unilateral origin; and (b) the same means for determining the existence of this criterion in practice, this chapter will demonstrate that these bodies actually treat international agreements and unilateral acts as belonging to the same genus of acts (juridical acts). Against this backdrop, the chapter continues by enquiring into the basis of the binding force of unilateral acts of States. It will be argued that good faith is the source of the binding nature of unilateral acts. Finally, the chapter revisits the debate on whether these acts are sources of law or simply sources of obligations. It is shown that the distinction between sources of law and sources of obligations is inspired by municipal legal reasoning and is not followed in practice at the international level. On this basis, the chapter concludes that unilateral acts can be viewed as sources of international law in the same way as international agreements.

 | DOI 10.1163/9789004300767_008

2 Unilateral Acts as Juridical Acts

2.1 *Intention as the Criterion for Distinguishing between Unilateral Juridical Acts and Unilateral Political Acts*

The previous chapter demonstrated that the element of the intention to be bound is the distinguishing element between binding and non-binding acts within the framework of the law of treaties. This section turns to unilateral acts and demonstrates that, both in judicial practice and in theory, the same criterion, *i.e.* the intention of the author to be bound, is used to differentiate between unilateral juridical acts and unilateral acts with no legal effects on the international plane.

In the *Nuclear Tests Case*,[1] the ICJ emphasised the importance of the element of the intention to create legal effects for the attribution of legal effects to such acts. In the words of the Court: "When it is the intention of the State making the declaration that it should become bound according to its terms, that intention confers on the declaration the character of a legal undertaking, the State being thenceforth legally required to follow a course of conduct consistent with the declaration."[2] In more recent case-law the element of intention has continued to play a major part in drawing the line between legal undertakings and mere political statements of unilateral origin. In the *Nicaragua Case*,[3] the US claimed that a resolution of the Nicaraguan Junta expressing its intention to hold democratic elections was legally binding upon the latter.[4] The Court refused to share this opinion; instead, it declared itself unable to identify anything in the documents and communications transmitting the Junta's declaration from which it could be inferred that any legal undertaking was intended to exist. Thus, the Court concluded that "it could not find an instrument with legal force, whether unilateral or synallagmatic, whereby Nicaragua has committed itself in respect of the principle or the method of holding elections."[5]

1 *Nuclear Tests Case*, New Zealand vs France, *ICJ Reports* 1974, p. 457, *Nuclear Tests Cases*, Australia vs France, *ICJ Reports* 1974, p. 253. The Court's judgments in these two cases are almost identical. Hereinafter, unless otherwise stated, all references made to the *Nuclear Tests Case* will concern the case between New Zealand and France.

2 *Ibid.*

3 *Case concerning Military and Paramilitary Activities in and against Nicaragua*, Merits, *ICJ Reports* 1986, p. 14.

4 *Ibid.*, para. 257.

5 *Ibid.*, para. 261.

Similarly, in the *Frontier Dispute Case*[6] the element of intention was central to the Court's decision. Here the act in question was a statement made by the Head of State of Mali who accepted – in advance – a report to be drawn up by the Mediation Committee concerning the territorial dispute between Mali and Burkina Faso. The Court, having cited both the *Nuclear Tests* and *Nicaragua* cases, asserted that such unilateral declarations might have the effect of creating legal effects for the State on whose behalf they are made.[7] The Court proceeded to emphasize that the intention of the declarant State is crucial in conferring on the declaration the character of a legal undertaking; in that respect, it was stated that "it all depends on the intention of the State in question."[8] Having examined the declaration of the Head of State of Mali, the Court finally concluded that there were not any grounds to interpret it as a unilateral juridical act.[9]

Apart from case-law originating from the International Court of Justice, there are decisions from other international adjudicating bodies in which the intention to be bound also features as the main determinant in attributing legal effects to unilateral acts. More particularly, in the *Case concerning Sections 301–310 of the Trade Act of 1974*,[10] a dispute settlement panel of the World Trade Organisation dealt with the legal significance of unilateral statements made by the US representatives in relation to a complaint filed by the European Union claiming that certain US legislation was incompatible with WTO commitments.[11] In addressing the question of the legal nature of the statements the WTO panel cited the abovementioned passages of the *Nuclear Tests* judgment relating to the element of intention and stated that the criterion of the obligation was the intention of the State to become bound by its unilateral pronouncements.[12] Having examined the statements made by the US Trade Representative, the panel concluded that they constituted legal commitments binding on the US.[13]

Apart from the ICJ and the WTO dispute settlement panel, the arbitral tribunal in the *Dispute concerning Access to Information under Article 9 of the OSPAR*

6 *Case concerning the Frontier Dispute*, *ICJ Reports* 1986, p. 554.

7 *Ibid.*, para. 39.

8 *Ibid.*

9 *Ibid.*, para. 40.

10 *Case Concerning Sections 301–310 of the Trade Act of 1974*, WT/DS152/R, Report of the Panel (22 December 1999), available at http://www.wto.org/english/tratop_e/dispu_e/cases_e/ds152_e.htm.

11 *Ibid.*, para. 1.4.

12 *Ibid*, fn. 692.

13 *Ibid.*, paras. 7.125–6.

Convention[14] also highlighted the decisive importance of the intention to be bound in determining the legal character of a unilateral act. The arbitral tribunal in that dispute was asked to determine whether the UK had violated its obligations under the Convention for the Protection of the Marine Environment of the North-East Atlantic[15] (OSPAR Convention) by failing to provide Ireland with certain information concerning the MOX plant (a mixed oxide plant) in Sellafield, UK, on coast of the Irish Sea.[16] Among others, the arbitral tribunal was faced with the question of assessing the legal effects of a statement made by the UK according to which no new commercial contracts would be accepted for reprocessing spent fuel at Dounreay, Scotland, with the result of future reductions in radioactive discharges in the maritime area.[17] The tribunal noted that "unilateral declarations accompanied by an intention to be bound may create binding obligations"[18] and quoted the relevant dictum of the ICJ in the *Nuclear Tests Case*. Although the tribunal explicitly accepted the possibility that the statement may have created an obligation for the UK, it refused to rule upon its bindingness since it considered that the statement was not relevant to the question of access to information about activities at Sellafield and thus, to the dispute.[19]

Finally, it is important to mention that the element of the intention to be bound features heavily both in the reports prepared by the Special Rapporteur[20] and in the 2006 Guiding Principles adopted by the ILC.[21] According to Guiding Principle 1: "Declarations publicly made and manifesting the will to be bound

14 *Dispute concerning Access to Information under Article 9 of the OSPAR Convention, ("OSPAR" Arbitration) (Ireland vs UK)*, PCA, Final Award, 02 July 2003, available at http://www.pca-cpa.org/showpage.asp?pag_id=1158.

15 *Convention for the Protection of the Marine Environment of the North-East Atlantic*, 22 September 1992, available at http://www.ospar.org/content/content.asp?menu=00340108070000_000000_000000.

16 For a case-commentary, see T.L. McDorman, Access to Information under Article 9 of the OSPAR Convention (Ireland v. UK), 98 *AJIL* 330 (2004).

17 *Dispute concerning Access to Information under Article 9 of the OSPAR Convention, supra* note 14, para. 87.

18 *Ibid.*, para. 89.

19 *Ibid.*, para. 90.

20 See for example V. Rodríguez Cedeño, First Report on Unilateral Acts of States, UN Doc. A/CN.4/486, p. 319.

21 Guiding Principles applicable to unilateral declarations of States capable of creating legal obligations in Report of the ILC on the Work of Its 58th Session, UN Doc. A/61/10, *Yrbk of the ILC* 2006, Vol. II. Hereinafter referred to as the 2006 Guiding Principles, or Guiding Principles.

may have the effect of creating legal obligations."[22] As far as the debate within the ILC is concerned, there was consensus among the members – who accepted unilateral acts as a legal institution in international law – that intention was the main condition for attributing legal effects to unilateral declarations.[23] Pellet, one the most vociferous proponents of the Commission's project to codify unilateral acts, stated during the 2002 debate that:

> International law was not based entirely on the expression of the will of the States but it was plain that, insofar as they were bound by treaty obligations and by unilateral acts, it was by their own individual or collective wish... Why were States bound under the treaty mechanism? It was because they wished to be bound and limit their freedom of action. The same was true when States formulated unilateral acts. It was indispensable to orderly relations between States that they should be bound by the expression of their will.[24]

2.2 *The Problem of 'Subjective' vs. 'Objective' Intention in the Context of Unilateral Acts*

The previous section demonstrated that, on a par with international agreements, the intention of the author State to be bound is widely accepted as the main criterion for distinguishing between unilateral juridical acts and unilateral political acts. However, intention in the context of unilateral acts creates the same problems encountered in the context of the law of treaties. Once again, the dilemma between 'subjective' or 'real' intention and 'objective' or 'manifest' intention rears its head. In other words, when called upon to establish the element of the intention to be bound, is one supposed to be looking for the real intention of the author State or for the intention that was manifested to the outside world?

The conundrum of 'subjective' versus 'objective' intention in the context of unilateral acts was intensely debated within the ILC. Koskenniemi adopted a subjective understanding of the notion and argued that unilateral acts do not constitute a legal institution because, conditioned by the subjective

22 *Ibid.*

23 See for example the statements made by Brownlie, Pambou-Tchivoudva, Chee and Addo in Summary Record of the 2772nd Meeting, UN Doc. A/CN.4/SR.2772, *Yrbk of the ILC* 2003, Vol. I, pp. 144–5.

24 See Summary Record of the 2722nd Meeting, UN Doc. A/CN.4/SR.2722, *Yrbk of the ILC* 2002, Vol. I, p. 75, para. 54.

will of States, they lack the objectivity necessary to qualify as one.[25] In his own words:

> The very concept of a unilateral act was fundamentally ambivalent… It was a sociological description of States acting… That process was impossible to describe in terms of a voluntary scheme in which States had the intention of creating legal effects and in which they formulated actions to that effect… The expression of will could not be decisive… : *it was impossible to know what the will of States was.*[26]

In Koskenniemi's opinion, the ICJ attributed legal effects to the French statements in the *Nuclear Tests Case*, not because it was France's intention to become bound by its unilateral statements, but because these statements had created expectations to other States. Thus, in his view, the only general rule that can be deduced from the *Nuclear Tests* judgment is that States sometimes "behaved in a particular way and then found themselves bound because that was the logic of the situation."[27]

However, Koskenniemi's position is flawed on two grounds. First, if we accept that unilateral acts are not a legal institution because the element of the intention to be bound cannot be objectively determined, then it is also necessary to accept that the same must be true for intention in the law of treaties. This would mean that international agreements, the legal character of which is also based on the existence of an intention to be bound, are not a legal institution. This is however not the case. In the previous chapter it was shown that the ICJ has, in its practice, interpreted the requirement of the intention to be bound objectively – according to the actual terms of the agreement and to the context surrounding it. Pellet also commented on the problems that Koskenniemi's conceptualisation of intention in objective terms would entail for the law of treaties: "Mr. Koskenniemi had also pointed out that there was no point in codifying promise, for example, because, by definition, it expressed the will to be bound. However, the same could be said of a treaty and it was nevertheless very useful to codify treaties."[28]

25 See the statements by Koskenniemi in Summary Record of the 2722nd Meeting, *ibid.*, p. 74, paras. 42–6.

26 *Ibid.* (Emph. added).

27 *Ibid.*, para. 45.

28 Summary record of the 2818th Meeting, UN Doc. A/CN.4/SR.2818, *Yrbk of the ILC* 2004, Vol. I, p. 182, para. 8.

More importantly, this subjective reading of the element of the intention to be bound is not supported by judicial practice. A close examination of the ICJ's judgment in the *Nuclear Tests Case* reveals that the Court indicated that, as with international agreements, what one is seeking when ascertaining the legal nature of a unilateral act is the 'objective' or 'manifest' will of the author. Two points in the judgment corroborate this view. The first one relates to the rules stipulated by the ICJ regarding the method of ascertaining the intention to be bound and the second to the references made by the Court to good faith and to other States' reliance on a unilateral act.

First, the Court, having proclaimed the general rule that a unilateral declaration may be binding if it expresses the intention of its author to be bound,[29] proceeded to state that: "intention is to be ascertained by interpretation of the act."[30] In a later part of the judgment, the method of interpreting the act was clarified: "It is from the actual substance of these statements and from the circumstances attending their making, that the legal implications of the unilateral act must be deduced."[31] The fact that the Court referred to the actual terms of the unilateral instrument and to the context surrounding its making as the means for ascertaining the intention to be bound points to an objective construction of the criterion of intent.[32]

Another part of the judgment that supports this proposition is the part in which the Court made reference to the role of good faith and to other States' reliance on a unilateral act. Directly after quoting the dictum in the *Temple of Preah Vihear Case*[33] relating to the normative effect of intention: "...the sole relevant question is whether the language employed in any given declaration does reveal a clear intention...",[34] the Court added that:

> One of the basic principles governing the creation and performance of legal obligations, whatever their source, is the principle of good faith. Trust and confidence are inherent in international relations... Thus interested States may take cognizance of unilateral declarations and place confidence in them, and are entitled to require that the obligation thus created be respected.[35]

29 *Nuclear Tests Case, supra* note 1, para. 46.

30 *Ibid.*, para. 47.

31 *Ibid.*, para. 53.

32 G. Fitzmaurice, The Law and Procedure of the International Court of Justice 1951–4: Treaty Interpretation and other Treaty Points, 33 *BYIL* 203 (1958), at p. 230.

33 *Case concerning the Temple of Preah Vihear, ICJ Reports* 1961, p. 17.

34 *Ibid.*, p. 32.

35 *Nuclear Tests Case, supra* note 1, para. 48.

By appealing to the principle of good faith and to the trust, confidence and reliance that other States may place in what was manifested to them by a unilateral act, the Court clearly supported an objective understanding of the requisite element of intention. Had the Court adopted the contrary view, *i.e.* that what matters is only what the author had in mind at the time of formulating the act, there would be no reason to refer to good faith and to other States' reliance. The same opinion, namely that intention in the context of unilateral acts refers to the objective intention of the author State to be bound, also finds widespread support in theory.[36]

2.3 *Ascertaining the Intention to be Bound in the Context of Unilateral Acts*

It was established in the previous section that, as with international agreements, the objective intention of the author State to be bound is the decisive factor in determining that a unilateral instrument gives rise to a binding legal obligation. However, how is one to ascertain that a given instrument of unilateral character does or does not express the objective intention of its author to create binding obligations?

It has already been mentioned that, as the Court enunciated in the *Nuclear Tests Case*, ascertaining the intention to become bound involves interpreting the intention of the author State in accordance with the actual content of the act and the context attending its making.[37] This is another similarity between the law of treaties and the law governing unilateral acts. As established previously, ascertaining the intention to be bound in the law of treaties also involves interpretation of the act in accordance with its actual terms and the context surrounding it. Thus, both types of legal acts share the same method of determining the existence of the element of intention.

The only difference – in terms of interpretation – is the standard of interpretation to be applied to unilateral acts. According to the ICJ, the standard of interpretation applicable to unilateral acts is restrictive: "Of course, not all unilateral acts imply obligation; but a State may choose to take up a certain position in relation to a particular matter with the intention of being bound… When States make statements by which their freedom of action is to be limited, a restrictive interpretation is called for."[38] Adopting a more rigid standard

36 A. Orakhelashvili, *The Interpretation of Acts and Rules in International Law*, (Oxford: Oxford University Press, 2008), p. 466; C. Eckart, *Promises of States under International Law*, (Oxford: Hart Publishing, 2012), pp. 208–211.

37 *Nuclear Tests Case*, *supra* note 1, para. 53.

38 *Ibid.*, para. 47.

of interpretation in the context of unilateral acts is understandable; the Court was anxious to ensure that obligations going beyond those intended by the declarant would not be opposable against it, thereby echoing a well-established principle of international law to the effect that States may not be bound against their will.[39] The same restrictive standard of interpretation was also adopted by the WTO Panel in the *Case concerning Sections 301–310 of the Trade Act of 1974*:

> Attributing legal significance to unilateral statements made by a State should not be done lightly and should be subject to strict conditions… A sovereign State should normally not find itself legally affected on the international plane by the casual statement of any of the numerous representatives speaking on its behalf in today's highly interactive and interdependent world…nor by a representation made in the heat of legal argument on a State's behalf.[40]

However, it is important to highlight that, apart from the standard of interpretation, which is stricter for unilateral acts, the method of ascertaining the legal nature of the act is the same for both unilateral acts and international agreements. More recent ICJ case-law verifies that the method of ascertaining the intention to be bound, first articulated in the *Nuclear Tests Case*, is still relevant today. In the *Armed Activities on the Territory of the Congo Case*, the Court was faced with the question of the legal effects of a unilateral statement made by Rwanda's Minister of Justice at the Sixty-first Session of the United Nations Commission on Human Rights, according to which, "[t]he few [human rights]

---

39 In the *Lotus Case*, the Permanent Court of International Justice stated that: "International law governs relations between independent States. The rules of law binding upon States therefore emanate from their own free will as expressed in conventions or by usages generally accepted as expressing principles of law and established in order to regulate the relations between these co-existing independent communities or with a view to the achievement of common aims. *Restrictions upon the independence of States cannot therefore be presumed.*" (Emph. added). *The Case of the S.S. Lotus, PCIJ Series A*, 1927, No. 10, p. 4, at p. 18. The restrictive standard of interpretation to be applied to unilateral acts is also mentioned in the 2006 Guiding Principles. According to Guiding Principle 7: "A unilateral declaration entails obligations for the formulating State only if it is stated in clear and specific terms. In the case of doubt as to the scope of the obligations resulting from such a declaration, such obligations must be interpreted *in a restrictive manner.*" (Emph. added.) See the 2006 Guiding Principles, *supra* note 21.

40 *Case Concerning Sections 301–310 of the Trade Act of 1974*, *supra* note 10, para. 7.118.

instruments not yet ratified"[41] by Rwanda at that date "will shortly be ratified" and reservations "not yet withdrawn will shortly be withdrawn."[42] The DRC argued that Rwanda, through that statement, had unilaterally committed itself to withdraw its reservation to Art. IX of the 1948 Genocide Convention[43] – a jurisdiction clause which allows the parties to the Convention to submit any disputes relating to its interpretation, application or fulfilment to the ICJ.[44] The Court considered that in order to determine the legal effects of the statement, it must "examine its actual content as well as the circumstances in which it was made."[45] Having analysed the statement made by the Rwandan Minister, the Court concluded that it did not create a binding obligation on Rwanda to withdraw its reservation.[46]

The same rule regarding the determination of the element of intention has been also enshrined in the 2006 Guiding Principles.[47] According to Guiding Principle 3: "To determine the legal effects of such declarations, it is necessary to take account of their content, of all the factual circumstances in which they were made, and of the reactions to which they gave rise."[48] Again, in Guiding Principle 7, it is stated that: "A unilateral declaration entails obligations for the formulating State... In interpreting the content of such obligations, weight shall be given first and foremost to the text of the declaration, together with the context and the circumstances in which it was formulated."[49] In the commentary to Guiding Principle 7, it is noted that the rule of interpretation enshrined therein, *i.e.* assessment of the intention to be bound on the basis of the text of the declaration and of the circumstances surrounding its making, reflects the same rule applicable in the law of treaties and the relevant jurisprudence of the ICJ.[50]

The above exposition established that it is well settled both in theory and in judicial practice that unilateral acts and international agreements have two basic elements in common: first, that the manifest intention to be bound is the

---

41 *Case concerning Armed Activities on the Territory of the Congo, New Application 2002, ICJ Reports* 2006, p. 6, at para. 45.

42 *Ibid.*

43 *Convention on the Prevention and Punishment of the Crime of Genocide*, 9 December 1948, available at http://www.icrc.org/ihl.nsf/full/357?OpenDocument.

44 See Article 9, *ibid.*

45 *Armed Activities Case, supra* note 41, para. 49.

46 *Ibid.*, para. 52.

47 2006 Guiding Principles, *supra* note 21.

48 Guiding Principle 3, *ibid.*, p. 371.

49 Guiding Principle 7, *ibid.*, p. 377.

50 Commentary to Guiding Principle 7, *ibid.*, p. 378.

determinant factor in attributing legal effects to both unilateral acts and international agreements. Second, that the same method of ascertaining the existence of the element of intention is applicable to both. The implications for the theory of juridical acts in international law are of utmost importance. The conclusions reached herein regarding the similarities between unilateral acts and international agreements substantiate, with reference to judicial authority, the theory of juridical acts first articulated by Verzijl and Lauterpacht decades ago. In the previous chapter, it was demonstrated that Verzijl and Lauterpacht attempted to develop a unified theory of juridical acts in international law which would bring together acts of both unilateral and bi/multilateral origin that were based upon the manifestation of a will to be bound. As previously explained, the theory did not gain much scholarly attention and remained underdeveloped. However, the analysis of judicial practice in this section proves the validity of the claim advocated by Verzijl and Lauterpacht: by applying the same criterion for determining their legal character and by having recourse to the same means for ascertaining the existence of that criterion, it has been established that international courts do indeed treat unilateral acts and international agreements as two aspects of the same phenomenon (juridical acts).

Confirming the validity of the theory of international juridical acts does not, however, solve the practical problems of ascertaining the intention to be bound in the context of unilateral acts. The relevant theory does not offer any guidance on how to identify the existence of the intention to be bound in practice. Similarly, the case-law of the ICJ is of limited assistance; apart from stipulating that intention is to be ascertained on the basis of the content of the act and of the context surrounding its making, the Court did not give any detailed instructions on how to identify intention. In light of the critical significance of the element of intention, the general guidance given by the ICJ is not enough. What specific content and circumstances indicate that a unilateral act was intended to create binding commitments?

The ILC Guiding Principles seem to simply repeat the relevant case-law of the ICJ without providing a definite answer to these crucial questions. As discussed above, Guiding Principles 3 and 7 merely reiterate the relevant dictum of the ICJ in the *Nuclear Tests Case*, namely that intention is to be ascertained on the basis of the actual content of the act and of the circumstances in which it was formulated, without adding much by way of explanation. Apart from a brief reference to the element of publicity and to the relevance of the reaction of the addressee of the act,[51] neither the text of the Guiding Principles, nor the

51 See Guiding Principle 3, *ibid.*

accompanying commentary provide any specific indicators of the manifest intent of a State to be bound by a unilateral act. The lack of practical guidance for establishing the intention to be bound necessitates the re-examination of the topic beyond the work of the ILC.

Thus, the following sections will examine the relevant jurisprudence of international judicial bodies with an aim to identify indicators of the manifest intent to be bound. These indicators will be arranged in two broad categories: indicators that refer to the actual content of a unilateral act and indicators that refer to the context surrounding the making of an act. It will be shown that the clear and specific wording of the act, its publicity, the authority which formulated the act on behalf of the State, the forum in which the act was made as well as registration under Art. 102 of the UN Charter may indicate the existence of an intention to create binding legal obligations. Furthermore, the indicator contained in the 2006 Guiding Principles, namely the reaction of the addressee of the act, will be analysed and rejected as not truly indicative of a manifest intent to be bound.

A Indicators of Manifest Intent to be Bound: The Content of the Act

A review of the relevant jurisprudence of the ICJ demonstrates that the wording used in formulating a unilateral act is one of the most reliable indicators of manifest intent. According to the *Nuclear Tests* judgment, a commitment phrased in clear and specific terms evidences the intention of the author State to be bound by its terms in law.[52] The importance of clear and specific wording for the purpose of inferring an intention to be bound was also stressed in the *Armed Activities Case*: "The Court recalls that a statement of this kind can create legal obligations only if it is made in clear and specific terms."[53]

Expressing an intention to be bound in clear and specific terms does not necessarily involve the use of particular phrases, such as "our State undertakes to…" or "we solemnly proclaim to…" Rather, the case-law of the ICJ indicates that it is sufficient that an intention to undertake a binding commitment can clearly be deduced from the text of the act. For example, the following statement, which was contained in a Communiqué issued by the office of the President of the French Republic, was found by the Court to clearly convey an intention to create legal effects in the context of the *Nuclear Tests Case*[54] – even though it fell short of a solemn proclamation:

52 *Nuclear Tests Case*, *supra* note 1, paras. 43, 46, 51 and 53.

53 *Armed Activities Case*, *supra* note 41, para. 50.

54 *Nuclear Tests Case*, *supra* note 1, para. 51.

> The Decree reintroducing the security measures in the South Pacific nuclear test zone has been published in the Official Journal of 8 June 1974. The Office of the President of the Republic takes this opportunity of stating that in view of the stage reached in carrying out the French nuclear defence programme France will be in a position to pass on to the stage of underground explosions as soon as the series of tests planned for this summer is completed.[55]

On the other hand, the use of broad terms and the absence of a precise time-frame for carrying out the commitment usually indicate a political act and not a binding undertaking. In the *Armed Activities Case*, the Court found that the statement made by the Rwandan Minister regarding the future withdrawals of reservations to human rights treaties was not made "in sufficiently specific terms" and lacked a "precise time-frame for such withdrawals."[56] Thus, it was concluded that the Rwandan statement was too indeterminate to be considered as a unilateral binding commitment.[57] Finally, the significance of clear and specific wording for ascertaining the existence of a legal commitment has also been enshrined in the 2006 Guiding Principles. According to Guiding Principle 7, "A unilateral declaration entails obligations for the formulating State only if it stated in clear and specific terms."[58]

B Indicators of Manifest Intent to be Bound: The Context in Which the Act Took Place

i) *The Publicity of the Act*

Apart from the content of a unilateral act, the circumstances in which the act was made can also be indicative of the author's manifest intention to become bound. One such indicator is the publicity of the act. The ICJ, in ascertaining the binding effects of the French statements in the *Nuclear Tests Case*, repeatedly referred to the fact that those statements were made in public. For example, in paragraph 46 of the *Nuclear Tests* judgment it is stated that: "An undertaking of this kind, if given publicly, and with an intent to be bound, even though not made within the context of international negotiations, is binding."[59] The Court went on to add that:

55 *Ibid.*, para. 35.

56 *Armed Activities Case*, *supra* note 41, paras. 50–1.

57 *Ibid.*, para. 52.

58 Guiding Principle 7, *supra* note 21.

59 *Nuclear Tests Case*, *supra* note 1, para. 46.

> The unilateral statements of the French authorities were made outside the Court, publicly and *erga omnes*... In announcing that the 1974 series of atmospheric tests would be the last, the French Government conveyed to the world at large, including the Applicant, its intention effectively to terminate these tests. It was bound to assume that other States might take note of these statements and rely on their being effective.[60]

The evidentiary value of publicity was also mentioned in the discussions within the ILC. In 1998, Brownlie noted that: "The criterion of publicity...was certainly relevant in terms of evidence and of the identification of those to whom the act was addressed."[61] Publicity also features in the 2006 Guiding Principles as the main indicator of the intention of the author to assume obligations of a legal nature. According to Guiding Principle 1: "Declarations publicly made and manifesting the will to be bound may have the effect of creating legal obligations."[62] The commentary to Guiding Principle 1 explicitly states that the public nature of declarations represents an important indication of their authors' intention to commit themselves.[63]

ii) *The Forum in Which the Act was made*

Next, the focus turns to the forum in which a unilateral act is made as an indicator of the manifest intention of the author to become bound. Two judgments decided by the Permanent Court of International Justice, the *Mavrommatis Palestine Concessions Case*[64] and the *Certain German Interests in Polish Upper Silesia Case*[65] are relevant here. A common feature of these cases is that they both concerned unilateral acts in the form of declarations made in the course of judicial proceedings. In both cases the Court upheld the binding character of the declarations and was keen to stress the added significance that making such declarations before a court entailed.

The *Mavrommatis Palestine Concessions Case* involved a dispute between the United Kingdom and Greece; the latter was, at the time, exercising diplomatic action on behalf of one of its citizens, Mavrommatis. The facts of the case originated from a series of pre-war concessions granted to Mavrommatis

60 *Ibid.*, paras. 52–3.

61 Summary Record of the 2527th Meeting, UN Doc. A/CN.4/SR.2527, *Yrbk of the ILC* 1998, Vol. I, p. 59, para. 15.

62 Guiding Principle 1, *supra* note 21, p. 370.

63 Commentary to Guiding Principle 1, *ibid.*

64 *The Mavrommatis Palestine Concessions Case*, PCIJ *Series A*, 1924, No. 2, p. 6.

65 *Case concerning certain German Interests in Polish Upper Silesia*, PCIJ *Series A*, 1926, No. 7, p. 4.

by the City of Jerusalem. After the end of World War I, the administration of Jerusalem was given to Great Britain on the basis of the terms of the Mandate for Palestine.[66] Subsequently, the UK proceeded to grant a number of concessions to another constructor, in defiance of the pre-existing contracts with Mavrommatis. According to the Greek Government, this amounted to a violation of the international obligations accepted by the UK as the mandatory of the said territory and, ultimately, to damage to Mavrommatis' interests.[67]

An issue closely related to the aforementioned question of damages concerned a clause in the contract between the UK and Rutenberg, according to which the latter had the right to request the expropriation of M. Mavrommatis' concessions. During the proceedings, the British agent made a declaration before the Court to the effect that even if a request of expropriation were received, the British Government would not comply with it.[68] More particularly, the British representative stated before the Court: "That explicit declaration I, as such authorized representative of H.M. Government, and a member of it, here repeat that we intend to carry out whatever obligations, if any, the Court says are imposed upon us by the terms of the Lausanne Protocol. That being so, there can be no question of our acting upon any request to expropriate M. Mavrommatis."[69] On the basis of this statement, which the Court considered as binding beyond any doubt, it was concluded that no question of expropriation of Mavrommatis' concessions could arise in the future.[70]

Another case, which involved a unilateral act in the form of a statement made during the proceedings of the Court, was the *Case concerning certain German Interests in Polish Upper Silesia*. In that case, the Permanent Court was called upon to adjudicate on the compatibility with international law of a Polish national decree, under which the properties of certain German nationals in Poland were to be expropriated.[71] At the beginning of the oral proceedings, the Polish representative declared before the Court that his Government did not intend to expropriate certain parts of the properties in question.[72]

---

66 See the *Mavrommatis Palestine Concessions Case, supra* note 64, pp. 11 *et seq.*

67 *Ibid.*, pp. 26–8.

68 In essence, the declaration made by the the representative of the British Government endorsed a previous declaration by Rutenberg, according to which the latter renounced the right to ask for the expropriation of Mavrommatis and would not oppose his being allowed to proceed with his concessions. See *ibid.*, pp. 36–7.

69 *Ibid.*, p. 37.

70 *Ibid.*

71 *Case concerning certain German Interests in Polish Upper Silesia, supra* note 65, p. 13.

72 *Ibid.*, p. 13.

The Permanent Court, in a similar vein to the *Mavrommatis Case*, noted that it could be "in no doubt as to the binding character of all these declarations."[73]

Not only the PCIJ, but also the ICJ, has acknowledged the fact that a declaration made during judicial proceedings usually evidences the manifest intention of its author to be bound. In the context of the *Pulp Mills Case*,[74] the facts of which were set out in the previous chapter, Argentina submitted a request for the indication of provisional measures in order to safeguard its rights deriving from the 1975 Statute of the River Uruguay.[75] During the oral proceedings, the agent of Uruguay expressly affirmed the latter's intention to comply in full with the Statute.[76] As a concrete expression of its intention Uruguay offered to conduct continuous joint monitoring of the River Uruguay with Argentina.[77] The Court took note of "these *commitments*" and concluded that there were no grounds for it to indicate the provisional measures requested by Argentina.[78]

In the *Questions relating to the Obligation to Prosecute or Extradite Case*,[79] Belgium instituted proceedings against Senegal before the ICJ. In its application, Belgium claimed that Senegal had breached its obligations under the 1984 UN Convention against Torture[80] by failing to either prosecute Habre, the former President of Chad, or to extradite him to Belgium for the purposes of criminal proceedings.[81] At the time that the application was filed, Habre was under house arrest by Senegalese authorities.[82] On 19 February 2009, Belgium filed a request for the indication of provisional measures asking the Court to "indicate, pending a final judgment on the merits, provisional measures requiring Senegal to take all steps within its power to keep Mr. Habre under the control and surveillance of the judicial authorities of Senegal."[83] In its request, Belgium indicated that the reason for requesting provisional measures was a

73 *Ibid.*

74 *Case concerning Pulp Mills on the River Uruguay*, *ICJ Reports* 2010, p. 14.

75 *Case concerning Pulp Mills on the River Uruguay*, Order of 13 July 2006, *ICJ Reports* 2006, p. 113, paras. 12–20.

76 *Ibid.*, para. 56.

77 *Ibid.*

78 *Ibid.*, para. 84. (Emph. added).

79 *Questions relating to the Obligation to Prosecute or Extradite*, *ICJ Reports* 2012, p. 422.

80 *United Nations Convention against Torture and other Cruel and Inhuman or Degrading Treatment or Punishment*, 10 December 1984, available at http://www2.ohchr.org/english/law/cat.htm.

81 *Questions relating to the Obligation to Prosecute or Extradite*, *supra* note 79, para. 1.

82 *Ibid.*, para. 17.

83 *Questions Relating to the Obligation to Prosecute or Extradite*, Order of 28 May 2009, *ICJ Reports* 2009, p. 139, para. 15.

statement made by the President of Senegal regarding the possibility of lifting Habre's house arrest in case Senegal failed to find the budget necessary in order to hold his trial.[84] Lifting the house arrest would mean that Habre would have the opportunity to flee Senegal and that, in Belgium's opinion, would cause irreparable prejudice to its rights to bring criminal proceedings against him.[85]

During the hearings, the Senegalese representatives asserted on several occasions that the statement made by the President of Senegal was taken out of context and that Senegal was not contemplating lifting the house arrest imposed on Habre.[86] At the end of the hearings and following a question by a member of the Court, the representative of Senegal solemnly declared that: "Senegal will not allow Mr. Habre to leave Senegal while the present case is pending before the Court. Senegal has not the intention to allow Mr. Habre to leave the territory while the present case is pending before the Court."[87] The Court highlighted the fact that this formal assurance was given before it and consequently concluded that there was no risk of irreparable damage to the rights claimed by Belgium.[88] The Court's decision verifies the importance placed upon the forum in which the act is made as an indicator of a State's manifest intention to become bound by a unilateral act.

By way of contrast, the assurances given by Nicaragua and Australia in the context of more recent case-law fell short of eliminating the risk of irreparable damage to Costa Rica's and Timor-Leste's rights respectively. It is important to note at the outset that, as it will be shown below, the Court did not question that the undertakings were binding on Nicaragua and Australia as a matter of international law. Rather, they were deemed insufficient since either they violated previous orders of the Court or, the intention of the author State was qualified by certain temporal and substantive reservations.

In the *Certain Activities Carried Out by Nicaragua in the Border Area Case*, Costa Rica instituted proceedings against Nicaragua for a number of actions including the construction of a canal (referred to in Spanish as *caño*) across Costa Rican territory.[89] By an order issued on 8th March 2011, the Court indicated that both parties "shall refrain from sending to, or maintaining in the disputed territory, including the *caño*, any personnel, whether civilian, police

84 *Ibid.*, para. 13.

85 *Ibid.*

86 *Ibid.*, para. 68.

87 *Ibid.*

88 *Ibid.*, paras. 72–3.

89 *Certain Activities Carried Out by Nicaragua in the Border Area*, Order of 22 November 2013, *ICJ Reports* 2013, p. 354, para. 1.

or security."[90] On 24 September 2013, Costa Rica filed a request for the indication of new provisional measures on the basis of satellite imagery showing that Nicaragua had commenced construction of two new artificial *caños* in the disputed territory.[91] During the oral proceedings, the Nicaraguan agent expressly stated that his government "considers itself bound not to undertake activities likely to connect any of the two new *caños* with the sea and to prevent any person or group of persons from doing so."[92] Although the Court took note of these assurances, it was not convinced that they removed the imminent risk of irreparable prejudice to Costa Rica's rights since, as Nicaragua conceded, persons under its jurisdiction had already violated the Court's previous order.[93] Thus, the Court indicated new provisional measures.[94]

Similarly, the written and oral assurances given by Australia in the context of the *Questions Relating to the Seizure and Detention of certain Documents and Data Case* did not suffice to prevent the risk of irreparable damage to Timor-Leste's rights. The dispute in question concerned the seizure and subsequent detention of certain documents and data from the Canberra-based office of a legal adviser to Timor-Leste by Australian agents in March 2013, allegedly pursuant to a warrant issued under the 1979 Australian Security Intelligence Organisation Act.[95] The seized material included documents, data and correspondence between Timor-Leste and its legal advisers relating to the pending arbitral proceedings between Timor-Leste and Australia under the Timor Sea Treaty of 20 May 2002.[96] On 17 December 2013, Timor-Leste filed an application with the Court asking it, *inter alia*, to adjudge and declare that the seizure of the documents and data violated the sovereignty of Timor-Leste and its property rights under international law.[97] On the same day, it also submitted a request for the indication of provisional measures asking the Court, among others, to order Australia to deliver into the Court's custody all seized

90 *Certain Activities Carried Out by Nicaragua in the Border Area*, Order of 8 March 2011, ICJ *Reports* 2011, p. 6, para. 86.

91 *Certain Activities Carried Out by Nicaragua in the Border Area*, Order of 22 November 2013, *supra* note 89, para. 13.

92 *Ibid.*, para. 50.

93 *Ibid.*

94 *Ibid.*, paras. 51–6.

95 *Questions Relating to the Seizure and Detention of Certain Documents and Data*, Order of 3 March 2014, available at http://www.icj-cij.org/docket/files/156/18078.pdf, para. 1.

96 *Ibid.* See also *Arbitration under the Timor Sea Treaty of 20 May 2002, (Timor-Leste vs Australia)*, PCA, available at http://www.pca-cpa.org/showpage.asp?pag_id=1403.

97 *Questions Relating to the Seizure and Detention of Certain Documents and Data*, Order of 3 March 2014, *supra* note 95, para. 2.

documents and data as well as "a list of any and all documents and data that it has disclosed or transmitted…to any person, whether or not such a person is employed by or holds office in any organ of the Australian State or of any third State."[98]

During the course of the proceedings pertaining to the provisional measures request, Australia gave a series of written and oral assurances to Timor-Leste regarding the seized material, the most important of which (and the one that the Court discussed at length) being a written undertaking made by Australia's Attorney-General on 21 January 2014.[99] The following declaration by the Attorney-General was included therein:

> Until final judgment in this proceeding or until further notice or earlier order of the Court:
> 1 I will not make myself aware or otherwise seek to inform myself of the content of the Material or any information derived from the material; and
> 2 Should I become aware of any circumstance which would make it necessary for me to inform myself of the Material, I will first bring that fact to the attention of the Court, at which time further undertakings will be offered; and
> 3 The Material will not be used by any part of the Australian Government for any purpose other than national security purposes which include potential law enforcement referrals and prosecutions; and
> 4 Without limiting the above, the Material, or any information derived from the material, will not be made available to any part of the Australian Government for any purpose relating to the exploitation of resources in the Timor Sea or related negotiations, or relating to the conduct of:
> (a) these proceedings; and
> (b) the proceedings in the Arbitral Tribunal [constituted under the 2002 Timor Sea Treaty].[100]

It is also worthwhile to note that, in its oral pleadings, Australia repeatedly stressed that the undertaking was binding upon it as a matter of international law. According to Australia's Agent, Mr Reid:

> Allow me to repeat what I said yesterday for the benefit of our friends. The Attorney–General of the Commonwealth of Australia has the actual

98 *Ibid.*, para. 5.

99 *Ibid.*, para. 38.

100 *Ibid.*

> and ostensible authority to bind Australia as a matter of both Australian law and international law. I need say no more. Again, as I said yesterday, Australia has made the undertakings. Australia will honour them.[101]

The Court had no difficulty in drawing the conclusion that the undertaking of 21 January 2014 was binding upon Australia, since the latter had expressly and repeatedly manifested its intention to become bound thereby: "The Court has no reason to believe that the written undertaking...will not be implemented by Australia. Once a State has made such a commitment concerning its conduct, its good faith in complying with that commitment is to be presumed."[102] However, what was problematic for the Court was that the intention of Australia was qualified by two reservations. The first was of a temporal nature; the Court noted that the commitment of Australia to keep the seized material sealed was only given until the Court's decision on the request for the indication of provisional measures.[103] Secondly, the Court was also concerned with the national security reservation contained in paragraph 3 of the written undertaking. The reservation opens up a possibility of making use of the seized material for national security purposes, thereby not completely eliminating the risk of disclosure of the highly sensitive information in question.[104] On this basis, the Court, while considering it beyond doubt that the undertaking of 21 January 2014 made "a significant contribution towards mitigating the risk of irreparable prejudice created by the seizure of the...material to Timor-Leste's rights", concluded that it did not remove the risk in its entirety.[105] Thus, the Court decided to indicate certain provisional measures including ordering Australia to ensure that the seized material will not in any way or at any time be used to the disadvantage of Timor-Leste until the case at hand has been concluded and to keep under seal the seized documents and data until further decision by the Court.[106]

Judge Cançado Trindade has been a vociferous critic of the Court's reliance upon unilateral acts in the course of international proceedings. Although the Judge accepts the binding nature of unilateral acts of States in the domain of

101 Statement by Mr Reid in *Questions Relating to the Seizure and Detention of Certain Documents and Data*, Public Sitting held on 22 January 2014, CR 2014/4, p. 8, at p. 27.

102 *Questions Relating to the Seizure and Detention of Certain Documents and Data*, *supra* note 95, para. 44.

103 *Ibid.*, para. 46.

104 *Ibid.*

105 *Ibid.*, para. 47.

106 *Ibid.*, para. 55.

inter-State relations, he argues that these acts are ill-suited to the realm of international legal procedure. In his view, the unilateral nature of such acts creates uncertainties that are inherently incompatible with international legal proceedings.[107] According to the Judge:

> Promises or assurances or "undertakings" have been relied upon in a distinct context, that of diplomatic relations. When they are unduly brought into the domain of international legal procedure, they cannot serve as basis for a decision of an international tribunal at issue, even less so when they ensue from an original act of arbitrariness... Judicial settlement was conceived as the most perfected means of dispute-settlement; if it starts relying upon unilateral acts of States, as basis for the reasoning of decisions to be rendered, it will undermine its own foundations, and there will be no reason for hope in the improvement of judicial settlement to secure the prevalence of the rule of law.[108]

In the light of the abovementioned orders indicating provisional measures in the context of the *Case concerning Certain Activities carried out by Nicaragua in the Border Area* and in the *Case concerning Questions Relating to the Seizure and Detention of certain Documents and Data*, this criticism seems somewhat unwarranted. It has been shown that the Court closely scrutinises both the content and circumstances surrounding the assurances given before making a determination as to their applicability to a given case. In any case, the practice of the ICJ clearly shows that, irrespective of the misgivings of individual judges, the fact that a unilateral act was made during judicial proceedings is a strong indication of the author State's intention to be bound thereby.

iii) *The Author of the Act*

The authority that formulated the unilateral act on behalf of the author State is also relevant in establishing whether the act expresses a manifest intention to become bound. The relevant jurisprudence of the ICJ makes it clear that declarations emanating from Heads of States carry a lot of evidentiary weight. In the *Nuclear Tests Case*, the Court stressed that: "Of the statements made by the French Government now before the Court, the most essential are clearly those

107 Separate Opinion of Judge Cançado Trindade in *Questions relating to the Obligation to Prosecute or Extradite*, *supra* note 79, p. 487, at paras. 73–8.

108 Separate Opinion of Judge Cançado Trindade in *Questions Relating to the Seizure and Detention of Certain Documents and Data*, Order of 3 March 2014, *supra* note 95, available at http://www.icj-cij.org/docket/files/156/18082.pdf, para. 14.

made by the President of the Republic."[109] Furthermore, in its Order of 28 May 2009 – in the context of the *Case concerning Questions relating to the Obligation to Prosecute or Extradite* – the Court indicated that it was understandable for Belgium to become concerned by the statement regarding the possibility of Habre leaving Senegal, since that statement came from the Senegalese Head of State,[110] before ruling that the statements made before it by the representatives of Senegal clarified the previous statement by the Head of State and unequivocally expressed Senegal's intention not to let Habre leave Senegal.[111]

The fact that statements made by Heads of States constitute an indicator of the manifest intention to become bound does not mean that declarations or acts stemming from other authorities are not valid unilateral acts. At this juncture, it is important to differentiate between the validity of a unilateral act and the question of proving a manifest intent to be bound. As far as validity is concerned, the Court made it clear in the *Armed Activities Case* that not only Heads of States, but also Heads of Government, Ministers for Foreign Affairs and other representatives of a State in specific fields may formulate binding unilateral acts in areas falling within their competences.[112] According to the Court:

> It is a well-established rule of international law that the Head of State, the Head of Government and the Minister for Foreign Affairs are deemed to represent the State merely by virtue of exercising their functions, including for the performance, on behalf of the said State, of unilateral acts having the force of international commitments... The Court notes, however, that with increasing frequency in international relations other persons representing a State in specific fields may be authorised by that State to bind it by their statements in respect of matters falling within their purview. This may be true, for example, of holders of technical ministerial portfolios exercising powers in their field of competence in the area of foreign relations, and even of certain officials.[113]

The ILC's Guiding Principles on Unilateral Declarations repeat almost verbatim the above dictum of the Court.[114]

109 *Nuclear Tests Case*, *supra* note 1, para. 51.

110 *Questions Relating to the Obligation to Prosecute or Extradite*, Order of 28 May 2009, *supra* note 83, para. 70.

111 *Ibid.*

112 *Armed Activities Case*, *supra* note 41, paras. 46–7.

113 *Ibid.*

114 See Guiding Principle 4, *supra* note 21, p. 372. Guiding Pirnciple 4 states that: "A unilateral declaration binds the State internationallly only if it made by an authority vested with the

However, the fact that a number of State officials may legally bind the State through their unilateral declarations as a matter of law, does not negate the claim made here, namely that international courts and tribunals – in determining whether a unilateral act evidences a manifest intention to be bound – will attach more evidentiary value to statements made by the upper echelons of a State. The judgment of the Court in the *Nuclear Tests Case* and the Court's Order of 28 May 2009 in the context of the *Case concerning Questions relating to the Obligation to Prosecute or Extradite* verify this claim.

C The Significance of Registration under Art. 102 of the Charter of the United Nations

Art. 102 of the UN Charter imposes on Member States the duty to register the international agreements they have entered into with the UN Secretariat: "Every treaty and international agreement entered into by any Member of the United Nations after the present Charter comes into force shall as soon as possible be registered with the Secretariat and published by it."[115] According to the second paragraph of Art. 102, the sanction for failing to fulfil this duty is that the Member State will not be allowed to invoke the non-registered treaty before any organ of the UN. Art. 102 of the UN Charter essentially reproduces – with minor changes – the duty of registration enshrined in Art.18 of the Covenant of the League of Nations.[116] The latter was adopted in the aftermath of World War I in order to satisfy the public demand for 'open diplomacy.'[117] The need to avoid secrecy in international relations was also stressed at the San Francisco Conference prior to the conclusion of the UN Charter. From a very early stage of the negotiations, it became apparent that the treaty registration system established under the Covenant of the League of Nations should be carried forward to the United Nations and thus, Art. 102 was adopted.[118]

---

power to do so. By virture of their functions, heads of State, heads of Governemnt and ministers for foreign affairs are competent to formulate such declarations. Other persons representing the State in specified areas may be authorized to bind it, through their delcarations, in areas falling within their competence." The commentary to Guiding Principle 4 expressly states that the Principle is directly inspired by the judgment of the Court in the *Armed Activities Case*. See Commentary to Guiding Principle 4, *ibid.*

115 Art. 102 of the *Charter of the United Nations*, 26 June 1945, San Francisco, 1 UNTS XVI (1945).

116 *Covenant of the League of Nations*, 28 April 1919, Paris, available at www.yale.edu/lawweb/avalon/leagcov.htm.

117 M.O. Hudson, The Registration and Publication of Treaties, 19 *AJIL* 273 (1925), at p. 273.

118 E. Hambro, L. Goodrich, A. Simons, *Charter of the United Nations: Commentary and Documents*, 3rd ed., (New York: Columbia University Press, 1969), p. 610.

On the face of it, Art. 102 has nothing to do with unilateral acts, since it expressly stipulates that it refers to international agreements. However, the fact that a well-known unilateral act, namely the 1957 Declaration made by Egypt on the Suez Canal and the arrangements for its operation,[119] was deposited and registered with the UN Secretariat under Art. 102 of the UN Charter raises the interesting question as to whether registration of a unilateral instrument could be considered as a reliable indicator of the manifest intention of the author State to be bound by it. This is especially so in light of the fact that registration under Art. 102 of the UN Charter is widely considered to be an indicator of the manifest intention of a State to be bound by an international agreement.[120]

In order to put the discussion in context, it is worthwhile to briefly revisit the 1957 Declaration and the circumstances surrounding its making. The Egyptian Declaration was made in the aftermath of the so-called 'Suez Crisis.' The 'Suez Crisis' arose after the Egyptian Government decided to nationalise the Suez Canal Company in 1956 and led to a failed military intervention by UK, France and Israel.[121] The following year, the Egyptian Government issued a Declaration under which it re-affirmed its intention to abide with the 1888 Constantinople Convention[122] and to ensure free and uninterrupted navigation through the Canal.[123] Apart from re-affirming pre-existing obligations, Egypt – though the Declaration – also undertook some news ones, such as the obligation to ensure that the Canal is maintained and developed in accordance with the progressive requirements of modern navigation and that an autonomous Suez Canal Authority would operate the Canal.[124] The Declaration ends with a solemn proclamation regarding its binding nature: "This Declaration, with the obligations therein, constitutes an international instrument and will be deposited and registered with the Secretariat of the United Nations."[125]

119 *Declaration on the Suez Canal and the arrangements for its operation issued by Egypt*, 24 April 1957, 265 UNTS 299. Hereinafter referred to as the 1957 Declaration or the Suez Canal Declaration.

120 See for example the literature cited in D.N. Hutchinson, The Significance of Registration or Non-Registration of an International Agreement in determining whether or not it is a Treaty, 46 *Current Legal Problems* 257 (1993), at p. 258, fn. 4.

121 A. Clapham, *Brierly's Law of Nations*, 7th ed., (Oxford: Oxford University Press, 2012), p. 212.

122 *Convention Respecting the Free Navigation of the Suez Maritime Canal*, 29 October 1888, 3(2) AJIL (Suppl.) 1909, pp. 123–7.

123 Art. 3 of the 1957 Declaration, *supra* note 119.

124 Art. 3(c) and Art. 4 of the 1957 Declaration, *ibid.*

125 Art. 10, *ibid.*

With few exceptions,[126] the majority of international lawyers consider the 1957 Declaration on the Suez Canal as a binding unilateral act and point to the fact that it was registered under Art. 102 of the UN Charter as further evidence that the Declaration was intended to create legal effects.[127] According to Degan, the Declaration "was probably the most formal and the most explicit unilateral act ever issued by a State in international practice."[128] The conclusions reached in doctrine regarding the evidentiary value of registration are also supported by the statements made by the UN Secretary General in a press conference announcing the registration of the 1957 Declaration. Addressing the press, the UN Secretary General stated the following:

> Then you may well ask: What does it mean that we register it [the Declaration]? In a case like this one, my interpretation is that it does mean that it is put on official United Nations record that the government – in this case the Government of Egypt – which submits the unilateral engagement, unilateral declaration, itself regards that declaration as an international engagement in relation to those who are the interested parties in the story.[129]

In light of the importance attached in literature to registration as evidence that the 1957 Declaration was binding on Egypt, would it then be correct to assume that registration under Art. 102 of the UN Charter is an indicator of the manifest intention of the author State to become bound by a unilateral act? Regrettably, the importance of registration as an indicator of intention is limited to the 1957 Declaration. Registration of unilateral acts is a rare occurrence and the 1957 Declaration is the only commonly cited example in the area. Thus, although in theory the possibility of registration of unilateral declarations exists, in practice this happens so rarely that it renders the usefulness of registration as an indicator of intention marginal.

---

126 See principally A. Rubin, The International Legal Effects of Unilateral Declarations, 71 *AJIL* 1 (1977), pp. 6–7.

127 See for example V.D. Degan, *Sources of International Law*, (The Hague: M. Nijhoff Publishers, 1997), p. 300; C. Eckart, *supra* note 36, pp. 108–14; A. Clapham, *supra* note 121, p. 212; T. Franck, Word Made Law: The Decision of the ICJ in the Nuclear Tests Case, 69 *AJIL* 612 (1975), pp. 615–6.

128 V.D. Degan, *ibid.*

129 A.W. Cordier, W. Foote, *Public Papers of the Secretaries General of the United Nations: 1956–7*, Vol. 3, (New York: Columbia University Press, 1973), pp. 567–8.

D The Reactions of the Addressee of the Act

As previously mentioned, one of the few indicators of manifest intent contained in the ILC Guiding Principles refers to the reactions of the addressee of the act. According to Guiding Principle 3: "To determine the legal effects of such declarations, it is necessary to take into account of their content, of all the factual circumstances in which they were made, and of the reactions to which they gave rise."[130] According to the accompanying commentary,[131] the wording of Guiding Principle 3 is inspired by the judgments of the ICJ in the *Nuclear Tests Case*, in the *Frontier Dispute Case* and in the *Armed Activities Case*.

However, the judicial practice cited in the commentary does not support the proposition that the reaction of the addressee is an element to be taken into account in determining the legal effects of a unilateral act. In none of these cases did the Court pay particular notice to the reactions of the addressee. On the contrary, in all three cases, the Court's determination of the legal effects of the unilateral acts in question was the exact opposite to what the addressees asserted. More particularly, in the context of the *Nuclear Tests Case*, the primary addressees of the French statements, Australia and New Zealand, expressly rejected the bindingness of those statements. Australia stressed that: "The recent French Presidential statement cannot be read as a firm, explicit and binding undertakings to refrain from further atmospheric tests",[132] while New Zealand noted that: "It should…be clearly understood that nothing said by the French Government, whether to New Zealand or to the international community at large, has amounted to an assurance that there will be no further atmospheric nuclear tests in the South Pacific."[133] Furthermore, the ICJ emphasised in its judgment that the opinions expressed by the addresses of a unilateral act – regarding the scope and meaning of such an act – can in no way

130 Guiding Principles applicable to unilateral declarations of States, *supra* note 21, p. 371.

131 Commentary to Guiding Priciple 3, *ibid.* It is noteworthy that the role of the reaction of the addressee of a unilateral act was not thoroughly discussed within the Commission. The Special Rapporteur made a specific reference to the reactions of the addressee as an indicator of a manifest intent to be bound for the first time in his Eight Report on Unilateral Acts- just a year before the Guiding Principles were adopted. See Rodríguez Cedeño V, Eighth Report on Unilateral Acts of States, UN Doc. A/CN.4/557, p. 119. However, the relevance of the reactions of the addressee was not really debated within the Commission. (See Report of the ILC on the Work of Its 57th Session, UN Doc. A/60/10, *Yrbk of the ILC* 2005, Vol. II, pp. 129–39). Despite the fact that the issue was not thoroughly discussed, the clause relating to "the reactions of the addressee" found its way in the 2006 Guiding Principles.

132 *Nuclear Tests Case*, Australia vs France, *ICJ Reports* 1974, p. 253, at p. 261, para. 27.

133 *Nuclear Tests Case*, *supra* note 1, at p. 465, para. 28.

impinge upon its legal status and that it is up to the Court to form its own interpretation. According to the Court: "The Court must however form its own view of the meaning and scope intended by the author of a unilateral declaration which may create a legal obligation, and cannot in this respect be bound by the view expressed by another State which is in no way a party to the text."[134]

Similarly, in the *Frontier Dispute* and in the *Armed Activities* cases, instead of attaching weight to the reactions of the addresses, the Court made its own determination of the legal effects of the relevant unilateral acts taking into account the content of the act and the circumstances in which these were made. In both cases, the addresses of the acts argued that the acts were binding upon the author States;[135] however, the Court disagreed with them and found that the acts in question were not of a juridical nature.[136] In light of the relevant case-law, the claim that the reactions of the addressee of the act may serve as an indicator of the manifest intent of the author State to be bound seems misguided.

3 The Basis of the Binding Force of Unilateral Acts

Having established the criterion for the binding nature of unilateral acts as well as the tools used in practice to ascertain the existence of this criterion, this section turns to the question posed in the first chapter of this book: what is the basis of the binding force of unilateral acts of States? Chapter 3 showed that theories invoking the presumed consent of the addressee, as well as estoppel, fail to explain the binding effects attributed to unilateral acts to the extent that they are incompatible with the strictly unilateral nature of these acts. In this light, this section examines the two most frequently encountered answers to the question of the binding force of unilateral acts, namely intention and good faith. It is argued that grounding the binding character of these acts in the will of the author State is conceptually problematic and finds no support in practice. The section claims that the binding force of unilateral acts derives from the general principle of good faith – a proposition that, as it will be shown below, finds widespread support both in practice and in the literature. Against this backdrop, the section continues by addressing some concerns that have been raised in theory in relation to the interplay between good faith and the binding character of unilateral acts. As it will be discussed, some international

134 *Ibid.*, para. 50.

135 *Frontier Dispute Case, supra* note 6, para. 38; *Armed Activities Case, supra* note 41, para. 45.

136 *Frontier Dispute Case, ibid.*, para. 40; *Armed Activities Case, ibid.*, para. 52.

lawyers are uncomfortable with the creative role given to good faith and, thus, they postulate the existence of a rule akin to *pacta sunt servanda* in order to justify the binding nature of unilateral acts. It will be argued that there is no reason to postulate such a rule. Good faith is a multifaceted concept: while some aspects of good faith refer to the performance of already existing obligations, it undeniably possesses some normative aspects too.

Next, the section turns to the question as to whether unilateral acts may be considered as a source of international law. It will be shown that, for some international lawyers, unilateral acts are only sources of obligations, but not sources of international law proper. According to this line of argumentation, the obligations borne out of acts of unilateral origin are too specific to qualify as 'law.' It will be argued that this proposition only holds true if one accepts the concomitant distinction between sources of obligation and sources of international law. Accordingly, international agreements and unilateral acts that do not create rules of general validity may only be considered as sources of obligations, but not as sources of law. It will be asserted that, although theoretically sound, this refined distinction is not made in practice. The section concludes that unilateral acts are sources of international law to the extent that they create obligations upon their authors in the same vein as international agreements.

3.1 *The Intention to be Bound as the Basis of the Binding Force of Unilateral Acts*

The view that intention forms the basis of the binding nature of unilateral acts was put forward by the Special Rapporteur of the ILC on unilateral acts of States in his very first report on the topic. Cedeño argued that "the State which formulates the declaration is bound to fulfil the obligation which it assumes, not because of the potential juridical interest of the addressee but because of the intention of the State making the declaration."[137] Sacasa also endorsed this view in the debate within the ILC following Cedeño's first report.[138] The idea that the intention of the author State is the justifying ground for attributing legal effects to juridical acts is reminiscent of the 'auto-limitation' theory propounded by Jellinek in the 1910s.[139] Jellinek perceived international law as a set

---

137 Rodríguez Cedeño V., First Report on Unilateral Acts of States, *supra* note 20, p. 319, at para. 160.

138 See the comments made by Sacasa in Summary Record of the 2527th Meeting, *supra* note 61, at p. 59, para. 14.

139 See generally G. Jellinek, *L'État Moderne et son Droit*, (Paris: V. Giard & E. Brière, 1911).

of rules by which a State limits itself.[140] Thus, the formal basis of all obligations in international law was, according to him, the will of the author State.[141]

As it was shown above, the intention of the author State is, indeed, the criterion for establishing the binding character of both unilateral acts and international agreements. However, there is a difference between the criterion for determining the legal character of a juridical act and the basis of the obligation assumed thereby. In other words, law-making and law-ascertainment are two distinct processes: while the former refers to the process of creation of a rule, the latter refers to the process of verification of a putative rule.[142] Thus, law-making criteria do not necessarily coincide with law-ascertaining criteria. The main problem with accepting intention as the basis of all legal obligations is that States would be free to release themselves from their obligations at will. However, this would jeopardise the stability and predictability of international relations. For this very reason, Jellinek's thesis has attracted considerable criticism. According to Brierly:

> However we may choose to define law, an essential part of the function of law must be to limit the wills of those to whom its precepts are addressed, and its binding force cannot possibly be derived from the wills that it limits. A self-imposed limitation is no true limitation at all, but a contradiction in terms.[143]

The Court in the *Nuclear Tests Case* expressly adopted the position that unilateral acts are not freely revocable: "The Court finds that the unilateral undertaking resulting from these statements cannot be interpreted as having been made in implicit reliance on an arbitrary power of reconsideration."[144] The ILC espoused the same position. Guiding Principle 10 stipulates that obligations assumed by means of a unilateral act cannot be revoked arbitrarily and lists several factors to be taken into account in assessing the revocability of a

---

140 For a detailed account of Jellinek's theory, see J. von Bernstorff, T. Dunlap, *The Public International Law Theory of Hans Kelsen: Believing in Universal Law*, (New York: Cambridge University Press, 2010), pp. 15–55.

141 J. von Bernstorff, Georg Jellinek and the Origins of Liberal Constitutionalism in International Law, 4 *GOJIL* 659 (2012), p. 668.

142 V.D. Degan, *supra* note 127, pp. 8–9; G. Fitzmaurice, The Foundations of the Authority of International Law and the Problem of Enforcement, 19 *The Modern Law Review* 1 (1956), p. 9.

143 J.L. Brierly, *The Basis of Obligation in International Law*, (Oxford: Clarendon Press, 1958), p. 14.

144 *Nuclear Tests Case, supra* note 1, para. 51.

particular act – including the *rebus sic standibus* clause.[145] According to the commentary accompanying Guiding Principle 10, "there can be no doubt that unilateral acts may be withdrawn or amended *in certain specific circumstances.*"[146] The fact that the Commission expressly stated that unilateral acts are to be rescinded in certain specific circumstances as well as the inclusion of the *rebus sic standibus clausula* militates in favour of the view that unilateral acts are not in principle revocable.[147] Thus, Jellinek's thesis is incompatible with the rules governing the revocability of unilateral acts. As Pellet aptly notes: "Once a State, by an apparent act of its free will has entered into a treaty or a unilateral commitment, the trap closes; its will is bound and it will be freed only through processes in which the will of an individual State will have nothing or very little to do."[148]

Furthermore, with the exception of Sacasa, no other member of the ILC shared Cedeño's position regarding the law-making role of intention. The majority of the members clarified from very early on that the binding force of unilateral acts "was to be found in the principle of good faith, as well as in the desirability of promoting conditions of security, confidence and trust in international relations."[149] It is noteworthy that, in his final report on the topic, the Special Rapporteur attempted to re-introduce intention through the back door. He suggested the adoption of a Guiding Principle under which the biding force of unilateral acts would be based both on the intention of the author State and on good faith.[150] However, the Commission refused to "delve into that theoretical jungle"[151] and dropped any references to intention in the final version of the Guiding Principles.

145 Guiding Principle 10, *supra* note 21.

146 *Ibid.* (Emph. added).

147 It is also noteworthy that in the jurisdictional phase of the *Nicaragua Case*, the Court, in assessing the revocability of declarations made under Art. 36.2 of its Statute, expressly referred to the *Nuclear Tests Case* and stated that "the unilateral nature of declarations does not signify that the State making the declaration is free to amend its scope and the content of its solemn commitments as it pleases." *Case concerning Military and Paramilitary Activities in and against Nicaragua*, Jurisdiction and Admissibility, ICJ *Reports* 1984, p. 392, para. 59. For a contrary position, see C. Eckart, *supra* note 36, p. 260.

148 A. Pellet, The Normative Dilemma: Will and Consent in International Law-Making, 12 *Australian YIL* 22 (1992), p. 35.

149 Report of the ILC on the work on its 50th session, UN Doc. A/53/10, *Yrbk of the ILC* 1998, Vol. II, p. 54, para. 150.

150 V. Rodríguez Cedeño, Ninth Report on Unilateral Acts of States, UN Doc. A/CN.4/569, p. 147, at para. 156.

151 C. Tomuschat, *Unilateral Acts under International Law*, in K. Meziou (ed.), *Droits et Culture: Mélanges en l' honneur du Doyen Yadh Ben Achour*, (Tunis: Centre de Publication Universitaire, 2008), p. 1487, at p. 1494.

3.2 *Good Faith as the Basis of the Binding Force of Unilateral Acts*

The Court in the *Nuclear Tests Case* made it abundantly clear that the binding force of unilateral acts resides in good faith. In an often-quoted passage the Court stated:

> One of the basic principles governing the creation and performance of legal obligations, whatever their source, is the principle of good faith. Trust and confidence are inherent in international co-operation, in particular in an age when this co-operation in many fields is becoming increasingly essential. Just as the very rule of *pacta sunt servanda* in the law of treaties is based on good faith, so also is the binding character of an obligation assumed by unilateral declaration. Thus interested States may take cognizance of unilateral declarations and place confidence in them, and are entitled to require that the obligation thus created be respected.[152]

With the exceptions discussed above, the ILC held the same view. Guiding Principle 1 expressly sets out that the binding character of unilateral declarations is based on good faith.[153] Mainstream legal thinking also shares the same approach.[154] In this sense, the promise to follow a certain line of conduct creates a legally relevant situation of trust between the author and the addresse/s. If the author State acts contrary to its expressed intent, then the confidence placed by the addresses in the maintenance of this situation would be impaired.

---

152 *Nuclear Tests Case*, *supra* note 1, para. 46.

153 Guiding Principle 1, *supra* note 21.

154 M. Lachs, The Development and General Trends of International Law in Our Time, 169 *RdC* 9 (1980), pp. 197–9; G. Fitzmaurice, *supra* note 32, p. 230; G. Schwarzenberger, The Fundamental Principles of International Law, 87 *RdC* 195 (1955), pp. 312–3; S. Carbone, Promise in International Law: A Confirmation of its Binding Force, 1 *Italian YIL* 166 (1975), p. 168; R. St. J. MacDonald and B. Hough, The Nuclear Tests Case Revisited, 20 *Germ. Yrb. I.L.* 337 (1977), p. 341; K. Zemanek, *Unilateral Legal Acts Revisited*, in K. Wellens (ed.), *International Law: Theory and Practice: Essays in Honour of Eric Suy*, (The Hague: M. Nijhoff, 1998), p. 209, at p. 217; W. Fiedler, *Unilateral Acts in International Law*, in R. Berhardt (ed.), *Encyclopaedia of Public International Law*, Vol. IV, (Amsterdam, Oxford, North-Holland, 1984), p. 1018, at p. 1020; D. Khosla, Nuclear Tests Cases: Judicial Valour v. Judicial Discretion, 18 *Indian JIL* 322 (1978), p. 342; K. Skubiszewski, *Unilateral Acts of States*, in M. Bedjaoui (ed.), *International law: achievements and prospects*, (Paris: UNESCO, 1991), p. 225, at p. 232; V.D. Degan, Unilateral Act as a Source of Particular International Law, 5 *Finnish YIL* 149 (1994), pp. 166–7; R. Kolb, Principles as Sources of International Law: (With Special Reference to Good Faith), 53 *NILR* 1 (2006), p. 19.

However, "trust and confidence are inherent in international relations"[155] and thus, it is in the best interests of the international community to protect and promote these values in any given situation. It is at this point that the general principle of good faith becomes operative: international law attributes binding effects to unilateral acts in order to protect other States that may have reasonably placed confidence in an expressed manifestation of will. As Fitzmaurice put it, a unilateral declaration:

> may or may not create binding legal obligations for the declaring party, according to its wording and intent, and the circumstances of its making; but it seems fairly well-settled that it can and will do so if clearly intended to have that effect and held out, so to speak, as an instrument on which others may rely and under which the declaration purports to assume such obligation.[156]

It is important to note that what matters here is abstract reliance rather than actual reliance. In other words, it is not necessary for the addressee to take action on the basis of the unilateral representation from which some sort of detriment would follow- as this would equate unilateral legal acts to estoppel. It is sufficient that the act has created abstract reliance, *i.e.* that the addressee *could have reasonably relied* on the representation made.[157] As Fiedler explains:

> It is, however, not generally necessary for the recipient State to have already been induced into taking action, from which adverse consequences would ensue... Rather it is sufficient if the declaring State has created a legally relevant situation of trust which in the specific circumstances of the case entails binding force.[158]

This proposition is also supported by the text of the *Nuclear Tests* judgment. The Court emphasised that the bindingness of unilateral acts is founded on the need to maintain trust and confidence in international co-operation, while at the same time it clarified that no acceptance or reliance on behalf of the addressee is needed for the act to produce legal effects.[159]

---

155 *Nuclear Tests Case*, *supra* note 1, para. 46.

156 G. Fitzmaurice, *supra* note 32, p. 230.

157 R. Kolb, *Le Bonne Foi en Droit International Public*, (Paris: Presses Universitaires de France, 2000), p. 335 and the translation provided by C. Eckart, *supra* note 36 p. 204, fn. 94.

158 W. Fiedler, *supra* note 154, p. 1021.

159 *Nuclear Tests Case*, *supra* note 1, paras. 43, 46.

One final point needs to be addressed here. Thirlway[160] has questioned the creative role attributed to good faith by the Court. For him, good faith governs the execution of already existing obligations, but cannot be the *ratio* justifying the creation of new ones. He argues that what the Court dubbed 'good faith' in its *Nuclear Tests* judgment is essentially a principle tantamount to *pacta sunt servanda*.[161] Since unilateral acts do not, by their very nature, involve the conclusion of a *pactum*, the putative principle is referred to as *acta sunt servanda* or *promissio est servanda* in the literature.[162] Some seemingly contradictory dicta lie at the heart of this argument. While in 1974 the Court expressly proclaimed that good faith is "one of the basic principle governing *the creation* and performance of legal obligations", in 1988 the same Court observed that good faith "is *not in itself a source of obligation* where none would otherwise exist."[163] Ten years later, the Court reaffirmed its 1988 pronouncement by declaring that good faith is a principle that relates only to the "fulfilment of *existing* obligations."[164]

Thirlway's position puts – in the opinion of the present author at least – undue emphasis on the way in which the Court has used good faith in its practice. It is true that the Court has the tendency to apply the principle mostly in situations where a legal obligation already exists. However, this is simply a tendency on the part of the Court in relation to its own practice and does not, as such, represent the position in international law more generally. Nor has the relevant practice of the Court escaped criticism. Judge Koroma disapproved of the Court's sweeping statement regarding the role of good faith in his Dissenting Opinion in the *Cameroon v. Nigeria Case*.[165] As Kolb[166] and Virally[167] explain, good faith is a multifaceted concept. Sometimes it operates as an open-ended legal standard, *i.e.* a standard of reasonableness, providing a measure for the

160 H. Thirlway, The Law and Procedure of the International Court of Justice 1960–1989 part I, 60 *BYIL* 1 (1989). See also C. Goodman, Acta Sunt Servanda? A Regime for the Unilateral Acts of States at International Law, 25 *Australian YIL* 43 (2006).

161 H. Thirlway, *ibid.*, pp. 9–10.

162 C. Goodman, *supra* note 160, pp. 53–9 S. Carbone, *supra* note 154, p. 167.

163 *Case concerning Border and Transborder Armed Actions, ICJ Reports* 1988, p. 69, at p. 105, para. 94.

164 *Case concerning the Land and Maritime Boundary between Cameroon and Nigeria, ICJ Reports* 1998, p. 275, at p. 304, para. 59.

165 Dissenting Opinion of Judge Koroma in the *Case concerning the Land and Maritime Boundary between Cameroon and Nigeria, ibid.*, p. 377, at p. 384.

166 R. Kolb, *supra* note 154.

167 M. Virally, Good Faith in Public International Law, 77 AJIL 130 (1983).

interpretation and application of already existing obligations.[168] However, good faith also has normative aspects as the basis of the binding force of a number of more precise rules including *pacta sunt servanda*,[169] estoppel[170] and normative acquiescence.[171] Through continuous usage, these 'concretisations' of good faith have come to acquire a separate legal identity. However, it remains the case that they were originally based on the overarching principle of good faith. In this light, fictional postulates, such as *acta sunt servanda*, seem superfluous. As Tomuschat notes:

> A formal proposition emulating *pacta sunt servanda*, in the sense of *declaratio est servanda* or *Acta sunt servanda*...lacks any intrinsic justification... [W]hat matters in the first place is the legal position. If a State generates confidence and trust so that the addressees rely on its declaration, it should not be free to revoke its promise without taking into consideration the expectations it has created.[172]

3.3 *Unilateral Acts as Sources of International Law/Obligations*

International lawyers who accept the binding force of unilateral acts are divided over whether these acts constitute a source of international law, or whether they are merely a source of obligations. The roots of this debate can be traced back to Fitzmaurice's seminal 1958 article on the formal sources of international law.[173] Inspired by municipal legal reasoning, Fitzmaurice argued that treaties are not sources of international law proper to the extent that they do not create rules of universal applicability.[174] Rather, he regarded them merely as sources of obligations since they create obligations only for States parties.[175] This distinction resonated with a number of international lawyers who have extrapolated it to the

---

168 R. Kolb, *supra* note 154, pp. 16–7; M. Virally, *ibid.*, p. 132.

169 B. Cheng, *General Principles of Law: As Applied by International Courts and Tribunals*, (London: Stevens & Sons, 1953), p. 113.

170 See generally D.W. Bowett, Estoppel before International Tribunals and its relation to Acquiescence, 33 *BYIL* 176 (1957).

171 R. Kolb, *supra* note 154, p. 19.

172 C. Tomuschat, *supra* note 151, p. 1495.

173 G. Fitzmaurice, *Some Problems Regarding the Formal Sources of International Law*, in F.M. van Asbeck (ed.), *Symbolae Verzijl*, (The Hague: M. Nijhoff, 1958), p. 153.

174 *Ibid.*, pp. 157–8.

175 *Ibid.*

field of unilateral acts. Thus, Bos[176] and Skubiszewski[177] treat unilateral acts as sources of obligations, rather than law, since these acts, by their very nature, may only create obligations for their authors.

Although the distinction between sources of law and sources of obligations is theoretically sound, its practical value is questionable – especially in such an open-textured system as international law. To be sure, the distinction is valid as far as domestic legal systems are concerned. While the central legislature enacts 'general law', other legal persons enter into contracts and thus, create 'particular law' that governs the legal relationship between them.[178] The absence of a central legislative authority makes it hard to sustain Fitzmaurice's distinction at the international level. Through their practice, States create both 'general' and 'particular' law and the neat distinction between sources of law and sources of obligations often becomes fuzzy.[179] As Pellet underlines: "why would 'law' necessarily be limited to rules of general validity?"[180] Art. 38 of the ICJ Statute expressly refers both to general and to particular conventions as sources of international law and the Court has, on numerous occasions, referred to treaties as sources of international law.[181]

If it is accepted that international law encompasses not only rules of general validity, but also more particular undertakings, there is no reason why unilateral acts cannot be viewed as sources of international law – on a par with international agreements. This view has been espoused by Pellet,[182] Virally,[183] Degan[184] and Zemanek.[185] Arguments that recourse to a source not expressly enumerated in Art.38 of the ICJ Statute would render the *Nuclear Tests* judgment – and thus the whole edifice of the theory on unilateral

176 M.S. Bos, *A Methodology of International Law*, (Amsterdam: T.M.C. Asser Institute, 1984), pp. 88–9.

177 K. Skubiszewski, *supra* note 154, p. 222.

178 R. Kolb, *supra* note 154, p. 11.

179 See generally M.H. Mendelson, *Are Treaties Merely a Source of Obligation?*, in W.E. Butler (ed.), *Perestroika and International Law*, (Dordrecht: M. Nijhoff, 1990), p. 81.

180 A. Pellet, *Article 38*, in A. Zimmermann, C. Tomuschat, K. Oelles-Frahm (eds.), *The Statute of The International Court of Justice: A Commentary*, 2nd ed., (Oxford: Oxford University Press, 2012), p. 731, at p. 761.

181 *Ibid.* See also the case-law mentioned therein, especially fn. 202.

182 *Ibid.*, p. 763.

183 M. Virally, *The Sources of International Law*, in M. Sorensen (ed.), *Manual of Public International Law*, (London: Macmillan, 1968), p. 116 at p. 154.

184 V.D. Degan, *supra* note 127, pp. 253 *et seq.*

185 K. Zemanek, *supra* note 154, p. 218.

acts – questionable[186] are overly formalistic, in the opinion of the present author. As Shahabuddeen stresses:

> Subparagraphs (*a*) to (*d*) of Article 38, paragraph 1, are not exhaustive of 'international law' as more generally referred to in Article 36, paragraph 2 (*b*). Since the Court's function is 'to decide in accordance with international law', if a principle can be shown to form part of international law the Court must decide in accordance with that principle where relevant, whether or not it falls under subparagraphs (*a*) to (*d*) of Article 38, paragraph 1. The structure of the provision encourages the view that these subparagraphs may be construed as a standing directive to the Court to apply certain elements… On that view, it is at least arguable that the Court is not prevented from discovering international law by other means if it can.[187]

Furthermore, in its practice, the Court has proven itself more flexible than it has been given credit for. It has not hesitated to apply decisions of international organisations as a separate source of law, although not included in Art.38.[188] Thus, arguments hinged on the exhaustiveness of Art.38, for the purpose of refuting that unilateral acts are a source of international law, fall short of convincing.

4 Conclusion

This chapter examined the legal nature of unilateral acts in order to establish whether and, to what extent, these acts may be considered as juridical acts. It was established that, as with international agreements, the manifest intention to be bound features both in theory and in judicial practice as the criterion for distinguishing between unilateral juridical acts and unilateral political acts. Moreover, analysis of the relevant case-law revealed that unilateral acts and

186 A. Rubin, The International Legal Effects of Unilateral Declarations, 71 *AJIL* 1 (1977), p. 28; H. Thirlway, *The Sources of International Law*, (Oxford: Oxford University Press, 2014), pp. 44–52.

187 M. Shahabuddeen, *Precedent in the World Court*, (Cambridge: Cambridge University Press, 2007), p. 81. For a contrary view, see H. Thirlway, *ibid.*, pp. 5–6.

188 A.J.P. Tammes, Decisions of International Organs as a Source of International Law, 94 *RdC* 265 (1958); A. Pellet, *supra* note 180, p. 763.

international agreements have another similarity: the same method of ascertaining the manifest intent to be bound, namely interpretation of the act in accordance with its content and the context surrounding it, is applicable to both. In doing so, the chapter proved that international courts, by applying the same criterion for determining their legal nature and the same means for ascertaining the existence of that criterion, treat unilateral acts and international agreements as belonging to the same genre of acts – thereby validating the theory of international juridical acts originally propounded by Verzijl and Lauterpacht.

Against this background, the chapter continued by inquiring as to whether any reliable indicators of the manifest intent of the author to be bound by a unilateral act may be deduced from the relevant judicial practice – a question that was not tackled within the work of the ILC on the topic. In this respect, it was argued that the content of the act, its publicity, the forum in which the act was made and the authority who made the act on behalf of the State may be relied upon in practice to facilitate the determination of the existence of a manifest intent to be bound.

Finally, the chapter turned to the question of the basis of the binding force of unilateral acts. It was shown that according to the prevailing view good faith is the source of the binding effects attributed to unilateral acts. The chapter also enquired whether and to what extent unilateral acts may be considered as sources of international law, or merely as sources of obligations. It was argued that the distinction between sources of law and sources of obligations is, to a large extent, inapplicable at the international level. On this basis, it was concluded that unilateral acts can be regarded as sources of international law in the same way as international agreements.

CHAPTER 7

A Brief Excursus to Unilateral Declarations of Independence

1 Introduction

The previous chapters established a theoretical framework for determining the juridical nature of unilateral acts of States. It was shown that the manifest intention to be bound is the criterion for establishing whether a unilateral act is binding upon its author/s. Furthermore, on the basis of relevant practice, a list of contextual indicators of the manifest intent to be bound was compiled in order to facilitate the task of determining the existence of this element in practice. Within this framework, most well-known instances of unilateral acts were discussed. At the same time, the present study makes no pretence of exhaustiveness: the sheer volume of relevant material and the limitations of space would render any effort to analyse all existing unilateral acts practically impossible. This would also run counter to the purpose of this book which is to provide a coherent framework for conceptualising unilateral acts, rather than a detailed account of each individual unilateral act to be found in State and judicial practice.

However, there are two generic categories of unilateral acts that merit closer attention: unilateral declarations of independence and unilateral security assurances. As it will be shown in this and the following chapter, the question of the binding force of these two distinct types of unilateral acts is far from settled and thus, it is necessary to examine them in detail. For this purpose, this chapter will examine the juridical nature of unilateral declarations of independence, while the next will focus on unilateral security assurances. The *problématique surrounding unilateral declarations of independence, as well as the structure of this chapter, are set out in the following section.*

2 Unilateral Declarations of Independence: The *Problématique*

By virtue of their very nature – as acts born in the twilight zone between Statehood and nothingness – unilateral declarations of independence pose a number of conceptual challenges. Do they fall within the ambit of international law and are they, thus, governed by the regime applicable to unilateral

 | DOI 10.1163/9789004300767_009

acts of States? Or, do they fall outside the realm of international law altogether? The picture becomes more complicated in the light of the fact that the proclamation of a new State is often accompanied by solemn undertakings that the new entity will comply with specific obligations set out in the text of the declaration of independence. The 2008 Kosovar declaration of independence is a pertinent example. It is worth quoting the text of the declaration in full:

> 1. We, the democratically-elected leaders of our people, hereby declare Kosovo to be an independent and sovereign state. This declaration reflects the will of our people and it is in full accordance with the recommendations of UN Special Envoy Martti Ahtisaari and his Comprehensive Proposal for the Kosovo Status Settlement. 2. We declare Kosovo to be a democratic, secular and multi-ethnic republic, guided by the principles of non-discrimination and equal protection under the law. We shall protect and promote the rights of all communities in Kosovo and create the conditions necessary for their effective participation in political and decision-making processes. We welcome the international community's continued support of our democratic development through international presences established in Kosovo on the basis of UN Security Council resolution 1244 (1999). We invite and welcome an international civilian presence to supervise our implementation of the Ahtisaari Plan, and a European Union-led rule of law mission. We hereby undertake the international obligations of Kosovo, including those concluded on our behalf by the United Nations Interim Administration Mission in Kosovo (UNMIK),...We hereby affirm, clearly, specifically and irrevocably, that Kosovo shall be legally bound to comply with the provisions contained in this Declaration, including especially, the obligations under the Ahtisaari Plan...We declare publicly that all states are entitled to rely upon this declaration.[1]

It is quite clear from the text of the declaration that the Assembly of Kosovo not only proclaimed Kosovo's independence, but also expressly stated that Kosovo is legally bound to comply with certain obligations. Serbia, for its part, considered the act as a "unilateral act expressing the intention of its authors to

1 *Accordance with International Law of the Unilateral Declaration of Independence in respect of Kosovo, Advisory Opinion, ICJ Reports* 2010, p. 403, at para. 75. Hereinafter referred to as the *Kosovo Advisory Opinion*.

purportedly create a new State…[and] to undertake certain obligations…"[2] – albeit one that failed to produce any legal effects since it, allegedly, contravened international law.[3] Some international lawyers have also shared the view that, since a manifest intention to create legal effects is evidenced through the declaration, it should be considered a unilateral juridical act.[4]

The question arose squarely in the context of the 2010 *Advisory Opinion on the Accordance with International Law of the Unilateral Declaration of Independence in respect of Kosovo*.[5] Here, the General Assembly (GA) asked the Court to give its opinion on whether the 2008 Kosovar declaration was in accordance with international law.[6] The Court interpreted the question narrowly and opined that it was not asked to rule on whether or not Kosovo had achieved Statehood or on the validity and legal effects of the recognition of Kosovo by those States which had, at the time, recognised it as an independent State.[7] Thus, instead of examining whether international law confers a right upon the people of Kosovo to declare independence, the Court proceeded to ascertain whether or not the declaration violated any applicable legal rules.[8] Having examined the applicable rules of law, *i.e.* rules of general international law and the special regime created by Security Council (SC) resolution 1244 (1999),[9] it was concluded that: "the adoption of that declaration did not violate any applicable rule of law."[10]

The Court has come under considerable attack for what has been perceived by many as an overly restrictive interpretation of the question before it. More specifically, it has been suggested that the Court focused on the legality of the declaration of independence *per se* in order to avoid giving its opinion on the – politically sensitive – underlying question of the existence of a right to remedial secession.[11]

---

2 Written Comments by Serbia in the *Kosovo Advisory Opinion*, 14 July 2009, available at http://www.icj-cij.org/docket/files/141/15686.pdf, para. 193.

3 *Ibid.*, para. 313.

4 See for example M. Weller, *Contested Statehood: Kosovo's Struggle for Independence*, (Oxford: Oxford University Press, 2009), p. 231.

5 *Kosovo Advisory Opinion, supra* note 1.

6 *Ibid.*, para. 51.

7 *Ibid.*

8 *Ibid.*, paras. 78–121.

9 SC, Res. 1244, UN Doc. S/RES/1244 (1999).

10 *Ibid.*, para. 122.

11 This narrow approach adopted by the majority of the judges was severely criticised not only by academics, but also by some of the judges. See for example R. Howse, R. Teitel, Delphic Dictum: How Has the ICJ Contributed to the Global Rule of Law by Its Ruling in

However, it is submitted that even the (arguably) narrowly framed question regarding the accordance of Kosovo's declaration of independence with international law was not fully answered by the Court. More particularly, the Court simply stated that the 2008 Declaration was not against international law. However, this rather Delphic pronouncement did not resolve the question of the precise legal nature of unilateral declarations of independence. By simply focusing on the existence of prohibitive rules, the Court did not clarify whether it considered these declarations as legal, or as purely political pronouncements. More particularly, the pronouncement of the Court may simultaneously lend support to two (mutually exclusive) propositions: (a) by stating that a unilateral declaration of independence is not illegal, the Court could have implied that, under international law, unilateral declarations of independence are legal, *i.e.* that international law regulates unilateral declarations of independence; (b) by stating that a unilateral declaration of independence is not illegal, the Court could have implied that international law does not regulate unilateral declarations of independence, *i.e.* that they are mere political pronouncements.

It would be helpful to use an example here in order to elucidate the problems arising from the way in which the Court chose to answer the question. Let us assume that the question put forward to the Court was whether the use of nuclear weapons by a State in self-defence is in accordance with international law. Let us now assume that the Court examined this question by focusing exclusively on the existence of prohibitive rules and thus, ignoring the existence of any permissive rules offering States a positive entitlement to use nuclear weapons in self-defence. On the basis of this methodological approach, if the answer of the Court is that the use of nuclear weapons in self-defence does not violate international law, this does not automatically mean that there is a *right* to use nuclear weapons in the case of self-defence. It could also very well mean that the use of nuclear weapons in self-defence is not regulated by international law.[12] Thus, by failing to examine both permissive and

Kosovo? 11 *German LJ* 841 (2010); See also the Declaration by Judge Simma in the *Kosovo Advisory Opinion, supra* note 1, p. 478; Separate Opinion of Judge Yusuf, *ibid.*, p. 618.

12 Of course, this particular question did arise in the context of the *Legality of the Threat or Use of Nuclear Weapons, Advisory Opinion, ICJ Reports* 1996, p. 226. Hereinafter referred to as the *Nuclear Weapons Advisory Opinion*. The Court, in that case, answered the question by examining both prohibitive and permissive rules of international law. *Ibid.*, para. 52. The Court's methodological approach in the *Kosovo Advisory Opinion* stands in stark contrast to the one adopted in the *Nuclear Weapons Advisory Opinion*. In the latter case, the Court examined both prohibitive and permissive relevant rules before concluding that "in view of the current state of international law…the Court cannot conclude definitely

prohibitive rules of international law and by failing to examine whether international law is neutral towards unilateral declarations of independence, the Court's pronouncement is of little assistance in ascertaining their juridical nature. Judge Simma highlighted the methodological shortcomings in the Court's argumentation in his Declaration:

> The Court could have considered the scope of the question from an approach which does not, in a formalistic fashion, equate the absence of a prohibition with the existence of a permissive rule; it could also have considered the possibility that international law can be neutral or deliberately silent on the international lawfulness of certain acts...By reading the General Assembly's question as it did, the Court denied itself the possibility to enquire into the precise status under international law of a declaration of independence.[13]

A comprehensive treatment of the topic is also lacking in literature. Scarce references to unilateral declarations of independence can be found in scholarly works preceding the Court's Opinion.[14] Although the Opinion itself attracted much scholarly attention, most of the voluminous writing produced in its aftermath is mainly centred on the existence of a right to remedial secession under international law.[15] In this light, the following sections will endeavour to explore the juridical nature of unilateral declarations of independence as follows: first, claims that unilateral declarations of independence are (entirely or partly) regulated by international law will be examined. In this

whether the threat or use of nuclear weapons would be lawful or unlawful in an extreme circumstance of self-defence, in which the very survival of a State would be at risk." *Ibid.*, para. 105 (2) E.

13 Declaration by Judge Simma, *supra* note 11, pp. 479–80.

14 Most notably, J. Crawford, *The Creation of States in International Law*, 2nd ed., (Oxford: Clarendon Press, 2006), pp. 389–90. See also H. Lauterpacht, *Recognition in International Law*, (Cambridge: Cambridge University Press, 1947), p. 8.

15 See for example J.A. Frowein, *Kosovo and Lotus*, in U. Fastenrath (ed.), *From Bilateralism to Community Interest: Essays in honour of Bruno Simma*, (Oxford: Oxford University Press, 2011), p. 923; H. Jamar, M.K. Vigness, Applying Kosovo: Looking to Russia, China, Spain and beyond after the International Court of Justice Opinion on Unilateral Declarations of Independence, 11 *German LJ* 913 (2010); A. Orakhelashvili, Statehood, Recognition and the United Nations System: A Unilateral Declaration of Independence in Kosovo, 12 *Max Planc Yrbk of United Nations Law* 1 (2009); M. Kohen, K. Del Mar, The Kosovo Advisory Opinion and UNSCR 1244 (1999): A Declaration of 'Independence from International Law?' 24 *LJIL* 109 (2011).

section, two lines of argumentation will be scrutinised. The first draws mainly from the arguments put forward by Serbia before the Court in the context of the *Kosovo Advisory Opinion*. As it will be shown below, Serbia argued that international law regulates unilateral declarations of independence. According to this line of argumentation, the lawfulness of these declarations hinges on the existence of a positive entitlement to declare independence under international law.[16] A second line of argumentation may be found in Vidmar's work on unilateral declarations of independence.[17] Vidmar argues that although international law remains, in general, neutral in relation to unilateral declarations of independence, such declarations may be illegal if they are conjoined with a violation of a *jus cogens* norm. These two lines of argumentation have been classed together since they share a common thread: they both accept that international law regulates unilateral declarations of independence – albeit in varying degrees. It will be claimed that both arguments are misguided to the extent that: (a) they do not take into account the legal context within which these acts occur; (b) they ignore the identity of their authors as non-State actors; and (c) they are based on an erroneous reading of the relevant SC practice.

Against this backdrop, the next section will consider the claim that, under international law, declarations of independence are legally neutral acts – an argument made by the authors of the Kosovar Declaration that found support in the submissions of a number of States including the UK, France, Norway, Finland and Germany. It will be concluded that this argument is the most convincing since it comports with the widely held view that the creation of a State is a matter of fact, rather than law, and it is also supported in practice.

Before embarking on the analysis, it would be useful to explain briefly why the *Kosovo Advisory Opinion* is afforded a prominent place in the following sections. First, as discussed above, the literature offers limited insight into the question at hand. By way of contrast, the written and oral comments provided by different States during the proceedings offer a wealth of competing arguments that are worth exploring. Secondly, it is important to tackle the question at hand using the *Kosovo Advisory Opinion* as a point of reference in order to

16 Written Statement of Serbia in the *Kosovo Advisory Opinion*, 15 April 2009, available at http://www.icj-cij.org/docket/files/141/15642.pdf, pp. 189–243.

17 See generally J. Vidmar, Conceptualizing Declarations of Independence in International Law, 32 *Oxford JLS* 153 (2012); J. Vidmar, *Unilateral Declarations of Independence in International Law*, in D. French (ed.), *Statehood and Self-Determination: Reconciling Tradition and Modernity in International Law*, (Cambridge: Cambridge University Press, 2013), p. 60.

set the record straight in regards to its exact precedential value. More particularly, it is submitted that clarifying what the Court actually answered in its Opinion, and – more importantly – what it left unanswered, has far-reaching implications not only for the doctrine of unilateral juridical acts, but for the international legal order as such. Judge Yusuf, in his Separate Opinion, warned that the way in which the Court chose to answer the question, *i.e.* without assessing whether international law is legally neutral towards unilateral declarations of independence, "may be misinterpreted as legitimizing such declarations under international law, by all kinds of separatist groups or entities that have either made or are planning to make declarations of independence."[18] The 2014 Crimean Declaration of Independence echoed this warning. The preamble of the Crimean Declaration of Independence issued by the Supreme Council of Crimea and the Sevastopol City Council specifically mentions the *Kosovo Advisory Opinion* as authority for the proposition that a "unilateral declaration of independence by a part of the country does not violate any international norms."[19]

3 Claims that Unilateral Declarations of Independence are (Entirely or Partly) Regulated by International Law: Unilateral Declarations of Independence as Unilateral Juridical Acts

The argument according to which unilateral declarations of independence constitute unilateral juridical acts, may be summarised as follows: the emergence of a new State is not a fact of which international law merely takes note. Rather, international law governs the whole process of creation of new States.[20] Thus, in some cases, international law recognises the existence of a positive right, *i.e.* the right to self-determination, to create new States.[21] In these cases, the relevant declarations are viewed as lawful unilateral juridical acts to the extent that the intention of their authors to purportedly create a new State is compatible with applicable rules of international law.[22] However, where there is no right to self-determination, international law may function as a barrier to

18 Separate Opinion of Judge Yusuf, *supra* note 11, para. 6.

19 Declaration of Independence of the Autonomous Republic of Crimea and Sevastopol in Crimea Parliament Declares Independence From Ukraine Ahead of Referendum, *RT*, 11 March 2014, available at rt.com/news/crimea-parliament-independence-ukraine-086/.

20 Written Comments by Serbia, *supra* note 2, para. 174.

21 *Ibid.*

22 *Ibid.*, paras. 181–4.

the emergence of a new State – even if the material elements of the Montevideo Convention are fulfilled.[23] In these cases, the relevant declarations of independence are unlawful since the intention to create a new State is not founded on a positive entitlement to declare independence.[24] Finally, according to this line of argumentation, the critical date for assessing whether a new State has been lawfully created is the date that the declaration of independence is issued.[25] This was, in broad strokes, the argument made by Serbia before the ICJ, which was further endorsed by a number of other States, including Argentina, Spain and Russia.[26] Proponents of this view have pointed to the practice of the SC as evidence that international law is not neutral in relation to unilateral declarations of independence. In this respect, it has been claimed that the SC has treated declarations issued by entities that have no right to self-determination under international law as unlawful.[27] The SC resolutions in relation to Southern Rhodesia,[28] Katanga[29] and the Turkish Republic of Northern Cyprus[30] are cited in support of this view.[31]

Without dwelling on the existence of a legal right to remedial secession – something that would be outside the purview of the present work – it is submitted that the above thesis is untenable in any case – irrespective of whether one accepts that a right to remedial secession exists or not. This is so on a number of grounds. First, the proposition that unilateral declarations of independence can be viewed as unilateral juridical acts ignores the identity of the author of the declaration as a non-State entity. More particularly, this argument draws its appeal by invoking a schema familiar to international lawyers: if X has the intention to create Y legal effects and that intention does not

23 *Ibid.*, para. 174. *Montevideo Convention on Rights and Duties of States*, 26 December 1933, Montevideo, 165 LNTS 19 (1934).

24 Written Comments by Serbia, *ibid.*, paras. 313–36.

25 *Ibid.*, para. 313; See also the statements made by M. Shaw as representaive of Serbia in Verbatim Record of the Public Sitting held on Tuesday 1 December 2009, at 10 a.m., at the Peace Palace, in the *Kosovo Advisory Opinion*, CR 2009/24, available at http://www.icj-cij.org/docket/files/141/15710.pdf, para. 29.

26 Of course, Serbia's final submission was that since Kosovo did not have a right to external self-determination at the time that the Declaration was made, the Declaration was unlawful and did not create its purported legal effects, *i.e.* the creation of the Republic of Kosovo. Written Comments by Serbia, *ibid.*, paras. 313 *et seq.*

27 *Ibid.*, paras. 208–10.

28 SC, Res. 216, UN Doc. S/RES/216 (1965) and SC, Res. 217, UN Doc. S/RES/217 (1965).

29 SC, Res. 169, UN Doc. S/RES/169 (1961).

30 SC, Res. 541, UN Doc. S/RES/541 (1983).

31 Written Comments by Serbia, *supra* note 2, paras. 208–10.

contravene any applicable rules of international law, then it is logical to assume that X's declaration (manifesting the relevant intention) has, in fact, created the purported legal effects under international law. However, what this schema does not take into account is that, in this case, X is not a subject of international law. By arbitrarily transposing the doctrine of unilateral juridical acts to the sphere of non-State entities, this proposition assumes that international law bestows the ability to create international legal effects through an act of will on certain entities. However, there is no evidence that international law treats the intention of a sovereign State similarly to that of a non-State actor.[32]

Furthermore, viewing unilateral declarations of independence as unilateral juridical acts would not comport with the factual nature of the process of the formation of States. If it were accepted that Kosovo's declaration of independence, or indeed any declaration of independence, constitutes a unilateral legal act, then it would mean that the effects of the declaration – the creation of a State – would arise solely by means of the declaration. In other words, accepting declarations of independence as unilateral legal acts would necessarily lead to the conclusion that international law allows an entity to become a State, its subject *par excellence*, purely by means of an act of will. However, according to both practice[33] and doctrine[34] Statehood is a fact; either an entity satisfies the effectiveness-based criteria stipulated under the Montevideo

---

32 In fact, the Court itself, in the context of the *Kosovo Advisory Opinion*, was quick to draw the line between States and non-State entities and rejected an argument according to which the principle of respect for territorial integrity is applicable *mutatis mutandis* to non-State entities. See *Kosovo Advisory Opinion*, *supra* note 1, para. 80.

33 See Art. 1 of the Montevideo Convention, *supra* note 23. *Reference re Secession of Quebec*, 2 *SCR* 217 (1998), para. 142. Conference on Yugoslavia Arbitration Commission (Badinter Commission): Opinions on Questions Arising from the Dissolution of Yugoslavia, January 11 and July 4, 1992, 31 *ILM* 1488 (1992), Opinion No. 1, p. 1495: "The Committee considers… that…the existence or disappearance of the state is a question of fact." See also the Report of the Independent International Fact-Finding Mission on the Conflict in Georgia, September 2009, Vol. II, available at http://rt.com/files/politics/georgia-started-ossetian-war/iiffmcg-volume-ii.pdf, pp. 127–9.

34 M. Craven, *Statehood, Self-Determination, and Recognition*, in M. Evans (ed.), *International Law*, 4th ed., (Oxford: Oxford University Press, 2014), p. 201, at p. 215. J. Crawford, *supra* note 14, p. 5. Of course, a State is not, as Crawford notes, a fact "in the sense that a chair is a fact." It is rather "a legal status attaching to a certain state of affairs by virtue of certain rules or practices." *Ibid.* For a simliar approach, see also J. Vidmar, *Democracy and Statehood in International Law*, (Oxford: Hart Publishing, 2013), p. 47: "The emergence of a new state is not a simple matter of a self-evident fact, but rather a matter of an international legal acceptance of a certain territory having a specific legal status." See also T. Christakis, *The State as A 'Primary Fact': Some Thoughts on the Principle of Effectiveness*,

Convention at the time that a declaration of independence is made or it does not.[35] A declaration of independence may not confer the status of a State to an entity that was not a State before the declaration. As Norway stated during the proceedings before the Court: "Declarations of independence do not create or constitute States under international law. It is not the issuance of such declarations that satisfies the factual requirements, under international law, for Statehood or recognition."[36]

Secondly, by focusing on the date that the declaration of independence is issued as the critical date for assessing the legality and effectiveness of a claim to Statehood, the argument put forward by Serbia neglects the role of recognition in consolidating claims to Statehood. Although, in theory, recognition is of purely declaratory nature,[37] it cannot be seriously argued that a State is an

---

in M. Kohen (ed.), *Secession: International Law Perspectives*, (Cambridge: Cambridge University Press, 2006), p. 138.

35 This is not to suggest that an entity that fulfils the factual requirements enunciated in the Montevideo Convention will *necessarily* achieve Statehood. In practice, recognition by other States plays an important role in consolidating claims to Statehood, as it will be discussed below. In modern State practice, it seems that recognition is not solely based on the existence of the factual elements of Statehood. A whole host of additional considerations, such as the existence of democratic institutions, respect for human rights and the protection of minorities, may lead a State to grant or withhold recognition See for example the EC Guidelines on the Recognition of New States in Eastern Europe and in the Soviet Union, 16 December 1991, available at http://207.57.19.226/journal/Vol4/No1/art6.html. See also J. Vidmar, *supra* note 34, pp. 137–8. However, it would be unfair to assume that, because modern recognition practice goes beyond the traditional criteria for Statehood, these criteria have become redundant. Rather, this recent trend highlights the fact that recognition is determined by both legal and political factors. See C. Ryngaert, S. Sobrie, Recognition of States: International Law or Realpolitik? The Practice of Recognition in the Wake of Kosovo, South Ossetia and Abkhazia, 24 *LJIL* 467 (2011), pp. 483–4.

36 See the Oral Statements made by Norway in the Verbatim Record of the Public Sitting held on Wednesday 9 December 2009, at 10 a.m., at the Peace Palace, in the *Kosovo Advisory Opinion*, CR 2009/31, available at http://www.icj-cij.org/docket/files/141/15728.pdf, p. 46; the Oral Statements made by France, *ibid.*, p. 9; and the Oral Statements made by Finland in the Verbatim Record of the Public Sitting held on Tuesday 8 December 2009, at 10 a.m., at the Peace Palace, in the *Kosovo Advisory Opinion*, CR 2009/30, available at http://www.icj-cij.org/docket/files/141/15726.pdf, p. 57.

37 Art. 6 of the Montevideo Convention, *supra* note 23. See also Opinion No. 1 of the Badinter Commission, *supra* note 33, p. 1495: "The Committee considers...that the effects of recognition by other states are purely declaratory." On the different theories on recognition see T. Grant, *The Recognition of States: Law and Practice in Debate and Evolution*, (Westport: Praeger Publishers, 1999), pp. 1–18.

entity that can effectively enter into relations with other States when it has received recognition by none or very few States. This proposition has found support both in practice and in the literature. The Supreme Court of Canada, in its judgment in the *Quebec Secession Reference Case*, expressly declared that: "Although recognition by other states is not, at least as a matter of theory, necessary to achieve statehood, the viability of a would-be state in the international community depends, as a practical matter, upon recognition by other states."[38] Similarly, the Independent International Fact-Finding Mission on the conflict in Georgia stressed that "even if recognition has only declaratory value, the recognition of an entity as a state by other states can give a certain evidence of its legal status as a state."[39] The lack of widespread recognition was specifically mentioned in the Mission's Report as evidence that neither South Ossetia nor Abkhazia have acquired the status of a State under international law.[40] As far as doctrine is concerned, even avowed 'declaratorists', such as Crawford, have accepted that recognition plays an important role in solidifying claims to Statehood in modern State practice.[41]

The stark contrast between successful secessionist attempts, such as Kosovo and Bangladesh on the one hand, and unsuccessful ones, such as Abkhazia and Biafra on the other, evidences the crucial role played by recognition in modern State practice.[42] All four cases involved disputed claims to Statehood. In all these cases the granting or withholding of recognition tipped the balance

38 *Reference re Secession of Quebec, supra* note 33, para. 142.

39 Report of the Independent International Fact-Finding Mission on the Conflict in Georgia, *supra* note 33, p. 129.

40 *Ibid.* See also the decision of the Tribunal in *Caglar vs Billingham (Inspector of Taxes)* 108 *ILR* 510 (1996), at p. 545: "In view of the non-recognition of the Turkish Republic of Northern Cyprus by the whole of the international community other than Turkey we conclude that it does not have functional independence as it cannot enter into relations with other States."

41 J. Crawford, *supra* note 14, p. 74. See also J. Klabbers, *International Law*, (Cambridge: Cambridge University Press, 2013), p. 73.

42 It would be beyond the scope of the present work to provide a detailed account of these four instances of unilateral secession. However, all of them have attracted much scholarly attention and thus, the relevant territory is fairly well chartered. For Bangladesh see J. Dugard, D. Raic, *The Role of Recognition in the Law and Practice of Secession*, in M. Kohen (ed.), *supra* note 34, p. 94 at pp. 120–3; J. Crawford, *supra* note 14, p. 393. For Kosovo see P. Hipold (ed.), *Kosovo and International Law: The ICJ Advisory Opinion of 22 July 2010*, (Leiden: M. Nijhoff, 2012); J. Almqvist, *The Politics of Recognition: The Question about the Final Status of Kosovo*, in D. French (ed.), *supra* note 17, p. 165. For Abkhazia see J. Dugard, D. Raic, *ibid.*, pp. 113–9; G. Bolton, *International Responses to the Secession Attempts of Kosovo*, Abkhazia and South Ossetia 1989–2009, in D. French (ed.), *ibid.*, p. 109. For Biafra

either in favour or against the creation of new States.[43] However, to ignore the effects of recognition – by zooming in on the day that a given declaration of independence is made – would effectively mean that the legal status of Kosovo, which has been formally recognised by 110 States,[44] would have to be judged on an equal footing with that of Biafra, which at the time, received a mere five recognitions.[45]

This is not to say that recognition alone is sufficient for an entity to achieve Statehood. However, to completely remove recognition from the picture would be to divorce law from reality. From this divorce the only injured party would be the former. As shown in previous chapters, by way of contrast to other normative orders, such as religion and morality, the law derives its authoritativeness *inter alia* from the fact that it remains relevant and that it reflects the realities on the ground of practice.[46] From the moment law becomes an outdated system that has lost touch with reality there is no guarantee that States would feel compelled to obey to rules that do not actually reflect their own practice. In the words of Jennings: "*Ex factis jus oritur* is an expression of a truth that no law can ignore save at its own peril."[47]

Thirdly and more importantly, the thesis that unilateral declarations of independence constitute, in essence, unilateral juridical acts rests on shaky evidentiary grounds. As previously mentioned, proponents of this view have relied on the fact that, on a number of occasions, the SC has condemned particular declarations of independence as evidence that international law treats such declarations as unlawful in certain circumstances.[48] The language employed in the resolutions may, at first glance, imply that the declarations of independence in question were considered contrary to international law. For example, the SC referred to the declarations of independence by Southern Rhodesia and by the Turkish Republic of Northern Cyprus as "legally invalid."[49]

---

see J. Crawford, *supra* note 14, p. 406; D.A. Ijalaye, Was "Biafra" at Any Time a State in International Law? 65 *AJIL* 551 (1971).

43 J. Dugard, D. Raic, *supra* note 42, pp. 96–7.

44 According to 'Who Recognized Kosova as an Independent State? The Kosovar People Thank You!', available at: www.kosovothanksyou.com.

45 D.A. Ijalaye, *supra* note 42, pp. 553–6.

46 M. Koskenniemi, *The Politics of International Law*, (Oxford: Hart Publishing, 2011), p. 39.

47 R. Jennings, *Nullity and Effectiveness in International Law*, R. Jennings *et al.* (eds.), *Cambridge Essays in International Law: Essays in Honour of Lord McNair*, (London: Stevens, 1965), p. 64, at p. 74.

48 Written Comments by Serbia, *supra* note 2, paras. 208–10.

49 (Southern Rhodesia) SC Res. 216 (1965), *supra* note 28; (Turkish Republic of Northern Cyprus) SC Res. 541 (1983), *supra* note 30.

However, a careful examination of the context within which these resolutions were issued allows for different conclusions. At first, in none of the debates on the SC resolutions regarding Katanga, Southern Rhodesia or the Turkish Republic of Northern Cyprus was the illegality of the declarations of independence raised *per se*.[50] Loutfi, representative of the United Arab Republic, made the only reference to the issue of illegality of unilateral declarations of independence in the context of the debate on the resolution on Katanga.[51] However, Loutfi expressly stated that the Katangan declaration of independence was illegal as a matter of Congolese, and therefore domestic, law.[52] No single reference to international law rules prohibiting unilateral declarations of independence can be found in the records of the meetings that preceded the adoption of the SC resolutions in question.

Furthermore, the argument that the SC has, on occasion, treated specific unilateral declarations as unlawful *per se* under international law is paradoxical in the light of the aim of the resolutions in question. More particularly, if we accept that the SC considered that a particular entity was acting illegally under international law, then we need to accept that the SC considered that entity as a subject of international law. However, the very aim of the resolutions cited above was to deny these entities legal status under international law.[53] It would be odd if the SC accepted that an entity had legal personality as a subject – and was thus, able to commit an internationally wrongful act – when the aim of the resolutions was precisely to deny such entities the capacity to become subjects of international law.

The eminently political nature of the UN bodies needs to be also taken into account in interpreting the terms contained in the resolutions at hand.[54] The SC is not a court. Thus, the 'invalidity' attached by this body to certain unilateral declarations of independence does not necessarily coincide with the juridical concept of 'invalidity.' As Talmon aptly notes, SC statements "that a 'declaration of independence' is totally invalid must be viewed in the context

50 All verbatim records of SC meetings can be accessed here http://www.un.org/en/sc/meetings/searchrecords.asp.

51 Statement by Mr Loutfi (United Arab Republic) in SC, 974th Meeting, UN Doc. S/PV.974 (15 November 1961) paras. 34–5.

52 *Ibid.*

53 J. Crawford, *supra* note 14, p. 389.

54 M.C. Wood, The Interpretation of Security Council Resolutions, 2 *Max Planck Encyclopedia of United Nations Law* 73 (1998), at p. 80; A. Orakhelashvili, *The Interpretations of Acts and Rules in Public International Law*, (Oxford: Oxford University Press, 2008), pp. 487–93.

of other such pronouncements."[55] Talmon cites a number of other acts that have been characterised as 'invalid' by the SC such as certain legislative and administrative measures; elections and their results; all statements by a State repudiating its foreign debt; and all acts taken by a government on behalf of or concerning a territory.[56] In all these instances, as is the case with the resolutions at hand, the SC did not invoke a concrete legal basis to justify its pronouncement of 'invalidity.'[57] This however, does not accord with the stringent procedural safeguards associated with the concept of nullity in law.[58] Thus, it seems that where a sound legal basis is absent, it would be a bridge too far to assume that 'invalid' is tantamount to 'absolute invalidity' in the legal sense of the term. As Tancredi stresses: "A void character does not represent the automatic effect of the resolution which contains the declaration of invalidity and the demand for non-recognition, since there is no organ having compulsory jurisdiction, endowed with the power to annul wrongful acts (and certainly the UN organs are not empowered to do so)."[59] Rather, in such cases, the use of the term 'invalid' by the SC, or other UN organs, indicates that "*they* do not (or will not) treat as valid an act that has already taken place or will take place in the future."[60] In other words, rather than equating the above SC resolutions to judicial pronouncements of absolute nullity, the better view is that these simply reflect the SC's strong disapproval of certain acts.

Conversely, had these resolutions actually invalidated the declarations of independence by Katanga, Southern Rhodesia and the Turkish Republic of Northern Cyprus, there would be no need to insert therein any requests for

---

55 S. Talmon, The Constitutive versus the Declaratory Doctrine of Recognition: Tertium non Datur? 75 *BYIL* 101 (2004), at p. 142.

56 *Ibid.*

57 *Ibid.*

58 See Art. 62 of the Draft Articles on the Law of Treaties, with Commentaries, *Yrbk of the ILC* 1966, Vol. II, p. 262; R. Jennings, *supra* note 47; J.A. Frowein, Nullity in International Law, 3 *Encyclopedia of Public International Law* 743 (1997).

59 A. Tancredi, *A Normative 'Due Process' in the Creation of States through Secession*, in M. Kohen, *supra* note 34, p. 171, at p. 200.

60 S. Talmon, *supra* note 55, p. 143. (Emph. added). See also the comments made by J. D'Aspremont, as representative of Burundi in Verbatim Record of the Public Sitting held on 4 December 2009, at 10 a.m., at the Peace Palace, in *Kosovo Advisory Opinion*, CR 2009/28, available at: http://www.icj-cij.org/docket/files/141/15718.pdf, p. 29, fn. 24. "Whereas, on occasion, the Security Council has condemned the adoption of a declaration of independence...nothing justifies the conclusion that, in these cases, any judgment of validity was made...by condemning a declaration of independence, the Security Council is merely expressing its disapproval."

non-recognition. In other words, if the declarations in question were automatically null and void, there would be nothing left for States to recognise and, thus, no need to impose a duty of non-recognition. However, in all these resolutions, the SC invariably requested Member States not to recognise the entities in question and/or to refrain from rendering any assistance to them.[61] This argument was also made by D'Aspremont, in his capacity as representative of Burundi, during the *Kosovo Advisory Opinion* proceedings:

> It is indeed because the Security Council generally adds sanctions to its condemnation, that its action does not equate to any form of invalidation. If the Council had "invalidated" the declaration of independence which it condemned, the latter would have ceased to exist and it would not have been necessary to adopt any sanctions whatsoever.[62]

Another weakness of relying on the aforementioned practice of the SC in order to argue that international law prohibits unilateral declarations of independence is that such arguments tend to overlook the actual reasoning used in these resolutions to justify the finding of 'invalidity.' More particularly, it is logical to expect that if there is a rule of international law outlawing declarations of independence, the SC would have expressly invoked it in order to justify why certain declarations are invalid. However, any reference to a rule of international law prohibiting declarations of independence is patently absent from the resolutions in question. More particularly, the justification for declaring the declaration of independence by the Turkish Republic of Northern Cyprus legally invalid[63] was that it was incompatible with the 1960 Treaty concerning the establishment of the Republic of Cyprus[64] and with the 1960 Treaty of Guarantee.[65] In relation to the resolution on Southern Rhodesia, the SC determined that the situation *resulting* from the declaration

61 SC Res. 216 (1965), *supra* note 28, (Southern Rhodesia): "T*he Security Council…Decides to call upon* all States not to recognize this illegal minority regime in Southern Rhodesia and to refrain from rendering any assistance to this illegal regime."; SC Res. 541 (1983), *supra* note 30, (Turkish Republic of Northern Cyprus): "The Security Council…*Calls upon* all States not to recognize any Cypriot State other than the Republic of Cyprus."; SC Res. 169 (1961), *supra* note 29, (Katanga): "*The Security Council…Requests* all States to refrain from the supply of arms, equipment or other material which could be used for warlike purposes…"

62 Comments by J. D'Aspremont, as representative of Burundi, *supra* note 60.

63 SC Res. 541 (1983), *supra* note 30.

64 *Treaty Concerning the Establishment of the Republic of Cyprus*, 16 August 1960, Nicosia, 382 UNTS 215.

65 *Cyprus Treaty of Guarantee*, 16 August 1960, Nicosia, 382 UNTS 8.

of independence constituted a threat to international peace and security before concluding that it was legally invalid.[66] As far as the resolution on Katanga is concerned, the SC strongly deprecated the secessionist movement as contrary to the Congolese Constitution and as having been carried out with the aid of external intervention.[67]

To sum up: (a) the inability to reconcile the contention that the SC considered the declarations in question as unlawful *per se* with the overall aim of the SC resolutions; (b) the fact that the SC did not invoke a concrete legal basis for invalidating acts emanating from a non-State actor; (c) and the actual reasoning used to justify the condemnation of these declarations all corroborate the view that the relevant practice of the SC cannot serve as evidence that international law prohibits such declarations in certain circumstances. What the text of the relevant SC resolutions shows is that, on occasion, the SC has attempted to regulate the *acceptance* of such declarations by imposing on its Member States the obligation not to recognise certain entities and/or to refrain from rendering any assistance to them.[68]

Vidmar has questioned this proposition, arguing that, under certain circumstances, a declaration of independence itself (and not only its acceptance) is illegal under international law.[69] Vidmar's argument can be broken down as follows: first, he draws a distinction between declarations of independence issued by "random groups" and those issued by representatives of an entity which meets or is capable of meeting the effectiveness criteria under the Montevideo Convention.[70] Only the latter, are in his view, acts regulated by international law and capable of being unlawful. Secondly, he claims that such declarations of independence, *i.e.* the ones issued by a (potentially) effective entity, are unlawful where they attempt "to consolidate an effective territorial situation created in breach of a norm of [*jus cogens*] character."[71]

In order to substantiate his argument, Vidmar relies on the abovementioned practice of the SC and on a passage from the *Kosovo Advisory Opinion*. More particularly, he suggests that the independence of the Turkish Republic of Northern Cyprus and of Southern Rhodesia would consolidate an otherwise

66 SC Res. 217 (1965), *supra* note 28.

67 SC Res. 169 (1961), *supra* note 29.

68 See commentary to Art. 41 in Draft Articles on Responsibility of States for Internationally Wrongful Acts, with Commentaries, UN Doc. A/56/10, *Yrbk of the ILC* 2001, Vol. II, p. 59, at p. 289, para. 8.

69 J. Vidmar, Conceptualising Declarations, *supra* note 17.

70 *Ibid.*, p. 159.

71 *Ibid.*, p. 177.

unlawfully created territorial situation.[72] Thus, the fact that the SC characterised them as invalid means that it perceived them as having been issued in violation of a fundamental norm of international law.[73] He further contends that the following observation made by the Court in the *Kosovo Advisory Opinion* confirms his argument:

> The illegality attached [to some other] declarations of independence thus stemmed not from the unilateral character of these declarations as such, but from the fact that they were, or would have been, connected with the unlawful use of force or other egregious violations of norms of general international law, in particular those of a peremptory character (*jus cogens*).[74]

This position is riddled with logical inconsistencies and rests on thin evidentiary foundations. First, there is something intrinsically problematic in suggesting that a prohibition only applies to entities that "meet or are likely to meet the Montevideo criteria." How would we know that an entity has reached that threshold? As shown above, in the absence of a central authority that would objectively determine Statehood, recognition serves as evidence that an entity has fulfilled the Montevideo criteria. How would this be extrapolated to Vidmar's schema? Would States recognise an entity simply for the purpose of attributing an internationally unlawful act to it? Would the SC be tasked with determining the effectiveness of every single group claiming independence and on what legal basis? Furthermore, making the applicability of a prohibition contingent upon the effectiveness of a subject would insert a degree of subjectivity to the prohibition incompatible with the objectivity expected of legal rules.[75] Vidmar fails to explain *why* declarations of independence stemming from effective entities are the only ones that come within the purview of international law. The position that international law contains a limited prohibition of such declarations was also challenged by Crawford, as representative of the UK, during *the Kosovo Advisory Opinion* proceedings: "But does international law only condemn declarations of independence when made by representative bodies and not, for example, by military movements? Does

72 *Ibid.*, pp. 171–4.

73 *Ibid.*

74 *Kosovo Advisory Opinion, supra* note 1, para. 81.

75 On the objectivity of legal rules, see M. Koskenniemi, *From Apology to Utopia: The Structure of International Legal Argument*, reissued with new epilogue, (Cambridge: Cambridge University Press, 2007), p. 24.

international law only condemn declarations of independence that are likely to be effective?"[76]

Secondly, even if it is accepted that non-State actors are bound by *jus cogens* rules – a highly disputed proposition in itself that Vidmar omits to justify[77] – the link between the breach of the rule and the conduct of the entity is too tenuous to justify attributing liability to the latter. More particularly, Vidmar argues that the declaration of independence by the Turkish Republic of Northern Cyprus was illegal because it resulted from Turkey's illegal use of force.[78] This would, however, amount to attributing liability to an entity for a breach committed by another subject and it would be at variance with the rules of attribution under the law of State responsibility.[79]

Thirdly, Vidmar's argument is predicated on the allegedly breached norm having attained the status of a *jus cogens* norm at the time that the declaration of independence is made. However, there is little evidence to suggest that at the time that the declaration of independence of Southern Rhodesia was issued in November 1965,[80] self-determination had attained that status. The discussions in the ILC during its 1966 session evidence that the right to self-determination was not one of the most "obvious and settled rules of *jus cogens*"[81] and it was not until well into the 1970s that it was widely recognised as having attained the status of a *jus cogens* norm.[82]

76 Comments by J. Crawford, as representative of the UK, Verbatim Record of the Public Sitting held on Thursday 10 December 2009, at 10 a.m., at the Peace Palace, in *Kosovo Advisory Opinion*, CR 2009/32, available at http://www.icj-cij.org/docket/files/141/15734.pdf, p. 47.

77 For the difficulties of holding non-State actors bound by international law obligations, see J. Klabbers, *(I Can't Get No) Recognition: Subjects Doctrine and the Emergence of Non-State Actors*, in J. Klabbers, J. Petman (eds.), *Nordic Cosmopolitanism: Essays in International Law for Martti Koskenniemi*, (Leiden: M. Nijhoff, 2003), p. 351.

78 J. Vidmar, Conceptualising Declarations, *supra* note 17, pp. 171–2.

79 See Art. 2 of the Draft Articles on Responsibility of States for Internationally Wrongful Acts, with Commentaries, *supra* note 68, pp. 34–6.

80 On Southern Rhodesia's declaration of independence, see C.P. Watts, *Rhodesia' Unilateral Declaration of Independence: An International History*, (New York: Palgrave Macmillan, 2012), p. 1.

81 S. Talmon, *supra* note 55, p. 131; see also Report of the ILC on the Work of Its 18th Session, UN Doc. A/CN.4/SER.A/1966/Add.l, *Yrbk of the* ILC 1966, Vol. II, p. 248.

82 S. Talmon, *ibid.*; M. Pomerance, *Self-Determination in Law and Practice: The New Doctrine in the United Nations*, (The Hague: M. Nijhoff, 1982), pp. 70–2; S.P. Sinha, Has Self-Determination become a Principle of International Law Today? 17 *Indian JIL* 332 (1974), at pp. 332–56.

All in all, it seems that Vidmar's thesis is only supported by the abovementioned dictum of the Court in the context of the *Kosovo Advisory Opinion*. However, upon closer inspection, it seems that even this dictum is open to interpretation. More particularly, in the text of the judgment directly preceding the dictum in question, the Court indicated that the SC has, on occasion, condemned particular declarations of independence, but that "in all those instances the Security Council was making a determination as regards *the concrete situation existing at the time* that those declarations of independence were made."[83] This shows that, in the Court's view, the SC, in condemning particular declarations of independence, was primarily concerned with the circumstances surrounding the making of the declarations, rather than with the declarations themselves. Furthermore, the use of the word "condemning" instead of "invalidating" evidences that the Court was cautious in ascribing legal effects to these resolutions.

4 The Claim That Unilateral Declarations of Independence are Not Regulated by International Law

The previous section established that claims according to which unilateral declarations of independence are, entirely or partly, regulated by international law fall short of convincing to the extent that they ignore the legal context within which these declarations are made, they do not take into account the identity of their authors as non-State entities and they rest on shaky logical and evidentiary grounds. Against that background, this section will explore the claim that these declarations fall outside the ambit of international law. It will be argued that this claim carries more persuasive force than the ones described above and is supported by relevant practice.

The position that unilateral declarations of independence are not regulated by international law comports with the widely held view that the creation of a State is a matter of fact, rather than law. According to this schema, declarations of independence are a means by which an entity puts forward a claim of Statehood, that other States may accept or reject, but are not in and of themselves a means of creating a State under international law. As Crawford noted in the proceedings before the Court: "A declaration issued by persons within a State is a collection of words writ in water; it is the sound of one hand clapping. What matters is what is done subsequently, especially the reaction of the

83 *Kosovo Advisory Opinion, supra* note 1, para. 81. (Emph. added).

international community."[84] A number of States (including Norway, France, Jordan, the United States and Croatia) also shared the view that declarations of independence are mere political pronouncements and as such they are not regulated by international law.[85] Most importantly, the authors of the 2008 Kosovar Declaration of Independence themselves did not consider the Declaration to produce any legal effects:

> Although the declaration of independence doubtless aimed at that result [Statehood], it was not the declaration that achieved it under international law. Therefore, it is wrong to maintain that the declaration has an effect under international law, and consequently is subject to that law, because the representatives of the Kosovo people expressed their wish to create a sovereign State.[86]

State practice also supports the aforementioned proposition, namely that declarations of independence, far from constituting unilateral legal acts, are not regulated by international law. Although – as it was shown above – it is true that the SC has condemned specific declarations of independence in the past, those declarations were never characterised as unlawful *per se*. Rather than treating them as internationally wrongful acts, as it would have been the case if declarations of independence were regulated by international law, the SC merely obliged other States not to recognise the entities in question and /or to refrain from rendering any assistance to them.[87]

An overview of modern declarations of independence yields the same results. The numerous proclamations of independence made in the early 1990s by entities that wished to secede from the then Socialist Federal Republic of Yugoslavia are further examples of the political, rather than legal, nature of unilateral declarations of independence.[88] The claims of Statehood made by Slovenia, Croatia, Bosnia and Herzegovina *etc.* were the object of close scrutiny

84 See the comments made by J. Crawford, as representative of the UK, *supra* note 76, p. 47.

85 See the statements made by Norway, *supra* note 36; the statements made by Jordan, *supra* note 36, p. 38, para. 42; the statements made by France, *supra* note 36, p. 5, para. 12; the statements made by the US in Verbatim Record of the Public Sitting held on Tuesday 8 December 2009, *supra* note 36.

86 See the statements made by the authors of the 2008 Declaration of Independence, in Verbatim Record of the Public Sitting held on Tuesday 1 December 2009, *supra* note 25, p. 37.

87 See *supra*, fn. 61.

88 J. Crawford, *supra* note 14, pp. 395–401.

both by the UN and the EU.[89] However, these claims were never discussed in terms of 'lawful' and 'unlawful.' The Arbitration Commission of the Conference on Yugoslavia (more widely known as the Badinter Commission) was set up by the EU Council in 1991 to provide legal advice to the Conference on Yugoslavia and delivered a number of opinions regarding the requests for recognition by entities in the territory of the SFRY.[90] However, the Badinter Commission never discussed or even raised the question of the lawfulness or unlawfulness of the relevant declarations of independence.[91] In the same vein, the Independent International Fact Finding Mission on the conflict in Georgia did not treat the Abkhazian and the South Ossetian declarations as wrongful acts, although it concluded that the entities in question did not have a right to remedial secession.[92]

Moreover, apart from the *Kosovo Advisory Opinion*, the question of illegality of unilateral declarations of independence also arose in the context of the *Application of the Convention on the Prevention and Punishment of the Crime of Genocide Case.*[93] Yugoslavia contended in its preliminary objections that, "Bosnia and Herzogovina...has never been established in the territory and in the form in which it pretends to exist since its illegal declaration of independence."[94] However, the Court treated the declaration as a matter of fact and rejected that objection.[95]

The argument that international law does not regulate unilateral declarations of independence is also supported by the opinions of the international law experts[96] in the context of the *Reference re Secession of Quebec Case.* According to the experts, secession is a matter that falls within the domestic jurisdiction of the metropolitan State and is not regulated by international

89 *Ibid.*

90 Badinter Commission Opinions, *supra* note 33.

91 See the comments made by J. Crawford, as representative of the UK, *supra* note 76, p. 49, para. 14.

92 Report of the Independent International Fact-Finding Mission on the Conflict in Georgia, *supra* note 33, pp. 144–7.

93 *Case concerning Application of the Convention on the Prevention and Punishment of the Crime of Genocide, ICJ Reports* 1996, p. 595.

94 *Ibid.*, pp. 604–5.

95 *Ibid.*, p. 623, para. 47; see also the comments made by J. Crawford, as representative of the UK, *supra* note 76, para. 16.

96 The opinions of the experts have been reproduced in A.F. Bayefsky (ed.), *Self-Determination in International Law: Quebec and Lessons Learned: Legal Opinions*, (The Hague, M. Nijhoff, 2000).

law.[97] If secession is not regulated by international law, then it is safe to assume that the act by which an entity secedes from the metropolitan State, *i.e.* the declaration of independence, is not regulated by international law either. According to Franck: "It cannot seriously be argued that international law *prohibits* secession. It cannot be seriously argued that international law *permits* secession…the law imposes *no duty* on any people not to secede."[98] Similarly, Abi-Saab noted that "but while international law does not recognize a right of secession outside the context of self-determination, this does not mean that it prohibits secession. The latter is basically a phenomenon not regulated by international law."[99] In this light, it becomes apparent that the view that unilateral declarations of independence fall outside the purview of international law is well-grounded in practice.

5 Conclusion

This chapter explored the question of the juridical nature of unilateral declarations of independence. It was shown that the ICJ's *Kosovo Advisory Opinion* left more questions unanswered than answered. The chapter demonstrated that, by failing to examine whether international law is neutral towards unilateral declarations of independence, the ruling of the Court is of little assistance is establishing the legal character of unilateral declarations of independence. It was further shown that arguments according to which unilateral declarations of independence are (entirely or partly) regulated by international law are largely misguided to the extent that they do not take into account the context within which these declarations are made, they neglect the identity of their authors as non-State entities and they are based on an erroneous understanding of the relevant SC practice. It was claimed that the proposition that international law is legally neutral towards unilateral declarations of independence has more persuasive force since it accords both with the factual nature of the process of attaining Statehood and with the relevant practice.

97 J. Crawford, *Report by James Crawford: Response to Experts Reports of the Amicus Curiae*, in A.F. Bayefsky, *ibid.*, p. 161.

98 T.M. Franck, *Report by Thomas M. Franck: Opinion Directed at Question 2 of the Reference*, in A.F. Bayefsky, *ibid.*, p. 79.

99 G. Abi-Saab, *Report by George Abi-Saab: The Effectivity required of an Entity that Declares its Independence in Order for it to be Considered a State in International Law*, in A.F. Bayefsky (ed.), *ibid.*, pp. 72–3.

What does this conclusion about the non-legal nature of unilateral declarations of independence entail for the theory of unilateral acts propounded in the present work? If, in the case of unilateral declarations of independence, the intention to create legal effects does not actually produce the purported legal effects (Statehood), does this mean that one of the main arguments of the book – that intention confers legal character to a unilateral act – is erroneous? The present author emphatically argues that it is not. On the contrary, this conclusion validates the contextual approach adopted here. This work advocates that intention is indeed the criterion for distinguishing between legal and non-legal acts of unilateral origin *as long as that intention does not conflict with other pre-existing rules of international law*. Therefore, all conclusions reached in the previous chapters regarding the legal nature of unilateral acts are premised on the understanding that the act in question is in conformity with relevant rules of international law. Consequently, when judging the legal character of an act issued by an entity purporting to achieve Statehood one would need to take the applicable rules into account. Accordingly, such rules would not allow the creation of a State simply through an act of will.

CHAPTER 8

A Brief Excursus to Unilateral Security Assurances

1 Introduction

Having explored the question of the legal nature of unilateral declarations of independence, this chapter turns to unilateral security assurances. The legal nature of unilateral security assurances, namely unilateral guarantees in the form of oral or written declarations given by nuclear weapon States (NWS)[1] to non-nuclear-weapon ones (NNWS), under which the former undertake to assist them in case of a nuclear attack (positive security assurances) or not to use or threaten to use such weapons against them (negative security assurances), has been the subject of fierce debate since the 1970s. While some international lawyers consider them legally binding and on a par with the French guarantees given in the context of the *Nuclear Tests Cases*,[2] others perceive them as mere political statements and thus, incapable of producing any legal effects.[3] In the same vein, international jurisprudence is of little avail in clarifying the legal status of these assurances. The ICJ, in its *Advisory Opinion on the Legality of the Threat or Use of Nuclear Weapons*, took note of such assurances, but refrained from drawing specific legal consequences from them.[4] At the same time,

1 According to the definition of 'nuclear-weapon States' under Art. 9.3 of the *Treaty on the Non-Proliferation of Nuclear Weapons*, 1 July 1968, 729 UNTS 161 (NPT), the NPT NWS are: Russia, France, the UK, the US and China. India and Pakistan are not parties to the NPT but have openly declared that they posses nuclear weapons. See S. Khan, *Nuclear Weapons and Conflict Transformation: the case of India-Pakistan*, (New York: Routledge, 2008), p. 84. Israel is widely believed to have nuclear weapons, although it maintains a policy of 'nuclear opacity.' See A. Cohen, *Israel and the Bomb*, (New York: Columbia University Press, 1998). North Korea, which withdrew from the NPT in 2003, has also openly declared that it has manufactured nuclear weapons. See http://www.washingtonpost.com/wp-dyn/articles/A12836-2005Feb10.html. My analysis will focus on the security assurances given by the NPT NWS since these have triggered – and remain at the center of – the relevant debate.

2 See for example C. Eckart, *Promises of States under International Law*, (Oxford: Hart Publishing, 2012), p. 165.

3 See for example, B. Fihn, The Conference on Disarmament and Negative Security Assurances, March 2011, available at http://www.unidir.org/files/publications/pdfs/the-conference-on-disarmament-and-negative-security-assurances-369.pdf; J. Goldbat, *Negative Security Assurances*, in A. Nikitin (ed.), *Lessons to be Learned from Non-Proliferation Failures and Successes*, (Amsterdam: IOS Press, 2009), p. 64, at p. 67.

4 *Legality of the Threat or Use of Nuclear Weapons, Advisory Opinion*, *ICJ Reports* 1996, p. 226.

 | DOI 10.1163/9789004300767_010

the need to shed light on the juridical nature of these assurances is as great as ever. Although NNWS have long insisted on the incorporation of such assurances in international agreements,[5] NWS have not yielded much ground over the years. The relevant discussions both within the context of the Conference of Disarmament (CD) and of the Non Proliferation Treaty (NPT) Review Conferences have reached a deadlock and efforts to persuade NWS to provide assurances by means of regional agreements have had limited success.[6]

In this light, this chapter purports to revisit the question of the legal nature of unilateral security assurances and more particularly the question as to whether and under which circumstances these assurances may be considered as binding upon their author States. The long and complex history of unilateral security assurances has been set out in detail elsewhere.[7] It suffices to mention here that the relevant debate largely revolves around three sets of assurances, namely the ones given by the US, the UK and the USSR in 1968, the ones given by all five NPT NWS in the period between 1978 and 1982 and the ones given in 1995. Thus, the chapter will mainly focus on these three sets of assurances – with occasional references to subsequent declarations strengthening the already existing ones, such as the ones made by the US and the UK in 2010. For reasons of methodological clarity, the chapter is divided in two sections: the first section will analyse the juridical character of positive security assurances, whereas the second will deal with the same question in the context of negative

5 See for example the Memorandum circulated by Nigeria during the Fourth NPT Review Conference in 1990 and the Proposed Agreement contained therein in Consideration of Proposed Agreement on the Prohibition of the Use or Threat of Use of Nuclear Weapons Against Non-Nuclear-Weapon States Parties to the Treaty on the Non-Proliferation of Nuclear Weapons (Proposal by Nigeria), Fourth NPT Review Conference, UN Doc. NPT/CONF.IV/17 (1990), pp. 2 *et seq.*

6 A number of regional agreements have been concluded establishing Nuclear Weapon Free Zones (NWFZS). These agreements include protocols on security assurances for the NWS to sign and ratify. For an overview, see G. Venturini, Control and Verification of Multilateral Treaties on Disarmament and Non-Proliferation of Weapons of Mass Destruction, 17 *U.C. Davis J. Int'l L. & Pol'y* 345 (2011), pp. 359–62. However, only Additional Protocol II to the Treaty for the Prohibition of Nuclear weapons in Latin America and the Caribbean (Treaty of Tlatelolco) has been signed and ratified by all five NPT NWS. For the text of the Additional Protocol II, see *Additional Protocol II to the Treaty for the Prohibition of Nuclear Weapons in Latin America and the Caribbean*, 14 February 1967, available at http://disarmament.un.org/treaties/t/tlateloco_p2. For the text of the Treaty of Tlatelolco, see *Treaty for the Prohibition of Nuclear Weapons in Latin America and the Caribbean*, 14 February 1967, available at http://www.nti.org/media/pdfs/Treaty_of_Tlatelolco.pdf?_=1316643635.

7 See generally T. Bernauer, *Nuclear Issues on the Agenda of the Conference on Disarmament*, (Geneva: United Nations Institute for Disarmament Research Centre, 1991).

security assurances. It will be argued that, while their content and scope leaves much to be desired, unilateral security assurances may be validly considered as internationally binding instruments. The chapter will conclude by stressing the importance of conceptualising negative and positive security assurances within the framework of unilateral juridical acts for the purpose of enhancing their importance as a non-proliferation tool.

2 Positive Security Assurances: 1968–1995

As mentioned earlier, the term 'positive security assurances' is used in nuclear diplomacy jargon to connote promises of assistance made by NWS to NNWS in case of nuclear attacks. Such promises go as far back as the 1960s. Against the backdrop of China's first nuclear tests, US President Johnson stated in 1964 that "nations that do not seek nuclear weapons can be sure that if they need our strong support against some threat or nuclear blackmail, then they will have it."[8] This broadly construed and vaguely worded statement gave little by way of reassurance to NNWS but paved the way for the 1968 statements by the US, the UK and the USSR. The latter were made just a few days before the NPT opened for signature.[9] More particularly, they were provided as an incentive for NNWS to join the NPT – despite the fact that such assurances were not part of the treaty. As France expressed its intention not to join the treaty at the time and China was not as yet a member of the UN, the three remaining NWS chose not to incorporate such assurances into the text of the treaty itself.[10] At the same time they were very well aware of the fact that NNWS would not be amenable to forgoing nuclear weaponry without anything in return. In order to solve this conundrum, the UK, the US and the USSR made oral declarations before the UN Security Council (SC) providing positive security assurances to NNWS that would join the NPT.

Ambassador Goldberg made the following declaration on behalf of the US:

> The Government of the United States notes with appreciation the desire expressed by a large number of States to subscribe to the treaty on the

8 J.A. Simpson, *The Role of Security Assurances in the Nuclear Nonproliferation Regime*, in J.W. Knopf (ed.), *Security Assurances and Nuclear Nonproliferation*, (Stanford: Stanford University Press, 2012), p. 57 at p. 60.

9 G. Bunn, R. Timmerbaev, Security Assurances to Non-Nuclear Weapon States: Possible Options for Change, 7 *PPNN Issue Review* 1 (1996), at p. 1.

10 J.A. Simpson, *supra* note 8, pp. 61–2.

> non-proliferation of nuclear weapons,...The United States also notes the concern of certain of these States that, in conjunction with their adherence to the treaty on the non proliferation of nuclear weapons, appropriate measures be undertaken to safeguard their security...The United States affirms its intention, as a permanent member of the United Nations Security Council, to seek immediate Security Council action to provide assistance, in accordance with the Charter, to any non-nuclear-weapon State party to the treaty on the non-proliferation of nuclear weapons that is a victim of an act of aggression or an object of a threat of aggression in which nuclear weapons are used.[11]

Identical declarations were made by the USSR and the UK.[12] These declarations were then incorporated into SC resolution 255/1968.[13] According to Res. 255/1968, the SC "*welcomes* the intention expressed by certain States that they will provide or support immediate assistance, in accordance with the Charter, to any non-nuclear-weapon State party to the Treaty on the Non-Proliferation of Nuclear Weapons that is a victim of an act or an object of a threat of aggression in which nuclear weapons are used."[14]

First, it needs to be observed that viewing these declarations as anything but unilateral in origin would amount to stretching the limits of interpretation to a breaking point. Although they were related to the NPT treaty, they were not made within a context of negotiations, nor were they phrased as an offer the acceptance of which would render them effective. On the contrary, they were made as a 'stand-alone' commitment to NNWS party to the NPT after the failure of the latter to convince NWS to include a clause on assurances in the treaty itself.[15] Thus, the language of the declarations and the historical context within which they were made verify their unilateral character.

Turning to the question of the binding effects of the 1968 declarations, it seems that both their content and the context within which they were made indicate an intention to become bound, as this element was defined in

11 US Arms Control and Disarmament Agency, *Documents on Disarmament* (1968), available at http://www.un.org/disarmament/publications/documents_on_disarmament/1968/DoD_1968.pdf, pp. 439–40.

12 *Ibid.*, p. 439.

13 SC, Res. 255, UN Doc. S/RES/255 (1968). France along with India, Pakistan, Algeria and Brazil abstained from voting. *Ibid.*

14 *Ibid.*, para. 2.

15 G. Nustyen, T. Graff Hugo, *The Nuclear Non-Proliferation Treaty*, in G. Nystuen *et al.* (ed.), *Nuclear Weapons Under International Law*, (Cambridge: Cambridge University Press, 2014), p. 374, at p. 384.

Chapters 5 and 6. The clear and specific language employed; the forum within which the declarations were made, *i.e.* the SC; the fact that these were later incorporated in a SC resolution; and the fact that they were made by official representatives of the countries in question corroborate the view that, indeed, these statements expressed the manifest intention of their authors to become bound thereby. Thus, from an instrument perspective, the unilateral form of the assurances does not affect their binding force.

What is, however, problematic is the *scope* of obligations undertaken thereunder: the 1968 security assurances merely reaffirm already existing obligations of the author States under the UN Charter. This point was also stressed by the French representative before the SC in justifying France's voting abstention: "It is not the French delegation's intention that that abstention should constitute an obstacle to the adoption of a draft *that in no way changes the provisions of Chapter VII of the Charter*, as is clear from the very contents of the draft, from the declared intentions of its sponsors...."[16] The failure to go beyond already existing obligations also features in the literature as one of the main shortcomings of the 1968 assurances.[17] Other oft-cited shortcomings include: the fact that the resolution seems to have given NWS the freedom to take collective military action without consulting the target State;[18] the fact that the resolution did not specify what kind of assistance would be provided to the

16 US Arms Control and Disarmament Agency, *supra* note 11, p. 442. (Emph. added).

17 See for example N. Elaraby, *Some Reflections on Disarmament*, in C. Tomuschat (ed.), *The United Nations at Fifty: A Legal Perspective*, (The Hague: Kluwer Law International, 1995), p. 9 at p. 19; J.A. Simpson, *supra* note 8, p. 62; B. Tertrais, *Security Assurances and the Future of Proliferation*, in J.W. Knopf (ed.), *supra* note 8, p. 240 at p. 249; T. Bernauer, *supra* note 7, p. 4.

18 See for example the statements by Austria and Switzerland during the Second NPT Review Conference in 1980. According to Austria: "...a country like Austria, which had committed itself to a status of permanent neutrality, could not agree to confer upon an outside Power the responsibility for the maintenance of its own security. Austria had therefore expressed strict reservations concerning so-called positive security assurances. It must be stated clearly that it was for the Country which was the victim of an act of aggression, or of the threat of such act, to decide by itself whether, and to what extent, any assistance offered in that regard would be accepted." Summary Record of the 6th Meeting of Committee 1, Second NPT Review Conference, UN Doc. NPT/CONF.II/C.I/SR.6 (1980), p. 196. Similarly, Switzerland declared that "only so-called negative security assurances were acceptable to Switzerland as a neutral State. Positive assurances of assistance to a State attacked or threatened by nuclear weapons would not be compatible with Switzerland's status of neutrality." *Ibid.*, p. 189. N. Elaraby, *ibid.*; D. Fleck, Second Report on Legal Aspects of Nuclear Disarmament, International Law Association Committee on Nuclear Weapons, Non Proliferation and Contemporary International Law, Washington

target State;[19] and the fact that, in reality, any act triggering the obligation to assist a target State under the resolution could only emanate from a NWS and thus, the same State could veto any response to such act in its capacity as a permanent member of the SC.[20] The picture that emerges is that the widely acknowledged problems associated with the 1968 positive security assurances concern the substance and scope of the obligations undertaken thereunder, rather that the legal status of the instrument by means of which they were created.

The same observations can be made regarding the 1995 positive assurances given by NWS on the path to the extension of the NPT Treaty. Just a few days prior to the crucial 1995 NPT Review Conference, where the question of extending the treaty indefinitely would be decided, each of the official NWS made declarations containing both positive and negative security assurances. These were largely identical and were communicated as official UN documents.[21] For example, the UK stated that:

> In 1968 the United Kingdom declared that aggression with nuclear weapons, or the threat of such aggression, against a non-nuclear-weapon State would create a qualitatively new situation in which the nuclear-weapon States which are Permanent Members of the United Nations Security Council would have to act immediately through the Security Council to take the measures necessary to counter such aggression or to remove the threat of aggression in accordance with the United Nations Charter, which calls for taking "effective collective measures for the prevention

Conference Report (2014), available at http://www.ila-hq.org/en/committees/index.cfm/cid/1025, para. 16.

19 N. Elaraby, *ibid.*

20 B. Tertrais, *supra* note 17, p. 249.

21 See Letter dated 6 April 1995 from the Permanent Representative of the Russian Federation to the United Nations addressed to the Secretary-General, UN Doc. S/1995/261 (1995) for the Russian declaration; Letter dated 6 April 1995 from the Permanent Representative of the United Kingdom of Great Britain and Northern Ireland to the United Nations addressed to the Secretary-General, UN Doc. S/1995/262 (1995) for the British declaration; Letter dated 6 April 1995 from the Chargé d'affaires a.i. of the Permanent Mission of the United States of America to the United Nations addressed to the Secretary-General, UN Doc. S/1995/263 (1995) for the US declaration; Letter dated 6 April 1995 from the Permanent Representative of France to the United Nations addressed to the Secretary-General, UN Doc. S/1995/264 (1995) for the French declaration and Letter dated 6 April 1995 from the Permanent Representative of China to the United Nations addressed to the Secretary-General, UN Doc. S/1995/265 (1995) for the Chinese declaration.

> and removal of threats to the peace, and for the suppression of acts of aggression or other breaches of the peace." Therefore, any State which commits aggression accompanied by the use of nuclear weapons or which threatens such aggression must be aware that its actions are to be countered effectively by measures to be taken in accordance with the United Nations Charter to suppress the aggression or remove the threat of aggression. I, therefore, recall and reaffirm the intention of the United Kingdom, as a Permanent Member of the United Nations Security Council, to seek immediate Security Council action to provide assistance, in accordance with the Charter, to any non-nuclear-weapon State, party to the Treaty on the Non-Proliferation of Nuclear Weapons, that is a victim of an act of aggression or an object of a threat of aggression in which nuclear weapons are used.[22]

The SC adopted resolution 984/1995 repeating almost verbatim the relevant part of the corresponding 1968 resolution and, once again, welcomed "the intention expressed by certain States that they will provide or support immediate assistance, in accordance with the Charter, to any non-nuclear-weapon State Party to the Treaty on the Non-Proliferation of Nuclear Weapons that is a victim of an act of, or an object of a threat of, aggression in which nuclear weapons are used."[23] Again, the same conclusions drawn in relation to the 1968 declarations may be repeated here. While the language and the context within which the 1995 declarations were made lend support to the view that they evidence the manifest intention of their authors to be bound, the content and scope of obligations undertaken thereunder are problematic to the extent that they do not add anything to pre-existing obligations under the Charter.

3 Negative Security Assurances

3.1 *The 1978–1982 Negative Security Assurances*

The 1968 positive assurances fell short of NNWS expectations and the topic resurfaced during the 1975 NPT Review Conference. The statement made by the representative of Nigeria, Mr Clark, is characteristic of the mood prevailing among NNWS at the time: "The so-called guarantees of the three nuclear weapon States Parties to the Treaty supposed to be embodied in SC resolution 255 (1968) seemed to deceive no one. That resolution was now significant

22 See S/1995/262, *ibid.*

23 SC, Res. 984, UN Doc. S/RES/984 (1995).

only for its historical and sentimental value."[24] In the light of the reluctance of NWS to commit themselves to providing assistance beyond the Charter's prescriptions, it was felt that another type of assurances, namely negative ones, would prove more effective. The Finnish representative stated in this respect:

> From the beginning, a number of non-nuclear-weapon States had expressed misgivings about the effectiveness of the security assurances given in Security Council Resolution 255 (1968). Some of these States had expressed a preference for "negative assurances", whereby nuclear-weapon States would commit themselves never to use nuclear weapons against non-nuclear-weapon States.[25]

In the face of mounting pressure, the US, the UK, China and the USSR gave a first set of negative security assurances during the First Special Session of the UN General Assembly (GA) devoted to Disarmament in 1978. These were neither uniform, nor – with the exception of the Chinese declaration – unqualified. It is worth quoting the relevant passages in full. The Soviet Union declared that "it will never use nuclear weapons against those States which renounce the production and acquisition of such weapons and do not have them on their territories."[26] The British and the American assurances were similar in content. More particularly, the British representative made a pledge to:

> [N]on-nuclear weapon States that are parties to the Treaty on the Non-Proliferation of Nuclear Weapons and to other internationally binding commitments not to manufacture or acquire nuclear explosive devices: Britain undertakes not to use nuclear weapons against such States except in the case of an attack on the United Kingdom, its dependent territories,

24 Statement by the representative of Nigeria, Mr Clark in Summary Record of the 7th Plenary Meeting, First NPT Review Conference, UN Doc. NPT/CONF/SR.7 (1975), p. 84.

25 Statement by the Finnish representative, Mr Hyväriven, in First NPT Review Conference in Summary Record of the 4th Meeting of Committee 1, First NPT Review Conference, UN Doc. NPT/CONF/C.1/SR.4 (1975), p. 168. For similar statements see for example the statement by the Syrian representative, Mr El-Fattal in Summary Record of the 8th Plenary Meeting, First NPT Review Conference, UN Doc. NPT/CONF/SR.8 (1975), p. 98 and the statement by the representative of New Zealand, Mr Roberts in Summary Record of the 9th Plenary Meeting, First NPT Review Conference, UN Doc. NPT/CONF/SR.9 (1975), p. 108.

26 Statement by the USSR, May 1978, as quoted in T. Bernauer, *supra* note 7, p. 8.

> its armed forces or its allies by such a State in association or alliance with a nuclear-weapon State.[27]

In a similar fashion, the US stated that they:

> [W]ill not use nuclear weapons against any non-nuclear-weapon State party to the non-proliferation Treaty or any comparable internationally binding commitment not to acquire nuclear explosive devices, except in the case of an attack on the United States, its territories or armed forces, or its allies, by such a State allied to a nuclear-weapon State or associated with a nuclear-weapon State in carrying out or sustaining the attack.[28]

China was the only State to offer an unconditional assurance. It undertook that "at no time and in no circumstances will it be the first to use nuclear weapons."[29] France, at the time, did not follow the lead of the rest of the NWS and simply indicated its willingness to give such assurances in the future "in accordance with arrangements to be negotiated, to States which constitute non-nuclear zones."[30] However, in 1982, France gave an assurance that emulated the 1978 Anglo-American formulation: "For its part, [France] states that it will not use nuclear arms against a State that does not have them and that has pledged not to seek them, except if an act of aggression is carried out in association or in alliance with a nuclear-weapon State against France or against a State with which France has a security commitment."[31] The final document of the 1978 G.A. Session made a reference to the negative security assurances given by the NWS. Paragraph 59 of that document reads:

> In the same context, the nuclear-weapon States are called upon to take steps to assure the non-nuclear-weapon States against the use or threat of use of nuclear weapons. The General Assembly notes the declarations made by the nuclear-weapon States and urges them to pursue efforts to

27 As quoted in Developments with Regard to Effective International Arrangements to Assure Non-Nuclear-Weapon States Against the Use or Threat of Use of Nuclear Weapons, 1995 NPT Review and Extension Conference, UN Doc. NPT/CONF.1995/6 (1995), p. 8.

28 *Ibid.*

29 *Ibid.* In April 1982 China added the following to its 1978 declaration: "[China] undertakes unconditionally not to use or threaten to use nuclear weapons against non-nuclear countries and nuclear-free zones." As quoted in T. Bernauer, *supra* note 7, p. 7.

30 *Ibid.*, p. 7.

31 *Ibid.*, p. 8.

> conclude, as appropriate, effective arrangements to assure non-nuclear-weapon States against the use or threat of use of nuclear weapons.[32]

What is the legal status of the 1978 assurances? Were these assurances binding upon their authors, or were they mere political statements? The language of the G.A.'s final document is quite circumspect. The fact that NWS were urged to conclude 'effective arrangements' seems to suggest that their recipients did not consider the 1978 assurances 'effective' enough. However, ineffective does not necessarily mean non-binding. Thus, no definite conclusions about the legal status of the assurances can be drawn from the actual text of the 1978 final document.

George Bunn, in his commentary on the 1978 assurances, concludes that they are binding and ascribes their binding force to estoppel.[33] This position does not seem to be convincing. As mentioned in Chapter 4, estoppel in international law requires not simply reliance, but *detrimental* reliance on behalf of the addressee. According to Crawford: "The essence of estoppel is the element of conduct which causes the other party, in reliance on such conduct, detrimentally to change its position or to suffer some prejudice."[34] Here, there is little evidence to suggest that NNWS relied upon the 1978 assurances or, for that matter, that any such reliance was to their detriment. The cautious language of the GA's final document, whereby NWS were 'urged' to conclude effective arrangements to reassure NNWS, is an indication that NNWS were far from satisfied with the negative assurances provided. Furthermore, subsequent debates within the context of the NPT Review Conferences clearly demonstrate that the majority of NNWS did not consider the 1978 assurances as binding undertakings.[35]

There are also *de lege ferenda* reasons for disassociating the binding force of negative security assurances from any type of reliance or acceptance on the

32 GA, Final Document of the Tenth Special Session of the General Assembly, UN Doc. A/RES/S-10/2 (1978), para. 59.

33 G. Bunn, The Legal Status of U.S. Negative Security Assurances to Non-Nuclear Weapon States, 4 *The Nonproliferation Review* 1 (1997), p. 9.

34 J. Crawford, *Brownlie's Principles of Public International Law*, 8th ed., (Oxford: Oxford University Press, 2012), p. 420.

35 See for example the statements made by Nigeria, New Zealand and Kenya during the 1980 NPT Review Conference, in Summary Record of the 8th Plenary Meeting, Second NPT Review Conference, UN Doc. NPT/CONF.II/SR.8 (1980); Summary Record of the 9th Plenary Meeting, Second NPT Review Conference, UN Doc. NPT/CONF.II/SR.9 (1980); Summary Record of the 11th Plenary Meeting, Second NPT Review Conference, UN Doc. NPT/CONF.II/SR.11 (1980), respectively.

part of NNWS. As it is evident from their text and as it will be explained below, the 1978 negative security assurances contained a wide spectrum of qualifications. If the only way to view them as binding would be through the operation of estoppel, this would affect the negotiating power of NNWS: if such assurances are only binding to the extent that they have been relied upon, NNWS would have to show some element of reliance in order to be able to claim their binding effect later on. This would, however, mean in practice that NNWS would have to settle for much less than what they wanted – or even deserved, if one takes into account the obligations undertaken by these States under the NPT.

Turning back to the question of the legal status of the 1978 assurances, a perusal of relevant literature reveals that the debate has been obfuscated by the conflation of two distinct questions, namely the question of the content and scope of these assurances and that of their legal character.[36] However, this approach is not methodologically sound. Ascertaining the existence of an obligation and ascertaining the content of that obligation are two separate operations. As far as the content of the 1978–1982 declarations is concerned, this certainly leaves much to be desired. First, these declarations were not uniform in scope and, thus, not all NNWS could benefit from all of them simultaneously. Only the Chinese declaration was addressed to all NNWS. The Anglo-American declarations were addressed to NNWS parties to the NPT; the French one to NNWS that did not seek to acquire nuclear weapons; and the Soviet one to NNWS that did not seek to produce or acquire such weapons and did not have them on their territory.

A further weakness of the 1978–1982 assurances lies in the broad scope of the qualifications contained therein. More particularly, the permissibility of the use or the threat of use of nuclear weapons in case of an attack by a NNWS "in association or in alliance" with a NWS raises a number of problems. The term 'attack' is not clearly defined and it could be construed very broadly to include even conventional attacks.[37] Similarly, the words 'in association' or 'in alliance' with a NWS raise questions regarding the precise degree of involvement needed to allow nuclear retaliation. On the face of it, it seems that this formulation would allow nuclear retaliation in case of an attack by a NNWS allied to a NWS – even in the absence of knowledge of the attack by the NWS ally of the attacking State.[38] While the Soviet declaration did not

36 For an account of the different variables to be taken into consideration in addressing the question of negative security assurances, see A. Rosas, Negative Security Assurances and Non-Use of Nuclear Weapons, 25 *German YIL* 199 (1982), p. 204.

37 A. Rosas, *ibid.*, p. 207; T. Bernauer, *supra* note 7, p. 10.

38 C. Eckart, *supra* note 2, p. 162; A. Rosas, *ibid.*; T. Bernauer, *ibid.*, p. 18.

contain a 'non-attack' condition, it did contain a 'non-stationing' condition that is equally problematic. The difficulties raised by the Soviet condition were highlighted by the UK in a working paper submitted to the CD in 1981.[39] First, the Soviet declaration gave no indication as to how it would be possible to verify in practice the absence of nuclear weapons from the territory of a given State.[40] Secondly, a number of NPT NNWS, most notably Germany, would not be able to benefit from the Soviet assurance since they had nuclear weapons stationed on their territories on the basis of security arrangements with NATO.[41]

All in all, it seems that dissatisfaction with the content and scope of the 1978–1982 assurances is justified. With the exception of China, the assurances given by the remaining NWS were shaped by their respective nuclear military doctrines and allowed them ample room for manoeuvre. However, does this mean that the assurances in question, unsatisfactory as they may be, are not binding upon their authors? An examination of the wording and context within which they were made shows that this is not the case. First, the language of the declarations is the language commonly employed in the creation of legal obligations. The Chinese assurance expressly states that "China undertakes unconditionally not to use or threaten to use nuclear weapons."[42] Similarly, the British, American, Soviet and French assurances explicitly articulate a commitment not to use nuclear weapons except in certain scenarios envisaged thereunder.[43] Furthermore, the assurances were given before a UN body. This has significant evidentiary weight in establishing the element of the intention to be bound according to the Court's judgment in the *Armed Activities Case*. It also needs to be noted that the persons who offered the assurances on behalf of the NWS in question were all official representatives of their States to the UN and that the 1982 French assurance emanated from the Minister for Foreign Affairs of France.[44]

More importantly, two NWS, the US and the UK, have drawn attention to the fact that the formal status of their assurances would not be enhanced through the conclusion of an international agreement – thereby confirming

39 Working Paper Submitted by the UK, UN Doc. CD/177 (10 April 1981) as quoted in T. Bernauer, *ibid.*, pp. 72–5.

40 *Ibid.*, p. 74.

41 *Ibid.*

42 See *supra* note 21.

43 *Ibid.*

44 T. Bernauer, *supra* note 7, p. 8.

the binding character of their unilateral declarations.[45] During the 1980 NPT Review Conference, the US representative stated that he:

> [C]ould not agree with the view expressed by a number of delegations in the general debate that negative security assurances required further strengthening, in particular, through the negotiation of a common formula which could be embodied in a binding international convention. *So far as the United States declaration was concerned, no further steps were necessary to make it a credible and effective assurance. The declaration had been issued by the president of the United States after careful consideration of all its implications, and could and should be regarded as a firm and reliable statement*...The desire for greater uniformity in the assurances available to non-nuclear weapon States was understandable but the prospects for working out a common formula had to be gauged realistically.[46]

The US has repeatedly stressed the binding character of its 1978 assurance. In 1994 the US delegation at the CD stated that "the United States of America recalled its solemn and binding security assurances of 1978, a position that had been reiterated by every subsequent Administration."[47] Similarly, the UK, in its 1981 working paper on negative security assurances discussed within the context of the CD, stressed that:

> Much of the discussion about security assurances has been concerned with the possibility of making them "legally binding." The United Kingdom has always made it clear that its assurance was solemnly and formally given...*The United Kingdom doubts the need for any...enhancement of its own assurance since it already regards it as a solemn undertaking*. As has been constantly stressed, the assurance took effect immediately [at the moment] it was given. There is no requirement for Non-Nuclear-Weapon States, in order to benefit from the assurance, to conclude a bilateral agreement, to adhere to a yet-to-be-concluded convention, or for there to be some other form of joint action by the Nuclear-Weapon States.[48]

---

45 A. Rosas, *supra* note 36, p. 208.

46 Statement by the US Representative in Summary Records of the 6th Meeting of Committee 1, *supra* note 18, p. 191 (Emph. added).

47 Report of the Ad Hoc Committee on Effective International Arrangements to Assure Non-Nuclear-Weapon States Against the Use or Threat of Use of Nuclear Weapons, 1994 Conference on Disarmament, UN Doc. CD/1275 (1994), para. 25.

48 Working Paper Submitted by the UK, *supra* note 39, pp. 74–5. (Emph. added).

Again, in 1994, the UK stressed "the continued validity of their unilateral security assurances which were solemn and formal undertakings."[49]

Russia, France and China have also expressly declared that they consider their unilateral assurances binding. In discussions within the context of the CD, France stated that it "fulfilled its *obligations* since it already granted security assurances to non nuclear-weapon States which had undertaken to retain that status"[50] and China "reiterated its *commitment* that in no time, and under no circumstances, would it be the first to use nuclear weapons, and that it would not use nuclear weapons against non-nuclear-weapon States and nuclear weapon-free zones."[51] In the same context, Russia "reiterated the *legally-binding character* of the unilateral Russian declaration on NSA."[52]

The proposition put forward here, namely that, while the 1978 assurances left much to be desired content-wise, they did evidence the manifest intention of their authors to be bound is also shared by some NPT NNWS. Switzerland, Austria and Italy explicitly referred to the doctrine of unilateral juridical acts in explaining why, in their opinion, the 1978 assurances had binding force on the international plane. During the 1980 NPT Review Conference, Switzerland stated that:

> [T]he nuclear Powers have, through unilateral declarations, renounced the use or threat of use of nuclear weapons against non-nuclear weapon States. *These declarations are legal undertakings which are binding upon their authors.* The form of the unilateral undertaking is well-known in international law, as was confirmed by the International court of Justice in the case of nuclear explosions in the Pacific. It is desirable that these undertakings should be further strengthened and some of the texts concerned rendered more precise.[53]

In a similar fashion, the Austrian delegation took "note with satisfaction of the respective unilateral declarations issued by the Governments of nuclear weapon States…and joined Switzerland in regarding those declarations

49 1994 Report of the Ad Hoc Committee on Effective International Arrangements to Assure Non-Nuclear-Weapon States Against the Use or Threat of Use of Nuclear Weapons, *supra* note 47, para. 24.

50 *Ibid.*, para. 23. (Emph. added).

51 *Ibid.*, para. 26.

52 *Ibid.*, para. 28.

53 Statement by Switzerland in Summary Record of the 5th Meeting of Committee 1, Second NPT Review Conference, UN Doc. NPT/CONF.II/C.I/5 (1980) (Emph. added).

binding upon the respective Powers under international law."[54] In the framework of discussions within the CD on the legal value of the 1978 assurances, the Italian delegation quoted the judgment of the Court in the *Nuclear Tests case* and stated that "under international law, unilateral declarations might contain a binding obligation insofar as a clear commitment can be drawn by their wording."[55] Furthermore, this position has also found support in literature: Rosas,[56] Bernauer[57] and Eckart,[58] in their commentaries on the 1978–1982 assurances, have concluded that the main weaknesses of those assurances do not lie in their (lack of) binding force, but in their content and scope.

Finally, it is interesting to note that even negative security assurances contained in instruments of undoubtedly binding character, *i.e.* protocols attached to international agreements, raise problems in practice. A good example here is Additional Protocol II to the Treaty of Tlatelolco which has been signed and ratified by all five NPT NWS. Under Art.3 of the Additional Protocol, the five NWS have undertaken not to use or threaten to use nuclear weapons against the contracting parties to the treaty.[59] However, upon signing and ratifying the Additional Protocol, all NWS – with the exception of China – made certain interpretative statements that closely resemble the qualifications entered in their 1978–1982 unilateral assurances.[60] For example, in ratifying Additional Protocol II, the UK stated in 1969 that it would "in the event of any act of aggression by a Contracting Party to the Treaty in which that Party was supported by a nuclear-weapon State, be free to reconsider the extent to which they could be regarded as committed by the provisions of Additional Protocol II."[61] However, these statements seriously modify the scope of obligations undertaken under Art. 3 and thus, are more akin to reservations, rather than mere interpretative statements.[62] This, in turn,

54 Statement by Austria in Summary Record of the 6th Meeting of Committee 1, *supra* note 18, p. 195.

55 Report of the Ad Hoc Committee on Effective International Arrangements to Assure Non-Nuclear-Weapon States against the Use or Threat of use of Nuclear Weapons, 1993 Conference on Disarmament, UN Doc. CD/1219 (1993), para. 24.

56 A. Rosas, *supra* note 36, p. 208.

57 T. Bernauer, *supra* note 7, p. 9.

58 C. Eckart, *supra* note 2, p. 163.

59 Art. 3 of Additional Protocol II to the Treaty of Tlatelolco, *supra* note 6.

60 For the text of the interpretative statements in question, see T. Bernauer, *supra* note 7, pp. 8–9.

61 *Ibid.*, p. 9.

62 A. Rosas, *supra* note 36, p. 213.

raises its own set of problems to the extent that Art. 4 of Additional Protocol II prohibits reservations. This brief excursus to negative security assurances contained in treaties verifies the conclusions drawn above, namely that the problems pertaining to security assurances are essentially problems of content and not problems of form.

3.2 *The 1995 Negative Security Assurances*

In the aftermath of the GA's First Special Session on Disarmament the topic of negative security assurances lost some of its salience. The relevant debate was transferred to the CD and an ad hoc committee on negative security assurances was established. However, the ad hoc committee failed to make progress and it soon reached a stalemate.[63] The topic regained momentum on the eve of the NPT Review and Extension Conference. As mentioned above, in 1995 the nuclear powers circulated renewed positive and negative security assurances. The French, British, American and Russian assurances were practically identical, thereby alleviating some of the problems associated with the 1978 declarations. For example, the US assurance reads:

> The United States reaffirms that it will not use nuclear weapons against non-nuclear-weapon States Parties to the Treaty on the Non-Proliferation of Nuclear Weapons except in the case of an invasion or any other attack on the United States, its territories, its armed forces or other troops, its allies, or on a State towards which it has a security commitment, carried out or sustained by such a non-nuclear-weapon State in association or alliance with a nuclear-weapon State.[64]

China reaffirmed its no-first-use commitment[65] and added that it "undertakes not to use or threaten to use nuclear weapons against non-nuclear-weapon

63 See for example the conclusions of the 1993 Report of the Ad Hoc Committee on Effective International Arrangements to Assure Non-Nuclear-Weapon States against the Use or Threat of use of Nuclear Weapons where it is stated that "the complex nature of the issues involved, as well as, *inter alia*, differing perceptions of security interests continued to impede the work on the substance of the effective arrangements and the search for a common formula." *Supra* note 55, para. 26.

64 S/1995/263, *supra* note 21. For the text of the French, British and Russian negative assurances see *ibid.*

65 S/1995/265, *supra* note 21.

States or nuclear-weapon-free zones at any time or under any circumstances."[66] SC resolution 984/1995 took note with appreciation of the declarations.[67]

The 1995 declarations improved on existing assurances in so far as their contents were harmonised and the conditions contained therein clarified. More particularly, the 'non-attack' condition was narrowed down to attacks "carried out" or "sustained" in association with a NWS ally. This clarification ended the long-standing controversy over the degree of involvement needed to trigger nuclear retaliation. According to the 1995 formulation, the attack itself needs to be carried out by a NNWS in association with its NWS ally. Thus, mere knowledge of the attack by a NWS ally is not enough to precipitate nuclear reprisals. Furthermore, as a result of the harmonisation of the contents of the assurances, the 'non-stationing' condition was omitted from the text of the Russian declaration. However, the French, Russian, American and British assurances still left much to be desired. By way of contrast to the Chinese declaration, the rest of the assurances were neither unconditional, nor did they include a no-first-use commitment. As such, they failed to assuage the misgivings of NNWS.[68] The NNWS' discontent was reflected in the second decision adopted by the 1995 Conference. Decision 2 para. 8 reads:

> Noting United Nations Security Council resolution 984 (1995) which was adopted unanimously on 11 April 1995, as well as the declarations of the nuclear-weapon States concerning both negative and positive security assurances, further steps should be considered to assure

66 *Ibid.* China clarified that its "commitment naturally applies to non-nuclear-weapon States parties to the Treaty on the Non-Proliferation of Nuclear Weapons or non-nuclear-weapon States that have entered into any comparable internationally-binding commitment not to manufacture or acquire nuclear explosive devices."

67 S/RES/984 (1995), *supra* note 23.

68 See for example Working Paper Submitted by Egypt on Security Assurances to Non-Nuclear-Weapon States, 1995 NPT Review and Extension Conference, UN Doc. NPT/CONF.1995/MC.I/WP.4 (1995), p. 290: "However, resolution 984 (1995) and the unilateral declarations issued by the permanent members of the Security Council, with the exception of the declaration issued by the People's Republic of China, continue to fall short of the general expectations of non-nuclear-weapon States and leave much to be desired to bestow credibility on the assurances they offer." See also the statement made by Indonesia during the Conference: "The recent declarations issued by the nuclear Powers had failed to assuage the apprehensions of non-nuclear-weapon States, which had long demanded legally binding commitments…States which had renounced the manufacture or acquisition of nuclear weapons had the inherent right to receive unconditional and legally binding assurances." Summary Record of the 3rd Plenary Meeting, 1995 NPT Review and Extension Conference, UN Doc. NPT/CONF.1995/SR.3 (1995), pp. 34–5.

> non-nuclear-weapon States party to the Treaty against the use or threat of use of nuclear weapons. *These steps could take the form of an internationally legally binding instrument.*[69]

The text of Decision 2 leaves no doubt that the recipients of the 1995 assurances were not convinced of their binding force. *On this basis, Cedeño, the* Special Rapporteur of the ILC on unilateral acts, concluded that "the attitude of the authors and the positions of most States appear to reflect the political nature of these statements."[70] However, to what extent are the reactions of the addresses of a unilateral act relevant in establishing whether the act has legal effects? Would the attitude of the beneficiaries of the 1995 assurances preclude an international adjudicative body from concluding that the assurances have binding force? At this point it is worth recalling that in the *Nuclear Tests Case* the Court made it abundantly clear that unilateral acts do not need to be accepted by their addressees in order to have legal effects on the international plane.[71] Rather, as it was shown in Chapter 6, the determinant factor in attributing legal effects to unilateral acts is whether these acts manifest the intention of their authors to be bound according to their terms.

As far as the element of the intention to be bound is concerned, the remarks made in relation to the 1978 assurances are also pertinent here. The clear and specific wording of the 1995 assurances as well as the formal context within which they were made indicate that they are legal undertakings, rather than mere political statements.[72] The Court's *Advisory Opinion on the Legality of the Threat or Use of Nuclear Weapons* substantiates this proposition. Although the Court did not expressly pronounce upon the legal status of the 1995 assurances, it analysed them alongside relevant international agreements.[73] This approach shows that the Court considered the assurances on a par with applicable treaties.[74] The following unanimous finding also corroborates this view:

69 Decision 2: Principles and Objectives for Nuclear Non-Proliferation and Disarmament, 1995 NPT Review and Extension Conference, UN Doc. NPT/CONF.1995/32 (Part I), Annex (1995), para. 8 (Emph. added).

70 See V. Rodríguez Cedeño, Eighth Report on Unilateral Acts of States, UN Doc. A/CN.4/557, p. 119, at para. 115.

71 *Nuclear Tests Case*, Australia vs France, *ICJ Reports* 1974, p. 253.

72 The same view is also shared by C. Eckart, *supra* note 2, p. 166.

73 *Legality of the Threat or Use of Nuclear Weapons*, *supra* note 4, paras. 62–3.

74 C. Eckart, *supra* note 2, p. 166.

> A threat or use of nuclear weapons should also be compatible with the requirements of the international law applicable in armed conflict, particularly those of the principles and rules of international humanitarian law, *as well as with specific obligations under treaties and other undertakings which expressly deal with nuclear weapons.*[75]

Despite the fact that the Court placed unilateral assurances on the same footing as applicable international agreements, NNWS remain dissatisfied with the 1995 assurances. However, the problem lying at the heart of the debate on unilateral assurances appears to be the political, rather than the legal dimension of unilateralism. First, NNWS feel that they received very little in return for voluntarily renouncing their nuclear option. Secondly, the fact that these assurances were issued in the form of unilateral declarations has deprived NNWS from the opportunity of sitting at the negotiating table and shaping their contents alongside NWS. Repeated references to multilateralism in connection to negative security assurances reinforce this conclusion. For example, during the 1998 session of the CD, the governments of Brazil, Egypt, Ireland, Mexico, New Zealand, Slovenia, South Africa and Sweden issued a joint declaration stressing that "the maintenance of a world free of nuclear weapons will require the underpinnings of a universal and multilaterally negotiated legally binding instrument or a framework encompassing a mutually reinforcing set of instruments."[76] Similarly, in the 2012 working paper on negative security assurances submitted by Syria on behalf of member States of G-21, multilateralism was reaffirmed as the "core principle in resolving disarmament and non-proliferation concerns."[77]

However, it would be erroneous, in the opinion of the present author at least, to assume that assurances in the form of unilateral declarations are of minor importance in disarmament diplomacy. In hindsight, it seems that such instruments offered some level of reassurance at a time when the rigid nuclear postures of NWS precluded much else. Simultaneously, they provided a starting point for further discussion and debate. This allowed NNWS to exercise political pressure and, indirectly, to shape future assurances, as the harmonised

75 *Legality of the Threat or Use of Nuclear Weapons*, *supra* note 4, para. 105(2)(D).

76 Joint Declaration by the Ministers for Foreign Affairs of Brazil, Egypt, Ireland, Mexico, New Zealand, Slovenia, South Africa and Sweden, 1998 Conference on Disarmament, UN Doc. CD/1542 (1998), p. 2.

77 Working Paper Submitted by the Syrian Arab Republic on Behalf of Member States of G-21 on Prevention of an Arms Race in Outer Space, 2012 Conference on Disarmament, UN Doc. CD/1940 (30 August 2012), para. 7.

contents of the 1995 assurances evidence. This proposition is also verified by the latest British and American nuclear posture reviews, in which the 'non-attack' condition seems to have been dropped. According to the 2010 US Nuclear Posture Review:

> The United States is now prepared to strengthen its long-standing 'negative security assurance' by declaring that the United States will not use or threaten to use nuclear weapons against non-nuclear weapon states that are party to the NPT and in compliance with their nuclear non-proliferation obligations.[78]

In a similar vein, the British government stated in its 2010 Strategic Defence and Security Review that:

> We are now able to give an assurance that the UK will not use or threaten to use nuclear weapons against non-nuclear weapon States parties to the NPT. In giving this assurance, we emphasise the need for universal adherence to and compliance with the NPT, and note that this assurance would not apply to any State in material breach of those non-proliferation obligations.[79]

Finally, if one takes into account the problems pertaining to treaty-based security assurances as these were exemplified above, it is fair to say that, despite their shortcomings, unilateral assurances have proven to be a flexible and useful tool of non-proliferation policy.

4 Conclusion

This chapter explored the juridical nature of unilateral security assurances within the framework of the doctrine of unilateral acts of States. Both positive and negative security assurances were tested against the background of the

78 US Department of Defense, Nuclear Posture Review Report, April 2010, available at http://www.defense.gov/npr/docs/2010%20Nuclear%20Posture%20Review%20Report.pdf, p. viii.

79 UK Government, Securing Britain in an Age of Uncertainty: The Strategic Defense and Security Review, October 2010, available at https://www.gov.uk/government/publications/the-strategic-defence-and-security-review-securing-britain-in-an-age-of-uncertainty, p. 37.

doctrine of unilateral acts. It was shown that these assurances – despite their shortcomings in terms of scope and content – may be validly considered as binding undertakings to the extent that they express the manifest intention of their authors to be bound. On this basis, it was concluded that such assurances, when viewed from the perspective of unilateral juridical acts, play an important role in non-proliferation dynamics.

Conclusions

The main themes that the present book has examined revolve around the question of the legal nature of unilateral acts of States in international law: namely, the question as to whether and under which circumstances unilateral acts of States may produce binding effects in international law. From the outset, it was shown that providing answers to this question is of utmost importance in light of the widespread use of such acts in modern State practice and of the fact that the legal framework pertaining to them remains unclear.[1] This study reviewed the relevant judicial practice in order to identify, define and analyse the essential elements of the legal nature of unilateral acts. Moreover, it enquired into the validity and usefulness of examining the legal nature of unilateral acts within the framework of the theory of international juridical acts, as opposed to in the abstract, which has previously been the case. For this purpose, this work compared the ways in which international judicial bodies determine the legal nature of both unilateral acts and international agreements. By doing so, conclusions were drawn regarding the relevance of the theory of international juridical acts as a framework for analysis of all juridical acts.

The main argument propounded here is that unilateral acts can produce binding effects in international law if they possess two elements: (a) the element of unilateralism and (b) the element of the intention of the author State to become bound according to the terms of the act. Unilateral acts were defined, on the basis of these two elements, as acts that include the elements of unilateralism and intention to become bound.[2] In order to reach this definition, a number of definitions that have been proposed in the literature were reviewed and rejected on the grounds that they were too narrow to encompass all aspects of the phenomenon of unilateral acts and that they do not take into account the different legal environments in which such acts occur. By way of contrast, the book focused on the elements of the legal nature of these acts and produced the above definition that enjoys the benefit of accurately describing unilateral acts, while being broad enough to take into account the diverse legal environments in which such acts take place.

Turning to the essentials of the legal nature of unilateral acts, unilateralism was defined as the autonomy of an act to produce legal effects irrespective of acceptance or compliance by the addressee, based on the approach taken by

1 Chapter 1.
2 Chapter 2.

 | DOI 10.1163/9789004300767_011

international courts.[3] By doing this, this study gave a definitive answer to the question as to whether legal effects may be borne out of acts of a strictly unilateral nature. Furthermore, it provided a criterion – autonomy – in order to clearly distinguish between unilateral acts and other phenomena in international law, such as international agreements and estoppel.[4] It was also shown that unilateral acts are of a juridical nature when they manifest the intention of their authors to be bound. Thus, this work established the criterion of manifest intention as the criterion for differentiating between unilateral juridical acts and unilateral political acts.[5] Consequently, by focusing on manifest intention, the book (hopefully) provided new insight into the controversy surrounding the alleged subjectivity of the concept of unilateral acts.[6]

Owing to the difficulties associated with the task of determining whether a given act is a unilateral juridical one in practice, a main concern of this study was to provide practical tools for ascertaining the existence of the aforementioned elements of unilateralism and intention. This concern is highlighted by the weaknesses that were identified in the work of the ILC on unilateral acts and its final product, the 2006 Guiding Principles. The work of the ILC on the topic as well as the 2006 Guiding Principles were introduced and analysed and it was established that one of the major weaknesses of the Guiding Principles is the lack of practical guidance regarding the determination of the juridical character of a unilateral act.[7] It was argued that this weakness leaves the legal framework pertaining to unilateral acts disappointingly opaque.

In order to fill this gap, this study looked into the context in which these acts usually occur in practice and compiled a list of indicators of the elements of unilateralism and manifest intention.[8] As far as the element of unilateralism is concerned, it was claimed that the following indicators are of relevance: the absence of a treaty law context; the absence of a rule requiring reciprocity; the absence of a context of negotiations; the absence of a pattern of offer/acceptance; and the existence of circumstances that preclude the conclusion of an international agreement.[9] Moreover, it was argued that the content of the act, its publicity, the forum in which the act was made and the authority who made the act on behalf of the State may be relied upon to facilitate the

3 Chapter 4.
4 *Ibid.*
5 Chapters 5 and 6.
6 *Ibid.*
7 Chapter 3.
8 Chapters 4 and 6.
9 Chapter 4.

determination of the existence of the element of manifest intention.[10] It is envisaged that these indicators will be of significant assistance both to States and to practitioners in determining whether a given act may be considered as a unilateral act with legal effects on the international plane.

This study adopted the aforementioned contextual approach by way of a comparative analysis with the law of treaties. It was shown that the practical problem of establishing the juridical character of an act is one that permeates not only unilateral acts but also acts of a contractual nature: the proliferation of soft-law instruments and the declining importance of form in international law have made the distinction between legal and non-legal acts increasingly difficult for both unilateral acts and international agreements.[11] On this basis, this work examined the ways in which the problem of distinguishing between legal and non-legal acts has been tackled in the field of the law of treaties, since this is the area of law closest to that of unilateral acts in which this problem has arisen and resolved. It was shown that, in the field of the law of treaties, one way of solving the problem of establishing the manifest intention of the authors to be bound by an international agreement is by having recourse to the context in which the agreement occurred.[12] The same approach was applied to unilateral acts and it was asserted that the context in which a unilateral act occurs may provide significant evidence as to the existence of a manifest intent to be bound, as the aforementioned indicators demonstrate.[13] In doing so, this study proved the usefulness of the contextual approach as a tool for establishing the existence of international law obligations irrespective of their origin.

Furthermore, this work explored the juridical character of unilateral acts within the framework of the theory of international juridical acts; a theory which has attempted to bring together unilateral and bi/multilateral acts based upon the manifestation of intention to create legal effects and which has remained largely underdeveloped.[14] It was shown that international courts and tribunals not only apply the same criterion (intention) for determining the juridical character of both unilateral acts and international agreements, but also have recourse to the same means of establishing the existence of this criterion (interpretation of the act in accordance with its content and the context surrounding it).[15] Thus, it was argued that, in practice, international judicial

10 Chapter 6.

11 Chapters 5 and 6.

12 *Ibid.*

13 *Ibid.*

14 *Ibid.*

15 *Ibid.*

bodies treat unilateral acts and international agreements as two aspects of the same phenomenon, namely that of international juridical acts. In doing so, the book proved, through an examination of judicial practice, the validity of the theory of international juridical acts and thus, (hopefully) contributed to the development of this theory as a comprehensive framework for the analysis of juridical acts in international law.

Bibliography

Books

Abi-Saab G., *Report by George Abi-Saab: The Effectivity required of an Entity that Declares its Independence in Order for it to be Considered a State in International Law*, in A.F. Bayefsky (ed.), *Self-Determination in International Law: Quebec and Lessons Learned: Legal Opinions*, (The Hague, M. Nijhoff, 2000).

Almqvist J., *The Politics of Recognition: The Question about the Final Status of Kosovo*, in D. French (ed.), *Statehood and Self-Determination: Reconciling Tradition and Modernity in International Law*, (Cambridge: Cambridge University Press, 2013).

Attanasio J.B., Norton J.J. (eds.), *Multilateralism v. Unilateralism: Policy Choices in Global Society*, (London: British Institute of International and Comparative Law, 2004).

Aust A., *Modern Treaty Law and Practice*, 3rd ed., (Cambridge: Cambridge University Press, 2013).

Bayefsky A.F. (ed.), *Self-Determination in International Law: Quebec and Lessons Learned: Legal Opinions*, (The Hague, M. Nijhoff, 2000).

Beatson J., Burrows A., and Cartwright J., *Anson's Law of Contracts*, 29th ed., (Oxford: Oxford University Press, 2010).

Bernauer T., *Nuclear Issues on the Agenda of the Conference on Disarmament*, (Geneva: United Nations Institute for Disarmament Research Centre, 1991).

Bolton G., *International Responses to the Secession Attempts of Kosovo*, Abkhazia and South Ossetia 1989–2009, in D. French (ed.), *Statehood and Self-Determination: Reconciling Tradition and Modernity in International Law*, (Cambridge: Cambridge University Press, 2013).

Bos M.S., *A Methodology of International Law*, (Amsterdam: T.M.C. Asser Institute, 1984).

Boyle A., *Soft Law in International Law-Making*, in Evans M. (ed.), *International Law*, 4th ed., (Oxford: Oxford University Press, 2014).

Boyle A., Chinkin C., *The Making of International Law*, (Oxford: Oxford University Press, 2007).

Brierly J.L., *The Basis of Obligation in International Law*, (Oxford: Clarendon Press, 1958).

Brierly J.L., *The Law of Nations: An Introduction to the Law of Peace*, 6th ed., (Oxford: Oxford University Press, 1963).

Broelmann C., *The PCIJ and International Rights of Groups and Individuals*, in C. Tams, M. Fitzmaurice (eds.), *Legacies of the Permanent Court of International Justice*, (Leiden: M. Nijhoff, 2013).

Cappelletti M., Merryman J.H., and Perillo J.M., *The Italian Legal system: An Introduction*, (Stanford: Stanford University Press, 1967).

Carpentier J., *Engagements unilatéraux et engagements conventionnels: Différences et convergences*, in J. Makarczyk (ed.), *Theory of International Law at the Threshold of the 21st Century: Essays in Honour of K. Skubiszewski*, (The Hague: Kluwer Law International, 1996).

Carreau D., *Droit International*, (Paris: A. Pedone, 1988).

Cassese A., *International Law*, 2nd ed., (Oxford: Oxford University Press, 2005).

Chen T., *The International Law of Recognition*, (London: Stevens, 1951).

Cheng B., *General Principles of Law: As Applied by International Courts and Tribunals*, (London: Stevens & Sons, 1953).

Chorus J.M.J., Gerver P.H.M., and Hondius E.H., *Introduction to Dutch Law*, 4th rev. ed., (Deventer: Kluwer, 2006).

Christakis T., *The State as A 'Primary Fact': Some Thoughts on the Principle of Effectiveness*, in M. Kohen (ed.), *Secession: International Law Perspectives*, (Cambridge: Cambridge University Press, 2006).

Churchill R.R., Lowe A.V., *The Law of the Sea*, 3rd ed., (Manchester: Manchester University Press, 1999).

Clapham A., *Brierly's Law of Nations*, 7th ed., (Oxford: Oxford University Press, 2012).

Cohen A., *Israel and the Bomb*, (New York: Columbia University Press, 1998).

Combacau J., Sur S., *Droit international public*, (Paris: Montchrestien, 1993).

Cooke J., Oughton D., *The Common Law of Obligations*, 3rd ed., (Oxford: Oxford University Press, 2000).

Cordier A.W., Foote W., *Public Papers of the Secretaries General of the United Nations: 1956–7*, Vol. 3, (New York: Columbia University Press, 1973).

Craven M., *Statehood, Self-Determination, and Recognition*, in M. Evans (ed.), *International Law*, 4th ed., (Oxford: Oxford University Press, 2014).

Crawford J., *Report by James Crawford: Response to Experts Reports of the Amicus Curiae*, in A.F. Bayefsky (ed.), *Self-Determination in International Law: Quebec and Lessons Learned: Legal Opinions*, (The Hague, M. Nijhoff, 2000).

Crawford J., *The Creation of States in International Law*, 2nd ed., (Oxford: Clarendon Press, 2006).

Crawford J., *Brownlie's Principles of Public International Law*, 8th ed., (Oxford: Oxford University Press, 2012).

Cryer R., Hervey T., and Sokhi-Bulley B., *Research Methodologies in EU and International Law*, (Oxford: Hart Publishing, 2011).

D'Amato A., *The Concept of Custom In International Law*, (London: Cornell University Press, 1971).

D'Aspremont J., *Formalism and the Sources of International Law: A Theory of the Ascertainment of Legal Rules*, (Oxford: Oxford University Press, 2011).

Daillier P., Pellet A., *Droit International Public*, (Paris: LGDJ, 1999).

Danilenko G.M., *Law-Making in the International Community*, (Dordrecht: M. Nijhoff, 1993).

Degan V.D., *Sources of International Law*, (The Hague: M. Nijhoff Publishers, 1997).

Dugard J., Raic D., *The Role of Recognition in the Law and Practice of Secession*, in M. Kohen (ed.), *Secession: International Law Perspectives*, (Cambridge: Cambridge University Press, 2006).

Eckart C., *Promises of States under International Law*, (Oxford: Hart Publishing, 2012).

Elaraby N., *Some Reflections on Disarmament*, in C. Tomuschat (ed.), *The United Nations at Fifty: A Legal Perspective*, (The Hague: Kluwer Law International, 1995).

Fauchille P., *Traite de droit international*, Vol. I, (Paris: Rousseau et Cie, 1926).

Fauvarque-Cosson B., Mazeud, D. (eds.), *European Contract Law, Materials for a Common Frame of Reference: Terminology, Guiding Principles, Model Rules* (Munich: Sellier, European Law Publishers, 2008).

Fiedler W., *Unilateral Acts in International Law*, in R. Berhardt (ed.), *Encyclopedia of Public International Law*, Vol. IV, (Amsterdam, Oxford: North-Holland, 1984).

Fitzmaurice G., *Some Problems Regarding the Formal Sources of International Law*, in F.M. van Asbeck (ed.), *Symbolae Verzijl*, (The Hague: M. Nijhoff, 1958).

Fitzmaurice G., *The Law and Procedure of the International Court of Justice*, Vols. I & II, (Cambridge: Grotius, 1986).

Franck T.M., *Report by Thomas M. Franck: Opinion Directed at Question 2 of the Reference*, in A.F. Bayefsky (ed.), *Self-Determination in International Law: Quebec and Lessons Learned: Legal Opinions*, (The Hague, M. Nijhoff, 2000).

Frowein J.A., *Kosovo and Lotus*, in U. Fastenrath (ed.), *From Bilateralism to Community Interest: Essays in Honour of Bruno Simma*, (Oxford: Oxford University Press, 2011).

Grant T., *The Recognition of States: Law and Practice in Debate and Evolution*, (Westport: Praeger Publishers, 1999).

Goldbat J., *Negative Security Assurances*, in A. Nikitin (ed.), *Lessons to be Learned from Non-Proliferation Failures and Successes*, (Amsterdam: IOS Press, 2009).

Hambro E., Goodrich L., and Simons A., *Charter of the United Nations: Commentary and Documents*, 3rd ed., (New York: Columbia University Press, 1969).

Harris D.J., *Cases and Materials on International Law*, 6th ed., (London: Sweet & Maxwell, 2004).

Harris D.J., *Cases and Materials on International Law*, 7th ed., (London: Sweet & Maxwell, 2010).

Hart H.L.A., *The Concept of Law*, 2nd ed., (Oxford: Oxford University Press, 1961).

Heilborn P., *Das System Des Volkerrechts, Entwickelt aus den Volkerrechtlichen Begriffen*, (Berlin: Springer, 1896).

Higgins R., *Problems and Process: International Law and How We Use It*, (Oxford: Clarendon Press, 1994).

Hipold P. (ed.), *Kosovo and International Law: The ICJ Advisory Opinion of 22 July 2010*, (Leiden: M. Nijhoff, 2012).

Hyde C.C., *International Law, Chiefly as Interpreted and Applied by the United States*, Vol. II, (Boston: Little & Brown, 1951).

Jacque J-P., *Elements pour Une Theorie de l'Acte Juridique en Droit International Public*, (Paris: LGDJ, 1972).

Jacque J-P., *A Propos de la Promesse Unilaterale*, in P. Reuter (ed.), *Melanges Offerts a Paul Reuter: Le Droit International: Unite et Diversite*, (Paris: A. Pedone, 1981).

Jellinek G., *L'État Moderne et son Droit*, (Paris: V. Giard & E. Brière, 1911).

Jennings R., *Nullity and Effectiveness in International Law*, R. Jennings *et al.* (eds.), *Cambridge Essays in International Law: Essays in Honour of Lord McNair*, (London: Stevens, 1965).

Jennings R., Watts A. (eds.), *Oppenheim's International Law*, Vol. 1: Peace, 9th ed., (London: Longman, 1992).

Kadner Graziano T., *Comparative Contract Law: Cases, Materials and Exercises*, (Basingstoke: Palgrave MacMillan, 2009).

Kelsen H., Knight M. (tr), *Pure Theory of Law*, 2nd rev. and enlarged ed., (Clark, Lawbook Exchange, 2005).

Kelsen H., Tucker R.W. (ed), *Principles of International Law*, 2nd rev. ed., (New York: Holt Rinehart & Winston, 1966).

Kelsen H., Litschewski Paulson B. and Paulson S.L. (trs), *Introduction to the Problems of Legal Theory: A Translation of the First Edition of the Reine Rechtslere or Pure Theory of Law*, (Oxford: Clarendon Press, 1992).

Khan S., *Nuclear Weapons and Conflict Transformation: the case of India-Pakistan*, (New York: Routledge, 2008).

Klabbers J., *The Concept of Treaty in International Law*, (The Hague: Kluwer Law International, 1996).

Klabbers J., *(I Can't Get No) Recognition: Subjects Doctrine and the Emergence of Non-State Actors*, in J. Klabbers, J. Petman (eds.), *Nordic Cosmopolitanism: Essays in International Law for Martti Koskenniemi*, (Leiden: M. Nijhoff, 2003).

Klabbers J., *Law-Making and Constitutionalism*, in J. Klabbers, A. Peters, G. Ulfstein (eds), *The Constitutionalization of International Law*, (Oxford: Oxford University Press, 2009).

Klabbers J., *International Law*, (Cambridge: Cambridge University Press, 2013).

Kolb R., *Le Bonne Foi en Droit International Public*, (Paris, Presses Universitaires de France, 2000).

Koskenniemi M., *From Apology to Utopia: The Structure of International Legal Argument*, re-issued with Epilogue (Cambridge: Cambridge University Press, 2005).

Koskenniemi M., *The Politics of International Law*, (Oxford: Hart Publishing, 2011).

Lachs M., *Some Reflections on Substance and Form in International Law*, in Friedmann W., Henkin L., Lissitzyn O. (eds.), *Transnational Law in a Changing Society: Essays in honor of Philip C. Jessup*, (New York: Columbia University Press, 1972).

Lachs M., *Pacta Sunt Servanda*, in R. Berhardt (ed.), *Encyclopedia of Public International Law*, Vol. VII, (Amsterdam, Oxford: North-Holland, 1984).

Lauterpacht H., *Recognition in International Law*, (Cambridge: Cambridge University Press, 1947).

Lauterpacht H. (ed.), *Oppenheim's International Law*, Vol. I, 8th ed., (London: Longmans, Green & Co., 1955).

Lauterpacht H., *The Function of the Commission and the Selection of Topics for Codification*, in E. Lauterpacht (ed.), *International Law, Being the Collected Papers of Hersch Lauterpacht*, Vol. I, (Cambridge: Cambridge University Press, 1970).

Lauterpacht H., *The Function of Law in the International Community*, new ed., (Oxford: Oxford University Press, 2011).

McNair A., *The Law of Treaties*, (Oxford: Clarendon Press, 1961).

Mendelson M.H., *Are Treaties Merely a Source of Obligation?*, in W.E. Butler (ed.), *Perestroika and International Law*, (Dordrecht: M. Nijhoff, 1990).

Merryman J.H., Perez-Perdomo R., *The Civil Law Tradition: An Introduction to the Legal Systems of Europe and Latin America*, (Stanford: Stanford University Press, 2007).

Murphy J., *The Evolving Dimensions of International law: Hard Choices for the World Community*, (Cambridge: Cambridge University Press, 2010).

Nustyen G., Graff Hugo T., *The Nuclear Non-Proliferation Treaty*, in G. Nystuen *et al.* (ed.), *Nuclear Weapons Under International Law*, (Cambridge: Cambridge University Press, 2014).

O' Connell D.P., *International Law*, 2nd ed., (London: Stevens, 1970).

Orakhelashvili A., *The Interpretation of Acts and Rules in International Law*, (Oxford: Oxford University Press, 2008).

Parlett K., *The Individual in the International Legal System: Continuity and Change in International law*, (Cambridge: Cambridge University Press, 2011).

Pellet A., *Article 38*, in A. Zimmermann (ed.), *The Statute of the International Court of Justice: A Commentary*, (Oxford: Oxford University Press, 2006).

Pellet A., *Article 38*, in A. Zimmermann, C. Tomuschat, K. Oelles-Frahm (eds.), *The Statute of The International Court of Justice: A Commentary*, 2nd ed., (Oxford: Oxford University Press, 2012).

Podliska B.F., *Acting Alone: A Scientific Study of American Hegemony and Unilateral Use-of-Force Decision Making*, (Lanham: Lexington Books, 2010).

Pomerance M., *Self-Determination in Law and Practice: The New Doctrine in the United Nations*, (The Hague: M. Nijhoff, 1982).

Raz J., *Practical Reason and Norms*, (Oxford: Oxford University Press, 1975).

Reuter P., *Introduction to the Law of Treaties*, 2nd ed., (London: Kegan Paul, 1996).

Schachter O., *The Nature and Process of Legal Development in International Society*, in R. MacDonald, D. Johnston (eds.), *The Structure and Process of International Law: Essays in legal philosophy, doctrine and theory*, (The Hague: M. Nijhoff, Boston, 1983).

Schachter O., *International Law in Theory and Practice*, (London: M. Nijhoff Publishers, 1991).

Schwarzenberger G., *International Law as applied by International Courts and Tribunals*, Vol. 1, 3rd ed., (London: Stevens, 1957).

Shahabuddeen M., *Precedent in the World Court*, (Cambridge: Cambridge University Press, 2007).

Shaw M., *International Law*, 6th ed., (Cambridge: Cambridge University Press, 2008).

Shaw M., *International Law*, 7th ed., (Cambridge: Cambridge University Press, 2014).

Simma B. (ed.), *The Charter of the United Nations: A Commentary*, Vol. 1, 2nd ed., (Oxford: Oxford University Press, 2002).

Simpson J.A., *The Role of Security Assurances in the Nuclear Nonproliferation Regime*, in J.W. Knopf (ed.), *Security Assurances and Nuclear Nonproliferation*, (Stanford: Stanford University Press, 2012).

Simpson J.A., Weiner E.S.C. (eds.), *The Oxford English Dictionary*, 2nd ed., (Oxford: Clarendon Press, 1989, online version June 2011), available at http://www.oed.com.

Sinclair I., *Estoppel and Acquiescence*, in Lowe V., Fitzmaurice M. (eds.), *Fifty Years of the International Court of Justice: Essays in honor of Sir R. Jennings*, (Cambridge: Cambridge University Press, 1996).

Sivakumaran S., *The Law of Non-International Armed Conflict*, (Oxford: Oxford University Press, 2012).

Skubiszewski K., *Unilateral Acts of States*, in M. Bedjaoui (ed.), *International Law: Achievements and Prospects*, (Paris: UNESCO, 1991).

Stathopoulos M., *Contract Law in Greece*, 2nd rev. ed., (The Hague: Kluwer Law International, 2009).

Suy E., *Les Actes Juridiques Unilateraux en Droit International Public*, (Paris: LGDJ, 1962).

Tancredi A., *A Normative 'Due Process' in the Creation of States through Secession* in M. Kohen (ed.), *Secession: International Law Perspectives*, (Cambridge: Cambridge University Press, 2006).

Tertrais B., *Security Assurances and the Future of Proliferation*, in J.W. Knopf (ed.), *Security Assurances and Nuclear Nonproliferation*, (Stanford: Stanford University Press, 2012).

Thirlway H., *Customary International Law and Codification: An examination of the continuing role of custom in the present period of codification of international law*, (Leiden: Sijthoff, 1972).

Thirlway H., *The Sources of International Law*, in M. Evans (ed.), *International Law*, 2nd ed., (Oxford: Oxford University Press, 2006).

Thirlway H., *The Sources of International Law*, (Oxford: Oxford University Press, 2014a).

Thirlway H., *The Sources of International Law*, in M. Evans (ed.), *International Law*, 4th ed., (Oxford: Oxford University Press, 2014b).

Tomuschat C., *Article 36*, in A. Zimmermann (ed.) *The Statute of the International Court of Justice: A Commentary*, (Oxford: Oxford University Press, 2006).

Tomuschat C., *Unilateral Acts under International Law*, in K. Meziou (ed.), *Droits et Culture: Mélanges en l' honneur du Doyen Yadh Ben Achour*, (Tunis: Centre de Publication Universitaire, 2008).

Van Hoof G.J.H., *Rethinking the Sources of International Law*, (Deventer: Kluwer, 1983).

Verdross A., Simma B., *Universelles Völkerrecht: Theorie und Praxis*, 3rd Aufl., (Berlin: Duncker & Humblot, 1984).

Verzijl J.H.W., *International Law in a Historical Perspective, Vol. VI: Juridical Facts as Sources of International Rights and Obligations*, (Leiden: Sijthoff, 1971).

Vicuna O., *The Exclusive Economic Zone: Regime and Legal Nature under International Law*, (Cambridge: Cambridge University Press, 1989).

Vidmar J., *Democracy and Statehood in International Law*, (Oxford: Hart Publishing, 2013a).

Vidmar J., *Unilateral Declarations of Independence in International Law*, in D. French (ed.), *Statehood and Self-Determination: Reconciling Tradition and Modernity in International Law*, (Cambridge: Cambridge University Press, 2013b).

Virally M., *The Sources of International Law*, in M. Sorensen (ed.), *Manual of Public International Law*, (London: Macmillan, 1968).

Virally M., *Unilateral Acts of International Organisations*, in M. Bedjaoui (ed.), *International Law: Achievements and Prospects*, (Paris: UNESCO, 1991).

Von Bernstorff J., Dunlap T., *The Public International Law Theory of Hans Kelsen: Believing in Universal Law*, (New York: Cambridge University Press, 2010).

Watts C.P., *Rhodesia' Unilateral Declaration of Independence: An International History*, (New York: Palgrave Macmillan, 2012).

Weller M., *Contested Statehood: Kosovo's Struggle for Independence*, (Oxford: Oxford University Press, 2009).

Wittich S., *The PCIJ and the Modern International Law of Treaties*, in C. Tams, M. Fitzmaurice (eds.), *Legacies of the Permanent Court of International Justice*, (Dordrecht: M. Nijhoff, 2013).

Whiteman M., *Digest of international law*, Vol. III, (Washington: US Govt. Print. Off, 1963).

Zemanek K., *Unilateral Legal Acts Revisited* in K. Wellens (ed.), *International Law: Theory and Practice: Essays in Honour of Eric Suy*, (The Hague: M. Nijhoff, 1998).

Articles

———., Symposium on Soft Law, 25 *LJIL* 309 (2012).

———., Unilateralism in International Law: A United States – European Symposium, 11 *EJIL* 3 (2000).

Akehurst M., Custom as a Source of International Law, 47 *BYIL* 1 (1974–5).

Allott P., The Concept of International Law, 10 *EJIL* 31 (1999).

Baxter R., International Law in "Her Infinite Variety", 29 *ICLQ* 549 (1980).

Blutman L., In the Trap of a Legal Metaphor: International Soft Law, 59 *ICLQ* 605 (2010).

Bothe M., Legal and Non-Legal Norms – A Meaningful Distinction in International Relations?, 11 *Netherlands YIL* 65 (1980).

Boyle A., Some Reflections on the Relationship of Treaties and Soft Law, 48 *ICLQ* 901 (1999).

Bowett D.W., Estoppel before International Tribunals and its relation to Acquiescence, 33 *BYIL* 176 (1957).

Brandon M., The Validity of Non-Registered Treaties, 29 *BYIL* 186 (1952).

Bunn G., Timmerbaev R., Security Assurances to Non-Nuclear Weapon States: Possible Options for Change, 7 *PPNN Issue Review* 1 (1996).

Bunn G., The Legal Status of U.S. Negative Security Assurances to Non-Nuclear Weapon States, 4 *The Nonproliferation Review* 1 (1997).

Calleros C., Cause, Consideration, Promissory Estoppel, and Promises under Deed: What Our Students Should Know about Enforcement of Promises in a Historical and International Context, *13 Chi.- Kent J. Int'l & Comp. L.* 83 (2013).

Carbone S., Promise in International Law: A Confirmation of its Binding Force, 1 *Italian YIL* 166 (1975).

Chinkin C., The Challenge Of Soft Law: Development and Change in International Law, 38 *ICLQ* 850 (1989).

Cruz F.C., Costa Rica's Constitutional Jurisprudence, its Political Importance and International Human Rights Law: Examination of Some Important Decisions, 45 *Duq. L. Rev.* 557, 2007.

D'Aspremont J., Softness in International Law: A Self-Serving Quest for New Legal Materials, 19 *EJIL* 1075 (2008).

Degan V.D., Unilateral Act as a Source of Particular International Law, 5 *Finnish YIL* 149 (1994).

Dupuy P.M., The Place and Role of Unilateralism in Contemporary International Law, 11 *EJIL* 19 (2000).

Fastenrath U., Relative Normativity in International Law, 4 *EJIL* 305 (1993).

Fawcett J.E.S., The Legal Character of International Agreements, 30 *BYIL* 381 (1953).

Fitzmaurice G., The Foundations of the Authority of International Law and the Problem of Enforcement, 19 *The Modern Law Review* 1 (1956).

Fitzmaurice G., The Law and Procedure of the International Court of Justice 1951–4: Treaty Interpretation and other Treaty Points, 33 *BYIL* 203 (1957).

Fitzmaurice M., The Identification and Character of Treaties and Treaty Obligations between States in International Law, 73 *BYIL* 141 (2002).

Franck T., Word Made Law: The Decision Of the ICJ in The Nuclear Tests Case, 69 *AJIL* 612 (1975).

Frowein J.A., Nullity in International Law, 3 *Encyclopedia of Public International Law* 743 (1997).

Garbone S., Promise in International Law: A Confirmation of its Binding Force, 1 *Italian YIL* 166 (1975).

Garner J.W., The International Binding Force of Unilateral Oral Declarations, 27 *AJIL* 493 (1933).

Giganti A., The Effect of Unilateral State Acts in International Law, 2 *NYU J. Int'l L.& Pol.* 333 (1962).

Goldmann M., We need to cut off the head of the King: Past, Present and Future Approaches to International Soft Law, 25 *LJIL* 335 (2012).

Goodman C., Acta Sunt Servanda? A Regime for the Unilateral Acts of States at International Law, 25 *Australian YIL* 43 (2006).

Havel B., An International Law Institution in Crisis: Rethinking Permanent Neutrality, 61 *Ohio St. L.J.* 167 (2000).

Hillgenberg H., A Fresh Look at Soft Law, 10 *EJIL* 499 (1999).

Hogg M.A., Promise: the neglected obligation in European private law, 59 *ICLQ* 461 (2010).

Hollick A., US Oceans Policy: The Truman Proclamations, 17 *Va. J. Int'l L.* 23 (1976–7).

Howse R., Teitel R., Delphic Dictum: How has the ICJ contributed to the global rule of law by its ruling in Kosovo? 11 *German L.J. 841* (2010).

Hudson M.O., The Registration and Publication of Treaties, 19 *AJIL* 273 (1925).

Hudson M.O., Legal Effect of Unregistered Treaties in Practice, Under Article 18 of the Covenant, 28 *AJIL* 546 (1934a).

Hudson M.O., The Aftermath of the Permanent Court's Judgment in the Free Zones Case, 28 *AJIL* 322 (1934b).

Hutchinson D.N., The Significance of Registration or Non-Registration of an International Agreement in determining whether or not it is a Treaty, 46 *Current Legal Problems* 257 (1993).

Ijalaye D.A., Was "Biafra" at Any Time a State in International Law?, 65 *AJIL* 551 (1971).

Jamar H., Vigness M.K., Applying Kosovo: Looking to Russia, China, Spain and beyond after the International Court of Justice Opinion on Unilateral Declarations of Independence, 11 *German L.J.* 913 (2010).

Jennings R., What Is International Law and How Do We Tell When We See It?, 37 *Schweizeriches Jahrbuch für Internationales Recht* 59 (1981).

Khosla D., Nuclear Tests Cases: Judicial Valour v. Judicial Discretion, 18 *Indian JIL* 322 (1978).

Klabbers J., Informal Agreements in International Law: Towards a Theoretical Framework, 5 *Finnish YIL* 267 (1994).

Klabbers J., The Undesirability of Soft Law, 67 *Nordic JIL* 381 (1998).

Kohen M., Del Mar K., The Kosovo Advisory Opinion and UNSCR 1244 (1999): A Declaration of 'Independence from International Law?', 24 *LJIL* 109 (2011).

Kolb R., Principles as Sources of International Law: (With Special Reference to Good Faith), 53 *NILR* 1 (2006).

Lachs M., The Development and General Trends of International Law in Our Time, 169 *RdC* 9 (1980).

Larroumet C., Detrimental Reliance and Promissory Estoppel as the Cause of Contracts in Louisiana and Comparative Law, 60 *Tu. L. Rev.* 1209 (1986).

Leich M.N., Contemporary Practice of the United States relating to International Law, 79 *AJIL* 431 (1985).

Lenner P., Promises of Rewards in a Comparative Perspective, 10 *Ann. Surv. Int'l & Comp. L.* 53 (2004).

MacDonald R. St. J., Hough B., The Nuclear Tests Case Revisited, 20 *German YIL* 337 (1977).

McCorquodale R., An Inclusive International Legal System, 17 *LJIL* 477 (2004).

McDorman T.L., Access to Information under Article 9 of the OSPAR Convention (Ireland v. UK), 98 *AJIL* 330 (2004).

McGibbon I., Some Observations on the Part of Protest in International Law, 30 *BYIL* 293 (1953).

McGibbon I.C., Estoppel in International Law, 7 *ICLQ* 468 (1958).

McNair A., The Functions and Differing Legal Character of Treaties, 11 *BYIL* 100 (1930).

Orakhelashvili A., Statehood, Recognition and the United Nations System: A Unilateral Declaration of Independence in Kosovo, 12 *Max Planc Yrbk. Of United Nations Law* 1 (2009).

Pellet A., The Normative Dilemma: Will and Consent in International Law-Making, 12 *Australian YIL* 22 (1992).

Preuss L., The Dispute Between Norway and Denmark Over the Sovereignty of Eastern Greenland, 26 *AJIL* 469 (1932).

Regaldies F., Contribution à l'étude de l'acte juridique unilatéral et droit international public, 15 *Revue Juridique Themis* 417 (1980–1).

Roberts A., Sivakumaran S., Lawmaking by Nonstate Actors: Engaging Armed groups in the creation of International Humanitarian Law, 37 *Yale J. Int'l L.* 108 (2011).

Rosas A., Negative Security Assurances and Non-Use of Nuclear Weapons, 25 *German YIL* 199 (1982).

Rousseau C., Chronique des Faits Internationaux, 85 *RGDIP* 411 (1981).

Rubin A., The International Legal Effects of Unilateral Declarations, 71 *AJIL* 1 (1977).

Russel H.S., The Helsinki Declaration: Brobdingnag or Lilliput?, 70 *AJIL* 242 (1976).

Ryngaert C., Sobrie S., Recognition of States: International Law or Realpolitik? The Practice of Recognition in the Wake of Kosovo, South Ossetia and Abkhazia, 24 *LJIL* 467 (2011).

Sands P., 'Unilateralism', Values, and International Law, 11 *EJIL* 291 (2000).

Schwarzenberger G., The Fundamental Principles of International Law, 87 *RdC* 195 (1955).

Sinha S.P., Has Self-Determination become a Principle of International Law Today?, 17 *Indian JIL* 332 (1974).

Talmon S., The Constitutive versus the Declaratory Doctrine of Recognition: Tertium non Datur?, 75 *BYIL* 101 (2004).

Tammes A.J.P., Decisions of International Organs as a Source of International Law, 94 *RdC* 265 (1958).

Thirlway H., The Law and Procedure of the International Court of Justice 1960–1989, part I, 60 *BYIL* 1 (1989).

Thirlway H., The Law and Procedure of the International Court of Justice 1960–1989, part III, 62 *BYIL* 1 (1991).

Van Ommeslaghe P., L'engagement par Volonté Unilatérale en Droit Belge, 1982 *Journal des Tribunaux* 144 (1982).

Venturini G., Control and Verification of Multilateral Treaties on Disarmament and Non-Proliferation of Weapons of Mass Destruction, 17 *U.C. Davis J. Int'l L. & Pol'y* 345 (2011).

Verdross A., Austria's Permanent Neutrality and the United Nations Organization, 50 *AJIL* 61 (1956).

Vidmar J., Conceptualizing Declarations of Independence, 32 *Oxford JLS* 153 (2012).

Virally M., Good Faith in Public International Law, 77 AJIL 130 (1983).

Von Bernstorff J., Georg Jellinek and the Origins of Liberal Constitutionalism in International Law, 4 *GOJIL* 659 (2012).

Wagner M., Jurisdiction by Estoppel in the International Court of Justice, 74 *Cal. L. Rev.* 1777 (1986).

Weil P., Towards Relative Normativity in International Law?, 77 *AJIL* 413 (1983).

Widdows K., What is an Agreement in International Law, 50 *BYIL* 117 (1978).

Wood M.C., The Interpretation of Security Council Resolutions, 2 *Max Planc Encyclopedia of United Nations Law* 73 (1998).

Zemanek K., The Law-Making Processes of the International System, 266 *Hague Recueil* 131 (1997).

Index